THE HUMAN FACE
OF PSYCHOLOGY

THE HUMAN FACE OF PSYCHOLOGY

humanistic psychology in its historical, social and cultural contexts

HELEN GRAHAM

Open University Press

Milton Keynes *Philadelphia*

Open University Press,
Open University Educational Enterprises Limited,
12 Cofferidge Close, Stony Stratford,
Milton Keynes MK11 1BY, England
and
242 Cherry Street,
Philadelphia, PA 19106, U.S.A.

First published 1986
Copyright © 1986
Helen Graham

British Library Cataloguing in Publication Data
Graham, Helen
  The human face of psychology: humanistic
  psychology in its historical, social and cultural
  contexts.
  1. Psychology
  I. Title
  150   BF121

  ISBN 0-335-15332-1
  ISBN 0-335-15331-3 Pbk

Editorial and Production Services by
Fisher Duncan Ltd, 10 Barley Mow Passage, London W4 4PH
Phototypeset by Dobbie Typesetting Service, Plymouth
Printed in Great Britain at The Alden Press, Oxford

CONTENTS

Introduction.   ix

Chapter 1

The Ancient Wisdom:
the visionary origins of culture and its institutions   .   . 1

Man's earliest attempts to understand the universe   .   . 2
The visionary sources of civilization   3
    Western culture   3
    Eastern culture   4
Religion as an expression of cultural differences   .   . 5
Education as a reflection of religious tradition .   .   . 8
    Education in Eastern culture 8
    Education in Western culture   9

Chapter 2

Psychology East and West:
different cultural perspectives on man, nature and knowledge 11

Psychology in Eastern culture   11
    Buddhism   12
    Taoism   14
    Zen Buddhism.   15
    Sufism 15
Common themes in oriental psychological traditions   .   . 16
Psychology in Western culture   17
    Orthodox scholasticism   17
    Materialism   18
    Positivism   20

Chapter 3

Psychology, Politics and Protest:
twentieth century opposition to science and technology . 23

The blind eye of Western psychology 24
Man the machine 25
Psychology as engineering 26
A spanner in the works 28
From man the robot to man the pilot 31

Chapter 4

Cults and Counter Culture:
radicalism during the 1960s 32

Openness to unfamiliar answers 32
    Oriental philosophy goes West 33
Experimentation and the development of new possibilities . 34
    The psychedelic revolution 34
    Cults of unreason 35
    Guru hunger 36
    The occult revival 37
    The cult of Castaneda 37
    The magical mystery tour 40
    Experiment and innovation in education . . 41

Chapter 5

The Cult of Psychotherapy:
psychotherapy as religion 44

Psychotherapy—the cure of souls 45
Diagnosis of the human condition 46
Salvation as science. 47
The politics of psychotherapy (Kurt Lewin) . . . 49
    A psychology of being (Abraham Maslow) . . . 51
    The homeopathic model 53
    The psychology of becoming (Carl Rogers) . . . 53
    The counselling movement 56
The human potential movement 58
Patterns of being (Frederick Perls) 58
Encounter 61

Chapter 6

The Philosophy of Being Human:
towards a psychology of freedom 65

Third Force psychology 65
Philosophical and psychological sources of humanistic psychology. 67
Existentialism 67
    Freedom 68
    The acceptance of death 69
    Isolation 70
    Meaninglessness 71
    The ethical tradition of existentialism. . . . 73
    Existential psychology 74
    British existentialism (R. D. Laing) 76
    New World existentialism 79

Chapter 7

Technology or Tao?
methods in psychotherapy 83

The non-method of being 84
The method of doing 86
Psychosomatic techniques (Wilhelm Reich) . . . 89
    Bioenergetics (Alexander Lowen) 90
    Biodynamic therapy (Gerda Boyeson). . . . 90
    Structural integration (Ida Rolf) 91
    The Alexander technique 92
Dramatic techniques 92
    Psychodrama (Jacob Moreno). 92
    Gestalt therapy (Frederick Perls) 93
    Transactional analysis (Eric Berne) 94
    Primal therapy (Arthur Janov) 94
    Est (Werner Erhard) 95
    Co-counselling (Harvey Jackins) 96
Mystic techniques 96
Enlightenment intensive (Charles Berner) . . . 96
Psychosynthesis (Roberto Assaglioli) 97
Do the techniques work? 98

Chapter 8

**Hard and Soft Psychologies:
the maddening problem of method in psychological research**   101

Hard and soft psychologies   101
    The common sense approach   105
    The hermeneutic approach 107
    New paradigm research   109

Chapter 9

**Paradigms and Paradoxes:
science, psychology and the new physics**   .   .   . 112

The uncertain universe   114
Godel's Incompleteness Theorem   115
Bohr's Principle of Complementarity   116
Heisenberg's Uncertainty Principle   116
The Tao of physics   119
The holographic universe   120
The physics of maya   121
Faithing the facts   124
A conscious universe   125
A creative universe   126
From ancient myths to modern movements   .   .   . 128

Bibliography   132

Index   144

INTRODUCTION

It is my experience that most people are attracted to the study of psychology because of their desire to understand themselves and others. Such an interest, manifest in all cultures since antiquity, would appear to be as old as mankind itself. Indeed, the desire for understanding or meaning constitutes a fundamental activating principle in the human species.

This dimension, which is spiritual in the non-religious sense of the word, is a specifically human feature, and as such must be addressed by any science that purports to study man. It is ironic, therefore, that in the Western world at least, psychology—the literal meaning of which is the study of (*logos*) the spirit or soul (*psyche*)—has largely neglected this spiritual or 'humanistic' dimension in favour of the study of behaviour.

Nevertheless, interest in humanistic concerns has been sustained throughout the history of psychology and began to flourish during the 1950s when confidence in behaviourism began to falter, gaining further momentum during the following decade. By the late 1960s it had become formalized as a distinct movement within psychology and dignified with the title 'humanistic psychology'. As such it represents a particular attitude to psychology rather than a school, taking as its subject matter human being, that is, humanity in all its aspects. It recognizes not only outer, objective behaviour but also inner subjective life or experience, and thereby admits into the realm of its investigations all the kinds of phenomena typically excluded from study by twentieth century Western psychology; personal meanings, 'common sense', imagination, fantasy, religious belief, mystical and anomalous experience, and altered states of consciousness.

Many existing books on humanistic psychology have tended to focus on narrow and limited issues, giving rise to the impression that its concerns are diverse, diffuse and unrelated and that it lacks coherence as a discipline. In addition to the generous scope of humanistic psychology, popular enthusiasm for an approach which corresponds with what the average intelligent person in the street believes psychology should be about, has given rise to a proliferation of trends (some of which appear bizarre, trivial and cultic) and dispute among psychologists as to its validity and credibility.

However, the approach not only conforms with the concerns and interests of the lay person but also with current developments in science. Within the last few years scientists have drawn attention to a change of world view within the physical sciences that has profound implications for scientific thinking as a whole.

They have also emphasized the potentially disastrous consequences of ignoring this new perspective and adhering to an outmoded world view. Exponents of this school of thought have identified humanistic psychology as just one of several important new movements which are emerging or re-emerging and emphasizing aspects of a new vision of reality — a vision which seems to confirm the Ancients' vision of the universe and humanity's place in it.

It is thus that the development of humanistic psychology needs to be seen in its social, cultural and historical context if it is to be adequately accounted for. *The Human Face of Psychology* provides such a framework, and in so doing attempts a synthesis of trends within humanistic psychology, identifying its diverse concerns as manifestations of the human quest for meaning, and tracing their development from early civilization to the present day.

Chapter 1

THE ANCIENT WISDOM

the visionary origins of culture
and its institutions

*If the doors of perception were cleansed, everything would appear
to man as it is, infinite. For man has closed himself up, till he sees
all things through narrow chinks of his cavern.*

William Blake[1]

Homo sapiens is the specific name of modern man. Literally this means 'wise
man', and indicates the human ability to think and act utilizing knowledge,
experience, understanding, common sense and insight. One could say that being
a wise man is the result of asking the question 'why' and thus enquiring into
reason, purpose and cause. Certainly 'why' is an archetypal question, and it is
by asking and attempting to answer it that man has accumulated knowledge. This
process is nowhere more evident than in the verbal behaviour of young children
who endlessly question everything from why the sky is up, to why the goldfish
doesn't drown. All these questions demand answers which for the most part can
be provided, in principle at least.

Inevitably, however, questions arise for which there are no ready answers;
questions such as why we are born, why we die, and why we exist at all, and,
despite much endeavour channelled along these lines of enquiry since the earliest
times, answers to such questions still elude us. Man's fundamental desire to
understand his existence, or being, is thwarted because he is not born into what
the Ancient Greeks termed *kosmos* — a well-structured universe with an inherent
design or given meaning. Instead, man finds himself — an apparently
meaning-seeking creature — cast into an apparently meaningless and orderless
universe, or *khaos*; a situation which Camus (1955) has described as absurd, and
which man throughout history has striven to resolve.

[1]From *The Marriage of Heaven and Hell*. In: *William Blake: Songs of Innocence and of
Experience* 1970 (ed. R. B. Kennedy) p. 69, London: MacDonald and Evans.

MAN'S EARLIEST ATTEMPTS TO UNDERSTAND THE UNIVERSE

Primeval man attributed phenomena beyond his comprehension to supernatural forces which could be invoked to influence worldly events and human destiny by way of spells, incantations, and certain rituals. These arts, which were widely practised throughout the known world as a means of gaining mastery over universal forces, were known as magic or sorcery, and adepts of magic, referred to variously as magicians, sorcerers or shamans, were deemed to have access to the mysteries of the universe. Wheatley (1973) suggests that these arts were actually the application of scientific laws which are, for the most part, still unknown to our recognized scientists.

Ancient mythology has it that man's vision of the universe is blinkered by conventional reality, or certain learned ways of perceiving, and that beyond this realm of mundane phenomena there exists a far greater hidden or occult reality; an infinite, ever-changing and expanding universe of harmonious relationships and inter-relationships of which man is part, and which was represented symbolically as a luminous orb, web or mandala. Moreover, this expanded universe or occult reality could be perceived by those so attuned.

Those 'enlightened' beings who had insight into the true nature of the universe and were initiated into its mysteries were variously termed seers, visionaries or mystics, a term derived from the Greek verb *muo* meaning to close or complete. Mystics were therefore those with a complete picture of reality, or cosmic vision. Accordingly mysticism in all ages and parts of the world is, as Russell (1959) points out, characterized by certain beliefs: the concept of a reality beyond the world of appearance and utterly different from it — knowledge of which comes by way of revelation, insight or intuition, which is 'sudden, penetrative and coercive', commencing with 'the sense of a mystery unveiled, of a hidden wisdom, now suddenly become certain beyond the possibility of a doubt' (p. 9); together with awareness of the unity and indivisibility of all things, and the denial of the reality of time. Mysticism is thus the development of enhanced perception, awareness and sensitivity which enables the individual to penetrate the ultimate secrets of the universe, together with man's own nature and destiny, and to work with universal forces accordingly.

It was up to the men of vision and masters of the occult arts who perceived the overall pattern and harmony of the universe that others turned with their questions. These masters, or maharishis, tended to control access to knowledge inasmuch that they decided what was to be disclosed, and to whom, and the means of dissemination. However, given the ineffable quality of the mystic vision, conceptualization in ordinary thought or language is impossible. Masters taught by analogy, in itself inadequate, and through various practices aimed at enhancing and transforming consciousness in others so that they might apprehend ultimate reality directly. The process was essentially that of developing insight, and took the form of trying to draw forth or lead out (*educere* in Latin), and harness the individual's potential by developing their inner feelings and intuition. The occult masters were literally therefore the first educators, and their vision the basis of human civilization as we know it.

THE VISIONARY SOURCES OF CIVILIZATION

Western culture

Ancient Greece was indisputably the fountain-head of Western civilization. According to Bertrand Russell (1948), Pythagorus was intellectually one of the most important men of all time. His thinking represents the main current of the mystical tradition, albeit mysticism of a peculiarly intellectual kind. Similarly, the philosophies of Heraclitus and Empedocles are mystical in origin. However, the mathematics of Pythagorus were to prove the greatest single influence on Western thought.

As Russell points out, mathematics is the chief source of the belief in external and exact truth, as well as in a super-sensible and intelligible world. The exactness of geometry, which is not matched in the real world, suggests that all exact reasoning applies to ideal as opposed to sensible objects, and when taken further leads to the belief that the objects of thought are more real than those of sense perception. Such a view is quite contrary to that of mysticism.

However, by the Classical period in Greece the mystic vision of the Ancients had become distorted. It had become fragmented as a result of the concept of measure known as the Golden Mean or Section, and later referred to by Kepler as the Divine Proportion. As the latter name suggests this measure had mystical origins, being viewed not as an overt or even readily visible feature of a phenomenon but a deeper hidden harmony which was deemed to lie in the ratio of its inner proportions to each other and the whole. To understand ratio, and thereby 'have the measure' of something was a form of insight into its essential harmony or nature.

Maintaining a sense of proportion or right measure came to be central to the world view of the Greeks and to their way of life, for according to Platonic doctrine, human experience could best be described in terms of pairs of opposites, the balance or harmony between which constituted the soul or psyche. Moreover, when anything lost its right proportion, or went beyond its proper measure, it lost its overall balance, becoming fragmented, hence the literal meaning of *ratio*, to break into fragments. The tragic consequences of losing the sense of proportion—of human *irrationality*—were dramatically depicted in Greek theatre.

Gradually, however, the notion of measure lost its mystical significance. Bohm (1980) surmises that it became routinized and habitual as measure began to be learned by mechanical conformity to the teachings of masters rather than intuitively through the development of insight. Ratio came to be conceptualized as that point on a line which divides it into segments such that the smaller is to the larger as the larger is to the whole line, and measure became imposed as a rule; as an objective 'out-there' fact or absolute truth about reality. The only sense in which its original meaning is retained is in the phrase 'to get the measure' of something or someone, meaning to intuitively grasp their essence. Otherwise measure came to denote mainly a process of comparison with some arbitrary external standard, and as such it was handed down by the Greeks to Western civilization via the Romans who thereby inherited the notion that knowledge, or *scientia* (the Latin word from which the term 'science' derives), means objective fact, and that such facts constitute the only valid knowledge of the world.

The intellectual heritage of Western culture, of which science is generally viewed to be the greatest achievement, thus has its foundations in a linear model of knowledge, implicit in which is the notion of absolute truth or fixed reality, and from its concepts of measure and ratio it also derives its emphases on measurement and standardization, rationality and reason, all of which involve dissection. It is thus, as Toffler (1985) observes, that dissection—the reduction of problems into the smallest possible components—is one of the most highly developed skills of contemporary Western civilization, and most finely honed in science. Indeed, as he points out (p. xi), 'We are good at it. So good, we often forget to put the pieces back together again.'

In conceiving of an orderly, rational and lawful universe which man could explore and hope to comprehend through reason, the possession of which set man above and apart from the rest of creation, the Greeks made a profound contribution to the development of Western thought. Nevertheless, as Happold (1970) points out, the Greeks acknowledged two valid forms of reason; *ratio*, or discursive reason, by its nature analytic and reductionist; and *intellectus*, which was more akin to intuition in being holistic and integrative, and viewed as a higher faculty of mind than ratio, capable of bringing man to a more profound knowledge than could be gained by reason. Intuition thus held an acknowledged status in Greek thought, but wherever the mystic tradition was filtered through the sieve of Greek culture the enduring emphasis remained upon reason and rationality.

Eastern culture

The distortions introduced into the mystic vision by Classical Greek culture are not present, at least to the same extent, in civilizations which largely lack this influence. Consequently, thinking in those cultures remains close to its mystical origins. Rationality may therefore be thought of as a peculiarly Western characteristic.

In most Eastern cultures, most notably the Indian and Chinese, all phenomenal existence is deemed to be essentially transitory, impermanent, and in the process of change. All phenomena are viewed as being involved in a ceaseless cycle of becoming and ending which constitutes ultimate reality. Such a process is indivisible, and so all reduction into objective facts or forms is considered to be illusory. The realms of reason, rationality and analysis, so esteemed in the West, are regarded as 'blind guides leading to a morass of illusion' (Russell, 1959, p. 9) and obscuring ultimate truth. Rationality is described in Sanskrit as *maya*—the etymological root of which is closely allied to the word for 'measure'—and it refers to 'the superficial organization of a reality which is primarily, ultimately, and more significantly, something else' (Barnes, 1967, p. 237). Truth being immeasurable, therefore, maya is fundamentally illusion.

This view is clearly expressed by Radhakrishnan (cited by Patel, 1980):

> How do we come to think of things rather than of processes in absolute flux? By shutting our eyes to successive events. It is an artificial attitude that makes sections in the stream of change and calls them things . . . When we know the truth of things we shall realise how absurd it is for us to worship isolated products of the incessant series of transformations as though they were eternal and real. Life is no thing or state of thing, but continuous movement or change.

Eastern culture, in its concern with intangibles rather than 'facts', with emotionality rather than rationality, gives pre-eminence to the subjective and experiential, which qualify for deeper examination than any other branch of knowledge.

These fundamental differences in emphasis between East and West have profound and enduring implications for the subsequent development of thought in their respective cultures. The traditional question on which Western thought has focussed is 'What is man?'. Thus framed the question implies an objective and alienated stance consistent with its rational heritage. The same basic question is framed quite differently in the Orient, as 'Who am I?', reflecting the East's traditional concern with the subjective aspects of being. In the East, therefore, man's spiritual quest is for feeling, whereas in the West it is for fact. Each culture is the expression of a fundamentally different conception of the nature of reality; an idea which permeates all its institutions, but is perhaps most clearly reflected in their dominant religions.

RELIGION AS AN EXPRESSION OF CULTURAL DIFFERENCES

Religion derives from the Latin *religio*, meaning fear of the supernatural. With time, fear of the forces believed to be at work in the world and in control of human destiny gave rise to the notion that they required placation, supplication and reverent worship, rather than invocation. The practice of these sacred ritual observances became formalized as religion, and conventionally it is within this context that the human preoccupation with spiritual concerns has since been framed.

Institutionalized religion endeavoured to define ultimate causes, designating them as gods or spirits. Within Western culture these were distinctly separate from each other, from man, animals, birds, trees and other aspects of creation. Whereas in Eastern culture trees, plants, animals, man and gods were all one, and the perception of separateness an error. Accordingly, any separation of life from death also constitutes illusion. In Eastern religions therefore, the mystical tradition with its holistic, integrative emphasis is evident, whilst Western religions have a characteristic focus on the 'day of reckoning', when life's deeds must be accounted for.

These world views are fundamentally different, not only in their content but also in their prevailing attitude. This difference can be characterized as that between the mystical, on the one hand, and the religious on the other. The mystic's belief in his potential to alter consciousness at will and thus commune with, and influence, the forces of nature is at once active, arrogant and assertive; all of which, as Drury (1979, pp. 13–14) points out, is quite foreign to most religious traditions:

> There is no aggression here, no stealing of the fire from heaven. One waits passively until one is given.

Active encouragement and development of the human will therefore constitutes the major difference between the mystical and religious attitude. Maslow (1968) reminds us that the myth of Adam and Eve, who were punished for their wilfulness in eating the fruit of the Tree of Knowledge, is paralleled in many cultures, most notably in the West, reflecting a belief that ultimate knowledge is something reserved for the gods. Maslow indicates that as a consequence most religions have a marked thread of anti-intellectualism, and a preference for faith, belief and piety rather than knowledge, some forms of which are viewed as dangerous, and therefore either forbidden or the preserve of a chosen few. Accordingly 'in most cultures those revolutionaries who defied the gods by seeking out their secrets were punished heavily like Adam and Eve, Prometheus and Oedipus and have been remembered as warnings to others not to be god-like' (p. 61).

To the early Greeks this *hubris*, or manifestation of human pride, arrogance and wilfulness, was an affront to the gods which led to the withdrawal of their support and protection. In the later Christian tradition, Adam and all his descendants—the entire human race—were punished by their Fall from God's favour and consequent loss of Paradise. Moreover, they were all thereafter blemished with this original sin of disobedience. Accordingly, in order to be worthy of the Kingdom of God, they must be absolved of their sin, which is achieved primarily through baptism, or ritual symbolic cleansing with water. Otherwise humankind remains a bad lot who must be converted — literally turned into what is correct — through repression, control and total subjugation to God's will. Thus, as Fromm (1951) has pointed out, another feature of these religions is their authoritarianism; God being a symbol of supreme power and force over man, who is utterly powerless. Moreover, God is viewed as external to, or other than, man. As such God is a fact or truth; the Ultimate Fact or Truth, the very embodiment of Western thought. Indeed, Russell (1959, p. 56) claims that were it not for the Pythagorean concept of an external world revealed to the intellect but not to the senses the notion of God as it is known in the West might not have existed.

Fromm points to further implications of the 'externalization' of God. He suggests that man's projection of his own powers on to an external God results in his separation from his most valuable force and alienation from himself, which makes him feel not only slavishly dependent on God but also bad and sinful. Western authoritarian theology not only reflects the tradition of thinking established by the Greeks but also, according to Huxley (1976, p. 134), 'the state of its children's bottoms', by which he is referring to their essentially punitive nature. He suggests that wherever one finds authoritarian religion one traditionally also finds enthusiastic childbeaters — and he cites as cases in point Christians, Calvinists and Hebrews.

Authoritarianism is not, however, confined exclusively to Western religions, nor theistic traditions, but where it is found elsewhere the concept of sin, or knowing too much, is replaced by the notion of ignorance, or lack of knowledge, which is viewed as a stage that man can overcome or transcend. For the most part Eastern traditions, notably Buddhism, Taoism and Hinduism are characterized by their human attitude. Fromm (1951) identifies them as 'humanistic' religions in contradistinction to those with an authoritarian emphasis.

The concerns of humanistic religion centre around man's innate potential for transcendence, for inasmuch as they are theistic, God is viewed not as other, or external to man, but as residing within him. Man is viewed as a manifestation of God and emphasis is upon him realizing his own nature, godliness or godhead. In the sense that God exists at all, he is viewed as a symbol of man's own powers which he should strive to realize in his life, and not as a symbol of force and domination. The aim of such religion is to achieve the greatest strength, not the greatest powerlessness. Virtue is self-realization, not obedience; faith is conviction based on one's own experience rather than the propositions and dogma of others; and the prevailing mood is joy, rather than sorrow or guilt.

It is possible to distinguish therefore, a number of important and characteristic differences between authoritarian and humanistic religious traditions, the former being rooted in the intellectual tradition of Classical Greece, and the latter in the mystical tradition of the Ancient World. Inasmuch as the mystical attitude is intrinsic to humanistic religion, mysticism has flourished in the more sympathetic climate of Eastern culture. There masters were actively encouraged, and sought out rather than suppressed. Acknowledged masters include the Buddha, Siddhartha Gautama; Mohammed, Lao Tsu, Confucius, and Jesus Christ, together with various exponents of the martial arts. More contemporary masters include Gurdjieff, Krishnamurti, Ramakrishnan, Sai Baba and Bhagwan Shree Rajneesh.

By comparison, the only master traditionally recognized in the West is Jesus Christ, whose teachings were strikingly similar to those of the Eastern masters, and clearly humanistic, as reflected in his insistence that 'the Kingdom of God is within you'. Christianity only became authoritarian on being established as the dominant religion of the Roman Empire, whereupon its founder was elevated from the status of a mere master to that of God.

All practices which emphasized the development of *human* powers and potential were systematically eradicated in Western culture, and all bodies of knowledge were framed within the context of its dominant religious tradition, with the result that sources of occult knowledge and mysticism were eclipsed. Nevertheless, although obscured and fragmented, mysticism never fully disappeared but survived, being passed down through the ages in the tradition of various masters and secret schools of initiates.

Gradually, masters of the older traditions were superseded by masters of divinity, philosophy, arts and science, and as education became formalized, by school masters. Educational practices in both Eastern and Western cultures are thus inextricably linked with the respective religious traditions in which they originate, and reflect them in both content and form.

EDUCATION AS A REFLECTION OF RELIGIOUS TRADITION

Education in Eastern culture

Just as religions in the East are rooted in ancient mystical origins, so also their educational practices reflect the tradition of mysticism. As such their emphasis, historically, has been upon knowing rather than knowledge *per se*. Knowing is viewed as an active, dynamic process, or flux, synonymous with unfolding or becoming. Knowledge is emergent, rather than given, and fluid rather than fixed. It is essentially experiential and subjective, residing within the person, and accessed through the development of feelings, intuition, and self-awareness. The educational process is thus fundamentally humanistic and individualistic, and focusses upon self-growth, self-direction and self-expression. In such a process neither means nor ends can be specified, so it is necessarily divergent rather than convergent, and non-directive. The role of the teacher is therefore that of facilitator, as is clearly expressed by Gibran (1978, pp. 67–68):

No man can reveal to you aught but that which already lies half asleep in the dawning of your knowledge. The teacher . . . gives not of his wisdom but rather of his faith and lovingness. If he is indeed wise he does not bid you enter the house of his wisdom, but rather leads you to the threshold of your own mind . . . he cannot give you his understanding . . . For the vision of one man lends not its wings to another man. And even as each one of you stands alone in God's knowledge, so must each of you be alone in his knowledge of God and in his understanding of the earth.

Education in Western culture

Within Western cultures the philosophy of education has largely been concerned with maintenance of the *status quo* and the transmission of a fixed body of knowledge from generation to generation. Traditionally emphasis has focussed on objective assessment of the knowledge acquired thereby and the maintenance of standards. The dominant concern lay with the content of knowledge rather than the process of knowing. Authority is seen to reside both in the bodies of knowledge taught and in the teacher, and hence outside the learner. Knowledge is essentially objective, comprising a body of given facts, of which the learner is a passive recipient, and knowing is the attainment of a fixed state of knowledge which is deemed to be desirable, and measurable. The process of gaining knowledge is convergent, being directed to a given end or objective, and intellectual, emphasis being upon reason, rationality and analytical thinking, and also upon discipline and control, for this form of education is fundamentally authoritarian and punitive.

These approaches to education can be described as humanistic and authoritarian consistent with the cultural and religious traditions from which they derive, and as such they differ radically. What is being conditioned in each is not only different forms of knowledge, but also different ways of thinking and acting; different values and attitudes. Within the humanistic traditions of the East emphasis is upon humanity, on feeling, and upon religion and philosophy as means to wisdom. In the authoritarian traditions of the West the focus is upon matter, on fact, and upon science.

Such a characterization in terms of an East-West dichotomy necessarily leads to some generalization and oversimplification. Neither East nor West are unitary wholes, and to stereotype them as such as misleading. Nevertheless, it remains true to say that fundamental differences in philosophy have had a profound impact upon the development of understanding within the respective cultures, and for the consequent view of man and human nature. Ashe (1977, p. 13) sums up the situation as follows:

There is said far back in the past to have been an Ancient Wisdom . . . In the historical phase most familiar to us, the past few thousand years, we can see both our science and our religions originating as parts of this greater whole. They distil out, so to speak; they develop along their own lines; but the development has loss in it as well as gain, and, in the deepest sense, more of the former. The Ancient Wisdom in its fullness has passed into eclipse. Science and religion have gone astray, giving narrow, distorted, and often false views of the universe.

It is this divergence of science and religion which has profound implications for the development of contemporary psychology.

Chapter 2

PSYCHOLOGY EAST AND WEST

different cultural perspectives on man, nature and knowledge

What does it profit a man if he should gain the whole world but lose his own soul.   Matthew, 16, 26

All knowledge is fundamentally cosmology inasmuch that it is an attempt by man to explain the universe in which he finds himself, and to understand thereby his own existence and nature. In the sense that personality, intellect, will and emotions comprise the human self, essence, or soul, man's attempts to understand himself constitute the study of the soul, or literally (from the Greek, *logos*: study, and *psyche*: soul) psychology. Cosmology is thus intrinsic to psychology. It is not, however, a unitary concept. Cosmologies differ, often radically, with peoples and their cultures. Therefore, one might expect psychology to reflect the world view in which it is embedded, and to differ accordingly. That this is indeed the case is clear from an examination of the psychologies of Eastern and Western culture.

PSYCHOLOGY IN EASTERN CULTURE

Eastern culture and its institutions are traditionally humanistic in the sense that they are centred around the human potential for transcendence or becoming. The contemporary Indian mystic and scholar Rajneesh explains its motif thus:

> This whole life is a challenge to growth. That is true religion and true psychology—because a true religion cannot be other than a true psychology . . . it gives you a great challenge to be more than you are. It gives you a divine discontent. It makes you aflame with a desire to go higher and higher—not higher than others, but higher than yourself.
>
> (Preface to the *Orange Book*, 1983)

11

Rajneesh terms this attitude 'the psychology of the Buddhas' or enlightened ones. Indeed, throughout Eastern culture, religion and psychology are synonymous, both being concerned with exploring human potential. Hence Buddhism, Zen, Taoism and Sufism represent 'the traditional esoteric psychologies' (Ornstein, 1973b, 1975) or 'spiritual psychologies' (Tart, 1975) of the East.

Buddhism

Buddhism originated in the teachings of the Indian master Siddartha Gautama, the so-called Buddha or Enlightened One, during 6–5 BC. The cardinal principles of his philosophy were expounded in the Sarnath Sermon, and held by his followers to be fundamental truths which explain the human condition.

Buddha asserted that the individual lives in process, or continuous motion (*samsara*), and it is thus that life is experienced as change and flux. The impersonal law or force operating within this process and governing growth and development is termed karma, which initially appears to imply a deterministic view of man activated by uncontrollable external forces, and appearing to encourage a futile resignation to life's events. Such a view, according to Patel (1980) is a misrepresentation of karma, for in the teachings of Buddha, the mind of man has a dual aspect. One aspect creates its own bondage by its attachment to, and apparent inability to grow beyond, the mundaneness of things. This seduction by the appearance of things is viewed by Budhha to be a form of ignorance or *avidja*, which is not so much a not-knowing, as a not-seeing of things as they really are, and implies the human tendency to obscure and veil the true nature of the universe.

The other aspect of mind has the potential to transform karma into the pursuit of wisdom and enlightenment, implicit in which is the ability for transcendence which frees the individual from all desires and needs. Therefore, when the mind is turned inwards it is the cause of release and freedom, but when turned outward it is the cause of bondage. This outer aspect of mind is identified with ego—the thinking mind—and all its attachments to power and possessions; whilst the inner aspect is identified with essence or authentic being. The ego is characterized as a monkey that plays tricks on man by creating illusion. For the individual, freedom from the endless cycle of meaningless existence, which is traditionally symbolized as a wheel or *chakra*, lies in looking inward to one's centre. This self-awareness, or self-perception is literally therefore, insight, and emphasis is placed upon its development through meditation and the abandonment of ego, for in Buddhism the perfect man has no ego, or self, but fuses with the Ultimate Oneness, ground or unity of the universe, which is indivisible, formless and timeless.

Buddhism is present-centred, focussing on the here-and-now rather than the past or future, both of which are deemed to be illusory; and concerned essentially with the centreing process. Emphasis is upon the ability to grasp the immediacy of the present moment as it is experienced; upon direct experience rather than rational or intellectual understanding.

One of Buddha's most penetrating insights was his understanding of the role of sorrow, suffering or *dukka* in human experience. This concept is intimately linked with that of impermanence, or *anicca*, which is consequent upon living in process. Buddha recognized that sorrow is experienced because of the impermanence of things, or change, and that man suffers through his awareness of bodily, mental and emotional change and its consequences — illness, ageing, decay, disease, death and loss; changing relationships to persons and things, and separation. Buddha also recognized that the human hunger for security, permanence, and fulfilment of wishes — implying as they do, resistance to change — are also a manifestation of our suffering; as is clinging to the world of the ego, and our deep-seated fear of losing our identity or sense of self. Change, in creating instability and uncertainty, produces anxiety and fear, and it is only tolerated as long as it does not compromise identity. However, irrespective of man's intolerance of it, change is an ever-present condition of human life. Existence itself is the cause of all human sorrow, and not what man wants it to be. He therefore defends himself against change by clinging to the familiar and the habitual, which gives rise to a false sense of security, and a frail sense of identity.

Buddha saw possibility for transformation through acceptance of change, which requires attention to, and direct confrontation with those anxieties it generates. This is achieved primarily by meditation, of which there are many different forms, but which all have in common full concentration on the individual's subjectivity and the attempt to uncover its working.

Moreover, Buddha emphasized a mode of conduct for the relief of man's suffering; a Middle Way, avoiding extremes; a balance or moderation in all things, which he termed *majhim nikaya*, and which Confucius called the Golden Mean. Buddha taught that extremes are dangerous; that a wise man balances, and knows that life balances itself. This subtle balance is the meeting of extremes, tranquility, or *samyaktva*. Rajneesh (1978) explains:

> That subtle balance is the highest peace possible, the peak, the climax, the crescendo, because when two things balance — outer and inner, activity and passivity — suddenly you transcend them both. When they both balance you are no more this, no more that. Suddenly you are a third force.
>
> pp. 47–48

His advice is, therefore;

> Transcend extremes! Don't be a worldly man and don't be a so-called spiritual man. Don't be a theist, don't be an atheist. Don't be mad for outer wealth and don't be obsessed with inner tranquility. Balance — balance should be the motto . . . And this is the result: those who choose extremes fail in both, because if you go on being active and active and active, and no passivity is allowed, from where are you going to revitalize yourself? You will become

an empty shell—impotent, powerless, poor . . . If you choose one extreme, you will fail in both . . . Just be in the middle. This is the greatest skill and art—to be just in the middle; not choosing, not moving left, not moving right . . . if you are exactly in the middle you transcend the world.   (p. 48)

This notion of balance is also central to Taoism.

Taoism

Taoism is thought to have originated in early Chinese magical practices. However, in a formal sense it was expounded in the doctrines of Lao Tzu in about 600 BC, and later expanded by Chuang Tsu. Other than the *Tao Te Ching*, or *Book of Changes*, of Lao Tzu, which comprises only 5000 words, there are no other authentic texts; the book of Chuang Tsu being believed to be an expanded form of the original writings of Lao Tzu. These 'inner chapters' of the Tao Te Ching, together with the additional chapters by Chuang Tsu form the basis of classical Taoism.

As in Bhuddism, Taoism commences with an awareness that man's immediate experience of the world is characterized by continuous change or movement. Taoism asserts, however, that as the flux of the universe is experienced one becomes aware also of a certain immutability, constancy or fixity; a pattern of change which is non-random and has a particular kind of structural continuity. This pattern is represented as the interplay between the two great principles of the universe—Yang, the principle of movement, creativity and energy; and Yin, the principle of stasis, receptivity and rest. Thus, although in terms of its content man's experience of the world is ever-changing, the form of that change is constant. Tao, which is symbolized as a partially occluded circle, (see figure 1 below) represents this constancy. It is the Ultimate Unity, or background, against which the two opposite but complementary Yin-Yang forces are reconciled, and as such it gives coherence, continuity and unity to all things.

Figure 1.

According to Taoist thinking, within any situation a particular balance may be discerned between the Yin and Yang forces which comprise this unity. The balance in nature is deemed to be correct, but in human affairs it is influenced by individual choice and by the human will. The person is therefore the mediator between the two great powers, the centre of his own universe, and is seen as needing to maintain a balance between its forces, physically, mentally and emotionally.

Taoism, like Buddhism, adopts a cosmological rather than a theological perspective, seeing the person as infused with all the powers of the universe. Necessarily, therefore, man must look inward for wisdom, rather than to some external power. Similarly, the human quest in Taoism is to find and maintain one's centre. Its aim is that of balanced man. The more off-centre, or unbalanced the individual is the more dangerous his predicament becomes, as at the extremes the opposing forces become antagonistic and destructive. However, complete awareness, wakefulness or mindfulness—a mental and spiritual state of immediacy—transcends and dissolves all extremes, and provides liberation from the bondage of the illusory world. For Chuang Tsu teaches that:

> At the still point at the centre of the circle, one can see the infinite in all things.

Zen Buddhism

Buddhism reached China in, or some time before, the first century AD, and in time passed from China via Korea to Japan where it flourished in several different forms under the name of Zen, a Japanese term which is derived from a word meaning 'meditation' or 'contemplation'. As Wilson-Ross (1973) observes, Zen is a unique blend of Indian mysticism and Chinese naturalism sieved through the rather special net of Japanese character. It is based on specific exhortations of the Buddha—most notably 'Look within—thou art the Buddha' (cf. with Christian teaching); the notion that godhead resides within the individual.

The aim of Zen is enlightenment (*satori*), or awareness of an Ultimate Reality which is beyond words and reasoning. Zen denies that understanding of the universe can be achieved by conceptual thought, or ever fully communicated, but can best be accessed and expressed through wordless activities such as archery, flower arrangement and the preparation of tea. Wisdom is therefore derived from intuitive insight, which may be achieved by close attention to the performance of these mundane activities, or through *zazen*, or seated meditation, which is directed to riddles or *koans* which defy reason. It is in this respect that Zen is similar to Sufism, the mystic tradition of Islam.

Sufism

Sufi, or Sufism, is the tradition of mysticism practised by Moslems throughout the Middle East, and so called because of the woollen robe or 'suf' traditionally worn by ascetics. The aim of Sufism is to lead the individual to wisdom; to open their eyes to the unity and oneness of all things. Once again emphasis is upon experiential understanding of existence rather than intellectual or rational analysis.

There is no dogma in Sufism, its contents being solely individual experience, and its methods are variable, although basically meditation on tales or parables, some of which have been popularized in the West by Idries Shah (1973, 1975). Poetry is also used as a means of contemplation. The greatest of the Sufi poets, according to Scharfstein (1973), was the thirteenth century sage Jalal al-Din Rumi, who is believed to have taught his followers the ecstatic circular dance from which they gained the reputation of 'whirling dervishes'. This dance is itself a form of dynamic meditation, and one of the most forceful, in which the dancer 'loses' himself or herself, thereby communing with the unity of all things. This mystical vision of unity is clearly evident in Rumi's work:

> I have put duality away, I have seen that the two worlds are one; One I seek,
> One I know, One I see, One I call.   (quoted in Scharfstein, 1973, p. 8)

COMMON THEMES IN ORIENTAL PSYCHOLOGICAL TRADITIONS

All these traditions of the East can be seen to share common emphases on present-centredness, experience, direct apprehension of reality, subjectivity, enhanced consciousness, insight, choice, will, actualization of personal power and the development of a whole and balanced person.

A basic aim of all approaches is the attainment of centredness, or groundedness. This spiritual quest is likened by Cooper (1981) to the desire to return to the womb, or the quest for the Holy Grail, inasmuch as it is essentially a striving for oneself, which necessitates going a long way to find a place one has never left, or looking outside for what is within one.

In Buddhism this idea is conveyed by the notion of mundane life as a wheel, the object of which is to return to its hub or centre. In Sufism the same idea is expressed in the tale of Nasrudin who was searching for his housekey on the road outside his house, despite his having mislaid it indoors, in the belief that it afforded more light.

In Chinese mythology one finds this notion conveyed thus:

> A dunce once searched for fire with a lighted lantern. Had he known what
> fire was he could have cooked his rice much sooner.

The goal of each tradition is enlightenment, which is synonymous with the perception of Ultimate Truth or Reality. The spiritual quest is from darkness to light, from blindness to sight; and in each the master or spiritual teacher is seen as an enlightened guide or 'guru' (*guru* being a Hindi term which literally means 'from darkness to light').

There is also a common emphasis on meditation, which takes many different forms, all of which focus on uncovering the mind, going beyond thought, enabling true knowing, true seeing, which is enlightenment.

PSYCHOLOGY IN WESTERN CULTURE

Enlightenment has a somewhat different meaning in Western culture, it being the name given to an eighteenth century philosophical movement which stressed the importance of reason, and in which the psychological tradition established in Classical Greece reached its peak, only to decline rapidly thereafter.

As Fromm (1951) has pointed out, the philosophers of the Enlightenment, who were also students of the soul, spoke, not in the name of any revelation or mystical insight but with the authority of reason, about man's happiness and the unfolding of his soul. They asserted that happiness could be realized only when man achieved inner freedom, and urged man to abolish those conditions of existence which required the maintenance of illusions and ignorance, and to affirm his independence from political shackles.

However, within a very short period of time, the tradition in which psychology was the study of the soul was abandoned, and 'reason as the means of discovering the truth and penetrating the surface to the essence of phenomena . . . relinquished for intellect as a mere instrument to manipulate things and men' (Fromm, 1951, p. 13). This change had a profound impact on the development of psychology in the West, and in order to understand the nature of that change it is necessary to examine the development of psychology within the context of Western thinking about man and the cosmos throughout history.

Orthodox scholasticism

From the time of the Ancient Greeks until the Middle Ages science, or knowledge, was synonymous with philosophy, the aim of which was understanding the meaning and purpose of natural phenomena, and especially man, who was seen as the most significant subject matter of enquiry. The main focus of study was consciousness, or mental life, the various manifestations of which were viewed as emanations of the human soul, psyche or essence. Psychology was the study of the soul and its development, and as such was closely linked with religion.

Both were rooted in a cosmology on the authority of the Church, which viewed man as the centre of God's creation, earth as the centre of the heavens, and everything with a purpose relating to man. Aristotle based his systematization of the natural order on this cosmology, and in the thirteenth century the Jesuit scholar Thomas Aquinas combined it with Christian theology and ethics, thereby establishing the scientific framework that was to remain unaltered, and largely unquestioned, until the Middle Ages. The psychological tradition established in antiquity continued during the Renaissance, as is evident from the title of the first book to employ the term psychology, Rudolf Goekel's *Psychologia: Hoc est de perfectione Hominis*, printed in 1590, the sub-title of which means 'such is the perfection of man'.

This orthodox scholasticism was brought into question during the sixteenth century when Copernicus (1473–1543) challenged the biblical notion of the earth as the centre of the universe by suggesting that the planets circled the sun. This removed the earth from its geometrical pre-eminence and consequently made it difficult to attribute to man the cosmic significance assigned to him in Christian theology.

Copernican theory was subsequently confirmed by Kepler (1571–1630) who discovered the laws of planetary motion and in so doing created a new astronomy which challenged even further the validity of the old cosmology. It was left to Galileo (1564–1642) to finally discredit the orthodox world view by demonstrating that the earth itself revolves around the sun. His discovery, which displaced man and the world as the centre of God's creation, brought Galileo into direct opposition with the Church, and he was subsequently forced by the Inquisition to recant his support of the Copernican system. His legacy to Western science was twofold; an emphasis on empirical method, and the mathematical description of nature, both of which remained essential features of subsequent scientific enquiry.

Up until that time the aim of science was wisdom—understanding the natural order and living by it. Francis Bacon (1521–1626) altered the whole concept of science by emphasizing the notion that knowledge is power. His philosophy was directed towards man gaining mastery over the forces of nature by means of scientific discovery. Capra (1983) suggests that his emphasis on the exploitation of nature and its resources sanctioned the scientific 'rape of the earth' which has since come to characterize Western science and civilization. This concern with human power was essentially anti-theological. Indeed, Bacon insisted that philosophy and science should be kept separate from theology and not blended with it as in scholasticism. Bacon thus brought science into direct conflict with religion, and thereafter they began to move ever farther apart.

Materialism

Descartes (1596–1650) advanced the views of Galileo and Bacon still further. He based his view of the universe on a fundamental separation of nature into two discrete realms, that of the mind (*res cogitans*), and matter (*res extensa*). This division allowed scientists to treat matter as inert and completely distinct from themselves, which meant that the world could be described objectively without reference to the human observer. Objectivity subsequently became the ideal of science.

For Descartes the material world was comprised of objects assembled like a huge machine and operated by mechanical laws that could be explained in terms of the arrangements and movements of its parts. His outlook was mechanistic, materialist, and inasmuch that complex wholes were deemed to be understandable in terms of their constituent parts, analytic and reductionist. In his attempt to build a complete cosmology or natural science he extended this mechanistic view of matter to living organisms, comparing animals to clocks composed of wheels and springs, and he later extended this analogy to man.

To Descartes the human body was a machine, part of a perfect cosmic machine, governed, in principle at least, by mathematical laws. Yet, whilst fully mechanistic in his physiology, Descartes did not identify the mind with matter, and considered that the study of mind could only be approached by introspective scrutiny of the contents of consciousness; through looking inwards. Notwithstanding, his method of enquiry into the nature of the universe was based on profound scepticism as to the reliability of the senses. All knowledge had to be certain and evident, and he therefore rejected all knowledge other than that about which there could be doubt; a sceptical attitude which all scientific disciplines thereafter retained.

Newton (1643-1727) subsequently formulated the mathematical laws or mechanics which were thought to account for all the changes observable in the physical world. These laws lent support to the Cartesian notion of a mechanistic universe composed of particles of matter existing in space and time and impelled by force into motion or change of motion, created as such by God and set in motion at the beginning of time.

The acceptance of this mechanistic world view coincided with the rise of a factory civilisation in the Western world and the mechanical model of the universe subsequently guided all scientific endeavour for the next two hundred years. Its effect was to profoundly alter man's view of the universe and of himself.

Man had been displaced from the centre of the cosmos and was no longer considered to be the main focus of theoretical enquiry. As Russell (1948, p. 559) suggests this 'should have been humbling to human pride, but in fact the contrary effect was produced, for the triumphs of science revived human pride'. Moreover, science was not only anti-religious in contributing to, and encouraging man's greatest sin, but it was also anti-theological, for in elevating man it reduced the status of God.

Indeed, the existence of God was brought into question as it became increasingly doubtful as to whether the universe had any beginning in time. Science therefore made it increasingly difficult to believe in a Creator. Gradually the divine disappeared from the scientific world view, and by the nineteenth century Nietzsche could indeed declare that 'God is dead' in the sense that traditional meanings and values had been negated. Science had become the ultimate authority within Western culture.

Positivism

The secularization of science and philosophy had profound implications for the Western perspective on man. By the nineteenth century, thinking was essentially analytic, reductionist, objective, and positivistic in the sense that it was held that the only valid knowledge is scientific knowledge or positive fact which is objectively verifiable. Under the influence of positivism attempts were made to elevate psychology to the status of an objective natural science, and in order for this to be accomplished it was deemed necessary for it to adopt the methods and principles of physics, which in the tradition of Cartesian-Newtonian science, was the standard for scientific rigour and objectivity, and the branch of science concerned with the properties of matter. This demanded a radical change in both the subject matter and the methods of psychology, which throughout its history had been predominantly concerned with the exploration of non-material consciousness by way of subjective introspection.

The scientific research tradition is, however, empirical rather than theoretical, and defined by a method which emphasizes the rejection of all but objective or positive fact. Its basic premise is the belief in 'objective consciousness'; the notion that the only way to gain access to reality is by the cultivation of a state of consciousness cleansed of all subjective distortion and all personal involvement, and that what emerges from this state of consciousness qualifies as valid knowledge or 'fact'.

Unfortunately, as Laing (1983, p. 9) observes, 'No experiences, ordinary, everyday, usual or unusual, whether impressions, ideas, dreams, visions, memories, strange, bizarre, familiar, weird, psychotic or sane, are objective facts.' Thus, by adopting the scientific method and the total objectivity it implies, psychology precluded from the realm of its investigations human experience, senses, feelings, soul and consciousness, and in so doing alienated man from his experience, himself and his existence. Ornstein (1975) suggests that in the process of refining its methods psychology discarded its essence–consciousness—in much the same way that the essence of wheat is discarded in its refinement, and for the same basic reasons; convenience and expediency.

Except for the work of William James, Sigmund Freud, Carl Jung and a few others which retained concern with consciousness, psychology became the scientific analysis of behaviour. Man became, thereby, the aggregate of all his responses to situations, and little else.

By the early twentieth century, textbooks on psychology had lost virtually all reference to consciousness, emotions, and will. Indeed, psychology, in

> trying to imitate the natural sciences and laboratory methods of weighing and counting, dealt with everything except the soul. It tried to understand those aspects of man which can be examined in the laboratory, and claimed that conscience, value judgements, and knowledge of good and evil are

metaphysical concepts, outside the problems of psychology; it was often more concerned with insignificant problems which fitted the alleged scientific method than with devising new methods to study the significant problems of man. Psychology thus became a science lacking its main subject matter, the soul. (Fromm, 1951, pp. 13-14).

Bereft of its soul or psyche, psychology became an empty or hollow discipline; study for its own sake.

It can be seen therefore, that Western psychology, inasmuch as it is no longer faithful to its original subject matter, the soul, is in Rajneesh's terms not true psychology at all, whilst many Western psychologists would deny that the esoteric spiritual traditions of the East constitute psychology in anything other than the loosest sense. The point at issue here is, of course, considerably more than mere etymological dispute. It is a question of what constitutes the proper subject matter of psychology, and as such it reflects the different traditions of thought — indeed the very 'soul' — of those cultures in which it is embedded.

In the East, where psychology is rooted in the tradition of mysticism, emphasis is upon the spiritual, the subjective, and the individual, and its dominant ethos is necessarily humanistic, whereas in the West psychology is rooted in the tradition of science and its emphasis is upon the material, the objective and the general, and its predominant ethos is accordingly mechanistic and impersonal.

The fundamental difference between them, however, is that of perspective; psychology East and West representing respectively the polar extremes of mystical *insight* and scientific *outlook*. This dichotomy can be seen to correspond with the two aspects of mind as conceived in Indian thought; the inward looking aspect of which is directed towards the essential nature of man, and the outward looking aspect directed towards the world of things and external appearances. In the traditions of the Orient both aspects are viewed as complementary facets of one whole or unity, and virtue and harmony are deemed not to consist in an accentuation of one aspect to the detriment of the other, but in maintaining a dynamic balance between them. Nevertheless, it is the human tendency to divide and separate, rather than to see things in the round, and as Ornstein (1976) points out, this yields a condition like hemianopia, or blindness to half of the visual field. In the pursuit of understanding innermost being the cultures of the East, most notably India, have tended to ignore the material world, developing their spiritual, poetic, artistic and mystical traditions and cultivating thereby an attitude to life quite alien to Western eyes. For in the West, with its reverence for the intellect and rationality, and the outward appearances of things, the inner man is neglected as science and technology progress apace. Thus, as Ornstein suggests (1976, p. 31), whilst in the West we have developed one half of our ability and organized external reality to an unparalleled extent, we remain nonetheless 'blind', or at least hemianopic, to the other; an oversight which may prove to be particularly significant in the light of the Eastern injunction against single-minded attachment to the world of appearances which is held to lead to illusion, human bondage and folly.

Indeed, at the peak of scientific ascendency in the middle of the twenthieth century, there was increasing evidence of a dawning awareness in Western consciousness that scientific progress might not be commensurate with all that is wise or desirable, and that the attempt to understand the world whilst precluding any attempt to understand human nature might be the ultimate in folly.

Chapter 3

PSYCHOLOGY, POLITICS AND PROTEST

twentieth century opposition to science and technology

He who breaks a thing to find out what it is has left the path of wisdom.   J. R. R. Tolkein[2]

The historian Theodore Roszak (1970) indicates that prior to the mid-twentieth century, science had generally been viewed as an unquestionable social good, being associated in the popular mind with progress, the promise of affluence, longevity and health. It was not anticipated, therefore, that science might generate its own characteristic problems, nor that as a result of its processes man might find his existence more precarious and meaningless. Yet, Roszak argues, the reductionist outlook of science has produced an even greater sense of meaninglessness in life. He contends that the progress of scientific expertise is 'a bewilderingly perverse effort to demonstrate that nothing, absolutely nothing, is particularly special, unique or marvellous, but can be lowered to the status of mechanized routine. More and more the spirit of "nothing but" hovers over advanced scientific research; the effort to degrade, disenchant and level down' (1970, p. 229).

His views are echoed by Ashe (1977, p. 12):

> Thinking people tend to feel that science has cut Man down. It's explained away everything that matters in terms of smaller, meaner things that don't matter. Religion is 'nothing but' wish-fulfilling fairy tales. Love is 'nothing but' body chemistry. Art is 'nothing but' a surge of conditioned reflexes . . .

Ashe argues that science has made everything hollow and pointless, and rather than explaining anything, has explained away man and the cosmos. In addition,

[2]*The Lord of the Rings* 1968. London: Allen & Unwin.

the scientific culture has been recognized as a potentially lethal one, in which people live in dread of technological horrors about which they feel powerless to do anything.

World War Two, which was fought by means of science and technology, generating rapid acceleration of both, together with dramatic social and cultural change, had done much to alert people to the possible undesirable consequences of scientific progress. The possibility of science becoming a tool for world domination was given even greater emphasis by the cold war existing between the major world powers, Russia and the United States of America, and the 'space race', in which Russia nosed ahead of her great rival with the launching of the Sputnik satellite in 1957.

Moreover, the scientific 'rape of the earth' advocated by Bacon several centuries earlier, was occurring on an unprecedented scale, and the exhaustion of natural resources, despoilation of the environment, extinction of plant and animal species, and pollution, all testified to man's growing alienation from other species and the environment. As Maslow (1968) observed, science had come to a kind of literal dead end, and could be seen as a threat or danger to mankind, or at least to its highest and most noble aspirations. He suggested that many people were afraid 'that science besmirches and depresses, that it tears things apart, rather than integrating them, thereby killing rather than creating' (p. viii).

Furthermore, Viktor Frankl, a European psychologist and survivor of Nazi concentration camps was amongst those who insisted that these fears were not without due cause. He asserted his conviction that

> the gas chambers of Auschwitz, Treblinka, and Maidanek were ultimately prepared, not in some ministry or other in Berlin, but rather at the desks and in the lecture halls of nihilistic scientists and philosophers.(1969a, p. xxi).

Moreover, he indicated that psychology, in presenting man as an automaton; a mass of reflexes; a bundle of instincts; a pawn of drives and reactions; as a mere product of instinct, heredity and environment; as a mind-machine, played no little part in augmenting and supporting the mass dehumanization of that era.

THE BLIND EYE OF WESTERN PSYCHOLOGY

Psychology, East or West, like the god Janus, has a dual aspect. It has two perspectives, facing as it does two fundamentally different realities, for psychology is, as Hetherington (1983) observes, what people do and suffer. It is concerned with both the public world of outer behaviour and the inner world of experience, and whilst this awareness is central to the traditional psychologies of the East, psychologists in the West, Richer (1975, p. 342) suggests, have 'failed to comprehend fully this essential dualism in their subject and have not acted accordingly'.

It might be truer to say that psychologists in the West have turned a blind eye on human suffering, for it would seem that they have recognized and comprehended very clearly the bifurcation in the subject matter of psychology since its very beginnings, accepting it throughout history until the late nineteenth century when it became an inconvenience and an embarrassment to a discipline seeking scientific status alongside the natural sciences, which, in addressing solely public phenomena, had no such dilemma. Thereafter, in order to gain acceptance as a science it was seen as necessary to suppress the human face of psychology, thereby extinguishing its essence and, as Heather (1976) suggests, effectively murdering the man it claims to study. Moreover, this was carried out, for the most part, without remorse — as exemplified by Skinner's declaration (1973, p. 196): 'To man qua man we readily say good riddance' — and with a single-mindedness that might be admirable were it not so absurd.

Its absurdity lies in the fact that psychology has, as Wittgenstein (1922, reprinted 1978) observed, method but conceptual confusion. Indeed, its confusion is, in no small measure, a direct outcome of its method — the experimental method, which Richer defines as the method of having a theory first and then trying to find phenomena to fit it. As he points out (1975, p. 344):

> Failing to have an explanation for something is an everyday problem, but failing to have something to explain, yet having an explanation all the same (of what?) is a bizarre state of affairs.

Consequently, psychologists, in striving 'to know absolutely everything about absolutely nothing' (Minogue, 1980), have been accused of converting method into madness (Child, 1973), and much psychology has become the object of derision. Indeed, as Koch (1964, p. 20) has indicated 'When the ludicrousness of the situation is made sufficiently plain perhaps it will be laughed out of existence.' Yet far from being a laughing matter, psychology's folly has potentially alarming and insidious implications.

MAN THE MACHINE

Scientific method is implicitly reductionist. Reduction (from the Latin verb *reductio*) means to take away, and psychology, in reducing the study of man to those of his aspects which are 'objective facts' — his physical behaviours — and precluding any examination of his experience, takes away from man what is essentially and fundamentally his humanness. Man is thereby reduced to a mere thing or object, from which, Heather (1976) suggests, it is but a small step to accepting the idea that man is a machine, and nothing but a machine.

Psychology, in adopting the mechanistic formulations of nineteenth century physical science, did precisely that. Man came to be viewed as functioning like a clock or engine, the workings or mechanisms of which could be elucidated and regulated by psychological science, hence the notion that in identifying these mechanisms or laws of behaviour, psychologists are discovering what makes man 'tick'.

Examination of the dominant orientations within twentieth century Western psychology, namely psychoanalysis and behaviourism, reveals the same basic view of man as a machine activated by forces over which he has little or no control. In psychoanalysis, behaviour is held to result from the workings of the mind, which is reduced to three fundamental components, the ego, id and superego, interactions between which are regulated by innate, biological 'drives' or forces. Whereas in behaviourism man is viewed as a constellation of responses to external stimuli. Such a view 'dispossesses autonomous man and turns the control he has been said to exert over to the environment' (Skinner 1973, p. 200), and in so doing depicts man as a kind of mechanical puppet operated by environmental strings. He is thus denied personal agency or responsibility for his actions, being seen merely as a passive reactor to various circumstances rather than an active determiner of his own behaviour. This notion of man-the-machine is also evident in contemporary orientations such as sociobiology, Dawkins (1976, p. 157) asserting that 'A body is really a machine blindly programmed by its selfish genes.'

Koch (1964) has pointed out that modern psychology projects an image of man as demeaning as it is simplistic. Moreover, in so doing, it elevates its own status, not merely to that of science, but to that of technology, for irrespective of whether man is viewed literally as a machine, or metaphorically as if one, the net result is that man is reduced to something less than human, and the psychologist becomes an engineer.

PSYCHOLOGY AS ENGINEERING

> Wheels must turn steadily, but cannot turn untended. There must be men
> to tend them, men as steady as wheels upon their axles, sane men, obedient
> men, stable in contentment.   (Huxley, 1979, *Brave New World*)

The notion of scientists as engineers, controlling and manipulating a mechanistic universe, was Francis Bacon's legacy to the philosophy of science, and it is implicit in scientific method. Therefore, as Capra (1983) indicates, psychology, in its adoption of scientific method, reflects Western culture's preoccupation with manipulative technology designed for domination and control.

Watson, the founding father of behaviourism, which represents in extreme form the mechanistic view of man, insisted (1913) that the psychologist's interest in human behaviour is not merely the interest of a spectator, but an attempt to control his reactions in much the same way that physical scientists seek to manipulate natural phenomena.

His successor in the behaviourist tradition, B. F. Skinner, also advocated the application of scientific principles to the control of human behaviour—a theme he elaborated upon in his utopian novel *Walden Two* (1948 reprinted 1962). Subsequently, Eysenck addressed even more explicitly the engineering function of psychology, proposing that it should engineer a social consent, a technology of behaviour, which would make people behave in socially acceptable ways and maintain established patterns of social life and its institutions. In effect he was urging that psychology become, in Huxley's terms, a major instrument of social control, and thus a political tool.

Heather (1976) points to numerous ways in which psychology can be seen to engineer social consent and maintain the *status quo* in Western culture, and, in maintaining and legitimizing a positivistic and mechanistic view of man, to serve an ideological function whilst acting under the guise of an objective and value-free science. He argues that it is essential to the maintenance of social stability for people to think of themselves as automata, powerless to control their actions or effect social change, and that this belief is sustained by their alienation from their feelings and personal experience.

Scientific method achieves this by negating the senses, feelings and consciousness. It thereby not only alienates man from his innermost self, but in presenting a view of his fellow man and other creatures as mere things, alienates him from them and makes their exploitation easier and more inevitable. Accordingly, Roszak (1970, p. 232) claims that scientific method *is* alienated life, promoted to its most honourific status.

As a result of its exclusion of the subjective from the subject matter of psychology, behaviourism came to be seen in some quarters as epitomizing the alienation of man, and during the 1950s and 1960s it became increasingly the focus of criticism. One of its most outspoken critics was Koestler (1975) who viewed the exclusion of the subjective as the first ideological purge of such a radical kind in the domain of science, and likened the doctrines of behaviourism to 'a virus that first causes convulsions, then slowly parlayses the victim' (p. 5). Burt (1962, p. 229) took a similarly cynical view of the behaviourist manifesto, claiming that psychology 'having first bargained away its soul and then gone out of its mind, seems, now, as it faces an untimely end, to have lost all consciousness'.

Psychologists were not slow to retaliate to such criticism. Koestler (1975) observed that typically they reacted to this attack upon psychology's dominant school in two ways, either by defending the orthodoxy—asserting it to be correct and the critics wrong—or by agreeing that behaviourism is cracked and flawed, a dead horse which should no longer be flogged. The latter approach has been particularly prevalent in recent years since the emergence of cognitive psychology from beneath the skirts of behaviourism. As Koestler indicates (p. 4):

> This type of criticism is frequently voiced by psychologists who believe that they have outgrown the orthodox doctrines. But this belief is often based

on self-deception, because the crude slot-machine model, in its modernised, more sophisticated versions, has had a profounder influence on them — and on our whole culture — than they realise. It has permeated our attitudes to philosophy, social science, education, psychiatry. Even orthodoxy recognises today the limitations and short-comings of Pavlov's experiments; but in the imagination of the masses, the dog on the laboratory table, predictably salivating at the sound of a gong, has become a paradigm of existence, a kind of Promethean myth; and the word 'conditioning', with its rigid deterministic connotations, has become a key-formula for explaining why we are what we are, and for explaining away moral responsibility. There has never been a dead horse with such a vicious kick.

However, by the late 1950s, and early 1960s in particular, it was clear that certain factions in Western society were beginning to kick back, for at the peak of scientific acceleration, which coincided with the ascendency of behaviourism, confidence in science and its methods began to falter as people became increasingly aware of the personal and social consequences of scientific reductionism.

A SPANNER IN THE WORKS

During the 1950s science was viewed with increasing suspicion, and its objective methods, blind as they are to human experience, were challenged, for as Laing (1983, p. 9) observes, 'Such blind method, applied blindly to us, is liable to destroy us in practice, as it has done already in theory.'

Indeed many, like Roszak (1970), saw the scientific culture as 'fatally and contagiously diseased', the prime symptom of that disease being the constant threat of thermo-nuclear annihilation: 'an evil which is not defined by the sheer fact of the bomb, but by the total ethos of the bomb' (p. 47). This concern prompted the Campaign for Nuclear Disarmament, the express aim of which was to 'ban the bomb' and prevent escalation of the arms race.

The very attempt, however, brought with it yet another awareness, which was, that scientific progress, once achieved, is irreversible and virtually impossible to arrest. Science came to be viewed increasingly as contributing to human problems rather than providing any solutions to them, and the integrity of scientists was brought into question by their apparent disregard for the potentially undesirable effects of scientific advancement on man and the environment. During the late 1950s and throughout the following decade, a variety of issues became vehicles for protest. These included nuclear power, nuclear weapons, uranium mining, pollution, conservation, and human and animal rights. The main thrust of opposition, was, however, against the arms race and war.

Protest was nowhere more vocal than among young people, particularly students in American colleges and universities, many of whom faced draft into the armed forces engaged in fighting the bitter and futile war in Vietnam. Frankl (1969a) suggests that these students were experiencing a sense of emptiness and meaninglessness, a distaste for the way in which scientific findings were presented to them, and the mechanistic and reductionist view of man which they implied.

These feelings were no doubt heightened by the disinclination of many to become dispensable cogs in the American war machine. Yet although protesting under the banner of peace, and urging their elders 'to make love not war', Roszak (1970) suggests that the struggle of the young was not primarily against war *per se*. He argues that their paramount struggle was against the dehumanizing and alienating values of science, and the technocracy; that system, more highly developed in America than in any other society, in which government rests upon technical expertise and scientific forms of knowledge. Thus it was that the unobtrusive but all-pervading ethics of reason, intellect and control were opposed with passion, feeling and freedom, as the young urged their peers and elders alike to 'drop out' of this lethal culture, to reject its hard-headed conformity and 'do their own thing'; to 'lose their heads and come to their senses', and to turn away from science and back to Nature, thereby earning the 'Flower Power' label with which the media dubbed the movement.

Nevertheless, despite much trivialization and distortion by the media, the movement was undisputably forceful, and not confined merely to students in America. Throughout Western culture, and particularly in continental Europe where the writings of Sartre, De Beauvoir and Camus, which emphasized the values of human freedom, choice and responsibility, were influential, students campaigned for a free, non-repressive society, and for peace.

These aims, frequently represented by the media as advocacy of anarchy, irresponsibility and promiscuity, were sadly and ironically thwarted as protest led to confrontation with civil and military authorities, resulting in widespread violence on university campuses, and culminating in the deaths of several students. As Roszak observes, the scale of the movement and the depth of the antagonism it revealed more than justified its being termed a 'counter culture'. Indeed, the rejection of science and scientific culture by the young represented perhaps the most significant and widespread social and intellectual revolution in Western culture since the seventeenth century, for as Tart (1975, p. 11) observes, 'When a tool as useful as science is rejected by a large proportion of the most intelligent young people, we have a major cultural crisis.'

He suggests, however, that whilst the causes of this rejection of science are, as with any major social movement, complex and varied, the basic cause of the radical disaffiliation of youth from mainstream Western society during the 1960s and 1970s was the widespread use of drugs and psychedelics, and the fact that the spiritual experiences and altered states of consciousness associated with drug use were almost totally rejected by orthodox science.

This was of particular significance because according to Gallup Poll statistics cited by Tart, in 1971 half the student population in America had experimented with marijuana and many of them used it frequently. Similarly, the use of hallucinogens such as Lysergic Acid (LSD25) was widespread. Finding that science had no place for either spiritual experience or altered states of consciousness, many of the young turned their attention to religious and mystical traditions that did, and which as Drury (1979) observes, are clearly reflected in the popular music of the period, in which spiritual, mystical and visionary themes abound.

The counter culture represented not only a defection from the three hundred year old 'cult of the fact'—as Hudson (1972) has termed Western culture's obsession with reason, rationality, intellect and physicality—but also a return to the visionary, mystical and spiritual sources of antiquity, and a renewed interest in the occult, supernatural, magical and esoteric. It was, according to Drury, essentially spiritual in nature, despite its trivialization by the media. Indeed, even the media came to recognize it as such. The prestigious American magazine *Newsweek* ran a cover feature during 1976 in which it was claimed that the cultural revolution sweeping the country was 'a religion without a creed' which constituted a major transformation of general consciousness in Western society.

For the best part of a decade Western society was under the sway of this youthful, spirited and 'spiritual' influence, or 'consciousness movement', which was as exciting to some onlookers as it was disturbing to others. Nevertheless, as Roszak indicates, whilst the disaffected young have rocked their societies, without the support of adult forces they could not overturn the established order, and for the most part this support was not forthcoming. On the contrary, the adult social forces represented 'the lead-bottomed ballast of the *status quo*' (1970, p. 3). Much of the counter culture, especially the widespread use of drugs and the threat posed to science and the technocracy, was viewed with undisguised alarm by the older generation, particularly as the philosophical underpinnings of the alternative society became increasingly infused into mainstream culture. The principles of the counter culture were perceived by some as tantamount to heresy. As Tart (1975, p. 117) suggests:

> Because of the astounding success of physical science, and human attachment to what is successful, we have had a psychological overinvestment in the physical world view, such that for many people it has become a religion. Like most religions, it defames it rivals.

This is clearly evident in an editorial by P. H. Abelson which appeared in *Science* during the mid 1970s, and is quoted in its entirety by Story (1976, pp. 15-16):

> During the past few years elements of the public and particularly university students have turned increasingly to mysticism and what I would call pseudoscience . . . It is not pleasant to contemplate a situation in which our future leaders are being steeped in fantasy and exposed to a putdown of science without effective response. The university community has a special obligation which it has not been meeting very well. It should move toward providing antidotes to the new intellectual poisons. In meeting these challenges to

rationality, we should remember that although humanity is eager to accept mysticism, it is also capable of yearning for truth.

However, it is perhaps true to say that during the 1960s a certain humility also emerged in scientific circles, as it became recognized that the increasing concern with mysticism represented an expression of yearning, and both dissatisfaction and disillusionment with scientific 'truth'. Disappointed with the limited knowledge of the universe revealed by science, man increasingly turned toward himself. Thus what was witnessed during the 1960s and 1970s was a return to 'the problem of man'.

FROM MAN THE ROBOT TO MAN THE PILOT

The counter culture may be seen as an attempt to regain a lost perspective within Western culture, that of human experience. It prompted a return to fundamental concerns such as the nature of mind and consciousness, which had largely been ruled out of the realm of enquiry by the dominant paradigm of twentieth century science, and demanded a conceptual transition 'from the mechanics of behaviour—man the robot—to the properly human aspects of man the pilot' (Naranjo, 1974, p. 14). As Rogers (1964) indicated, psychology has room for such a philosophy of man. Indeed, during the 1960s and 1970s several trends were discernible within psychology which shared the common aim of restoring man and human consciousness to the central focus of psychological concern. These trends were notable because in their attempts to reinstate consciousness they drew upon the experience of students of consciousness, not only those within the tradition of psychology, such as William James (1892; 1902) and Carl Jung (1946), but also those outside psychology, mainstream society, and even Western culture. However, in order to fully appreciate the nature of these trends and their implications for psychology it is necesssary to view them against the background of developments within Western culture since 1960.

Chapter 4

CULTS AND COUNTER CULTURE

radicalism during the 1960s

*In a world of fugitives the person taking the opposite direction will
appear to run away.* T. S. Eliot[3]

The counter culture of the 1960s and 1970s was not merely a protest against
science and the technocracy but also an active search for new meanings and
answers. A growing number of people had come to view traditional forms of
authority within Western culture as obsolete. Consequently, traditional religion,
education and standards of morality were left behind, 'as a snake leaves behind
its old skin, unchanged and still beautiful perhaps, but too tight and therefore
not functional' (Naranjo, 1974, p. 4).

However, this questioning of traditional answers and departure from traditional
sources of authority created a vacuum, an emptiness and a meaninglessness, and
gave rise to a groping for orientation. Naranjo suggests that such a situation
typically leads to two different, albeit compatible reactions: an openness to
unfamiliar answers, such as those provided by other cultures; or experimentation
and the development of new possibilities. Certainly, both of these reactions were
clearly discernible in the wake of the iconoclasm of the 1960s.

OPENNESS TO UNFAMILIAR ANSWERS

G. K. Chesterton once observed that when men cease to believe in God they
then believe, not in nothing, but in anything. This grasping at straws was at
no time more evident than during the 1970s when intense interest developed
throughout the Western world in the books of Erich von Daniken (1969, 1970,
1973, 1974, 1975), which became international best-sellers.

[3] *The Family Reunion* 1939. London: Faber and Faber.

Sagan (1976) argues that the world-wide craze for von Daniken's writings represents a sober commentary on the credulousness and despair of the times, for it is von Daniken's thesis that the earth had at one time been visited by all-knowing and benign powers from outer space, which had established human culture as we know it, and will return at some time in the future to save us from ourselves.

Sagan suggests that in times when the immediate relevance of traditional religions to contemporary problems is no longer obvious, von Daniken's thesis represents, not merely a pseudo-science, but a pop religion. Indeed, following the iconoclasm of the 1960s, when all the 'gods' of religion, science and morality were torn down, the Western world and most notably North America, witnessed in the counter culture and its aftermath, a new eclectic religious revival, most, but by no means all of which, was rather more down to earth than the 'space gods' doctrine of von Daniken.

The shift away from traditional Western explanations was reflected in a growing fascination with alternative and unfamiliar views of the human predicament, not only those of other cultures, but also those of earlier epochs. Ancient texts, such as the *Bhagavad Gita*, were translated into English (Prabhupado, 1968), and astonishingly the *Bardo Thodol*, or *Tibetan Book of the Dead* (Evans-Wentz, 1976), and the *I Ching* (R. Wilhelm, 1978) became best-sellers in the United States.

The dramatic upsurge of interest in spiritual traditions of the East led to the names of Eastern writers such as T. Suzuki, Idries Shah, Gurdjieff, Bhagwan Shree Rajneesh, Swami Nikhilananda, and Krishnamurti becoming familiar in the West as their books, and books about them, found their way on to more and more bookshelves, as did those of Western interpreters of Eastern traditions such as Lama Govinda, Mircea Eliade, Alan Watts, Ram Dass, Christmas Humphreys, Karlfried Durckheim and Christopher Isherwood. In addition, the practice of these alternative disciplines flourished as more and more people explored Buddhism, Zen, Sufi, Yoga and various forms of meditation. According to a Gallup Poll (published in *Newsweek* magazine, 6th September 1976) by the mid 1970s no less than five million Americans practised yoga and six million meditated regularly, whilst two million were deeply involved in oriental religions.

Oriental philosophy goes West

Oriental philosophy had been brought to the attention of Americans in the writings of Theosophists such as Helena Blavatsky in the early twentieth century, and subsequently Zen Buddhism was popularized in the novels and poems of the so-called 'beat generation' of writers such as Jack Kerouac and Allen Ginsberg during the 1950s.

Zen was further promoted during the 1960s by Watts and Suzuki. However, much of the Zen literature which subsequently emerged, such as Pirsig's best-selling *Zen and the Art of Motorcycle Maintenance* (1974) can be thought of as 'pop' Zen, as such a distortion of the fundamental philosophy. Nevertheless, Roszak (1970) claims that even if this form of Zen was flawed by crude simplifications and vulgarized by the young, as formulated by writers such as Watts and Suzuki it embraced a radical critique of the conventional scientific conception of man and nature. Accordingly the young seized upon it, and what began with Zen subsequently proliferated rapidly into 'a phantasmagoria of exotic religiosity' (pp. 138-139).

EXPERIMENTATION AND THE DEVELOPMENT OF NEW POSSIBILITIES

The psychedelic revolution

The writings of Aldous Huxley, most notably *The Doors of Perception* (1954), were particularly influential in stimulating interest in the exotic and mystical during this period. Huxley was a student of Mayahana Buddhism but he also advocated the use of psychotrophic drugs as a means of enhancing consciousness. For Huxley, mescaline and LSD prepared for an expansion of consciousness more effectively than fasting and other rituals, and he advocated their use in the systematic exploration of consciousness or 'inner space'.

It was this advocacy of drug use that alienated Huxley from the orthodox Buddhist movement, as is clear from the correspondence after his death between Sir Julian Huxley and Swami Ranganathananda (published in 1971). Buddhists remain steadfast in their belief that meditation is the only path to transcendence, denying that the drug-induced experience is other than an aspect or *maya*, or illusion, and therefore self-indulgence rather than mysticism. They assert that the heightened sense of reality produced by psychotrophic drugs has little to do with any significant revelation of truth:

> In some rare cases, such experiences may land one on the shores of true religion and become a fortunate escape from the cheap escape from civilisation. But, by themselves, they are just psychic ones; not spiritual . . . The stimulus of spirituality is received from within, not from without. This is always a slow process, but sure and steady. This is the science of religion . . . , the other is the magic of pseudo-religion. A magic fruit cannot quench the physical hunger and thirst of man but a real fruit can. Similarly, a magic pseudo-religion cannot quench the spiritual hunger and thirst of modern man; but the science of religion can.   (Ranganathananda, 1971, pp. 38-39)

The use of drugs for altering consciousness was by no means a new phenomenon. Mescaline, peyote, cannabis, opium and numerous other substances have long been employed in the mystical and magical practices of many cultures, including those of the West (see: Aleister Crowley's *Diary of a Drug Fiend*, 1922).

Huxley's writings, however, stimulated widespread interest in drugs as a means of exploring consciousness, and his status lent legitimacy to experimentation with these substances on an unprecedented scale.

Timothy Leary, a Harvard psychologist, influenced by both Buddhism and Huxley and other esoteric sources such as the *Tibetan Book of the Dead*, began to conduct research into consciousness during the 1960s using the psychotrophic drug LSD25. However, Leary's psychedelic experiments were destined to become rather more than a form of exotic psychological research. They became instead a fundamental ingredient of the cultural revolution. Indeed, Leary was to emerge as the leading prophet of the counter culture, insisting that drugs were the new religion; 'dope' the only hope for mankind, and urging the young to opt out of conventional society and 'turn on' to the spiritual through drug use.

In his messianic *Politics of Ecstasy* (1970) he paid homage to Huxley and mapped out the ground plan of a psychedelic revolution by proposing a third amendment to the American Revolution—the 'Fifth Freedom', or 'right to get high'—thereby taking the notion of man the pilot to its logical conclusion, helped in no little way by the dramatic developments in the U.S. space programme.

Subsequently, there was a shift from von Daniken's notion of God the astronaut, to that of man the astronaut, as the exploration of inner space was paralleled with that of outer space, notably in Stanley Kubrick's film version of Arthur C. Clarke's *2001: A Space Odyssey*, which gained a cultic following, particularly among young drug users. Indeed the psychedelic revolution and the phenomenal popularity of Eastern religious traditions set the stage within American society, and to a lesser degree in other Western societies, for the proliferation of various esoteric cults, some of which were extreme.

Cults of unreason

As Roszak observes, the antidote to Western society's mad rationality seemed to lie in an assortment of mad passions. These included the Hare Krishna Foundation, The Children of God, The Unification Church of Sun Myung Moon, Scientology, The Divine Light Mission of Maharaj Ji, Transcendental Meditation and the Orange Movement.

Arising as they did in the wake of a reaction against the values of scientific culture, they focussed attention on the non-intellectual, spiritual aspects of man, and were thus termed by Evans (1974) 'cults of unreason'. Opposition to these cults has been widespread and voracious, especially among psychologists.

Llewelyn and Fielding (1984) indicate that popular treatment of some of these cults is unjustified. They suggest that rejection of the cults is not based on a rational analysis of any objective characteristic of the cult process: recruitment, content or consequences; but is based on their common opposition to convention. They suggest that a 'clue to this is given precisely by the fact that no distinction is made between the cults, i.e. it is precisely what they have in common that is the basis of this judgement. And what they have in common is an opposition to the *status quo*. Hence reaction to the cults can best be understood, not in terms of judgements of "psychological well-being" but in terms of social processes of competition and conflict.'

Indeed, as Whitehorn (1981) indicates, however bizarre some of these cults might appear, they are far from being unreasonable. She argues that people need to believe in something that is not rational 'because the bare bones of a totally material existence are just not enough to live on. Whether they flesh them out with voodoo or the Virgin Mary, Elvis or the Reverend Moon, it is the same need that is being answered' (p. 81). Naranjo likewise suggests that whilst fanatical adherance of some people to certain of these trends might be pathological, they represent nonetheless peripheral manifestations of a valid need for meaning in existence and reaffirmation of identity in a world from which humankind has come to feel alienated.

The need for meaning and a sense of belonging are indeed among several characteristic features of adherents of the more extreme cults identified by Enroth (1977). Others include the pursuit of enlightenment and the discovery of answers to fundamental human questions; rejection of the 'ways of the world'; deprecation of worldly knowledge, vocations and materialism; perceived persecution; the attraction of an exotic lifestyle; and a pervasive subjectivism. What Enroth fails to identify, however, but which is clearly of central importance, is the need for a master or guru. Indeed, Minogue (1980, p. 180) suggests that it is this 'great guru hunger which has led to the current spiritual Disneyland in the West'.

Guru hunger

The pursuit of gurus, or spiritual teachers, has a lengthy history even within Western culture, but during the 1960s and 1970s the quest assumed epic proportions, and as Minogue indicates, a complex and specialized industry grew up to supply the need. Numerous self-styled teachers, European, Asian and American, appeared 'on the market', competing with each other for acolytes, and in the ensuing 'antique and collectors' fayres' many old masters came to light.

One such was Giorgi Gurdjieff, a charismatic and enigmatic teacher, and undisputed rogue, who had attracted a cultic and international following among intellectuals during the early years of this century. His system of highly eclectic occultism, 'intelligently packaged for a technologically oriented public' (Minogue, 1980, p. 180), clearly owes much to Sufism, the influence of which is discernible in the meditation exercises he prescribed which were similar to those of the Dervishes, taking the form of repetitive movements and dancing. Gurdjieff took the view that man is machine-like, but unlike a machine can realize his own mechanisms by attending to the ritualistic, habitual nature of his behaviour, and through repetitive physical labour and activity can learn to transcend them. His system, like Zen, requires attention to one's actions and remembering them; paying precise attention to one's 'doing' at all times, and thereby achieving heightened awareness and altered states of consciousness.

Following Gurdjieff's death in 1949 his teachings were continued in the work of Pietr Ouspensky, A. R. Orage and the de Hartmanns, and in the writings of Fritz Peters (1964, 1965, 1978) and Margaret Anderson (1962, 1969). During the 1960s and 1970s the major works of Gurdjieff were published (Gurdjieff, 1974), his autobiography *Meetings with Remarkable Men* (1978) becoming the subject of a film. A Gurdjieff Foundation was established in Paris, and groups of followers flourished world-wide, as did various movements derived from his teachings, such as the Arica Institute founded by Oscar Ichazo. Gurdjieff's teachings were undoubtedly influential in stimulating research into altered states of consciousness, such as the work of Lilly (1973), and also a widespread renewal of interest in occultism.

The occult revival

Roszak (1975) interprets the upsurge of interest in the occult during the 1960s as an attempt to bring myth, magic and mystery back into twentieth century living. As he indicates, the magical and mysterious have been transformed over the centuries into science and technology and the end product of this transformation is a technocratic culture which focusses on the nature of man devoid of magical or mystical origins, and places scientific achievement ahead of cosmological explanation of reality. He argues, therefore, that in turning back to the occult and magic, Western culture is witnessing a return to its visionary origins.

The widespread use of psychedelic drugs, which traditionally are part of much esoteric ritual, also stimulated further interest in magical practices, and, ostensibly at least, it was an attempt to scientifically investigate the relationship between drug use and magical consciousness that prompted one of the most remarkable cults to emerge during the era, that surrounding Carlos Castaneda.

The cult of Castaneda

In the early 1960s, Carlos Castaneda, an anthropology student at UCLA, submitted as his Ph.D. thesis an account of how he had developed visionary insight into the nature of the universe through his twelve-year apprenticeship in sorcery, or shamanism, to the Yaqui Indian sorcerer, brujo, or magician, Don Juan Matus. Castaneda was awarded his doctorate and the virtually unaltered text was published in 1968 (reprinted 1970) under the title *The Teachings of Don Juan: a Yaqui way of knowledge*. Almost immediately Castaneda was seized upon as a new Western guru, or enlightened one, and elevated to the status of a god by some of his more fanatical readers. The elusive Don Juan, who could not be found outside the pages of Castaneda's book despite being the object of numerous searches and investigations in the desert of Sonora, was, nonetheless, included among other 'Modern Mystics and Sages' in Anne Bancroft's book of that name (1978). Elsewhere Castaneda was cited in authorative texts on religion, mysticism, anthropology and psychology, and his work was used, among other things, as a framework for sociological analysis by Silverman (1975). Three subsequent books (1973, 1975, 1976) by Castaneda elaborated further on the progress of his apprenticeship and were adopted as textbooks on anthropology in several US universities. *The Second Ring of Power* (1978), *The Eagle's Gift* (1982) and *The Fire Within* (1984) followed, but by that time doubt had descended on the whole Castaneda legend.

De Mille (1978, 1980) claimed that Castaneda's work was almost entirely fictional—the product of a vivid imagination and a tortuous journeying through various highly obscure anthropological and philosophical sources, and that he had never travelled beyond the UCLA libraries, much less roamed the Sonoran desert in the company of a sorcerer. Nevertheless, it was held by Castaneda's supporters that de Mille's critique cast more doubt on the validity of the UCLA examining board than on Castaneda's work, which even allowing for possibly fictitious content, remains an astonishing, and apparently accurate account of the development of mystical consciousness (cf. Chevalier 1976, *The Sacred Magician*).

Indeed, despite de Mille's endeavours, the authenticity of the works still remains in question, and is likely to remain so, but what is beyond doubt is the fascination they hold for the millions of readers throughout the world who appear to have found them meaningful. Their importance lies less in the veracity of the account, than in their impact on Western audiences, which has been considerable.

At one level they have emphasized the importance of the subjectivity of the researcher in understanding and interpreting his subject, and, in clearly identifying the limitations of the verbal, rational, logical approach, they have underlined the difficulties encountered by Western intellectuals in attempting to comprehend the esoteric traditions of other cultures. In so doing they have illustrated a new ethnomethodological framework which has since been widely adopted within anthropology, and helped to reinstate the phenomenological approach within social science research.

At a different level, others have found in Castaneda the elements of visionary and mystical experience, and recognized in it what appear to be universal truths. Drury (1978) identifies parallels between Don Juan's system as expounded by Castaneda and other systems of magic outside Mexico and Central America. In particular he draws attention to the similarities in the magical view of Don Juan with that found in contemporary Western magic, notably Cabbalism—an esoteric system of Judaic origin designed to induce a dramatic transformation of consciousness, and which may be viewed as the Judaic equivalent of Taoism and Zen. It entails a structured sequence of successive initiatory experiences leading to increasingly radical modifications of consciousness and cognition, which Baigent *et al.* (1982) liken to a kind of symbolic death and rebirth into a dimension of all-encompassing unity and harmony.

It is not necessary, however, to understand the complexities of Cabbalism, nor the details of Mexican sorcery, to see parallels between the Yaqui way of knowledge as depicted by Castaneda and other esoteric traditions. Whilst Don Juan's system is highly complex, and much of it remains obscure, several familiar themes emerge from Castaneda's writing.

The whole object of Castaneda's apprenticeship is seeing the world as it is, which involves 'stopping the world' of conventional reality. In order to control and direct consciousness to this end it is necessary for the individual to learn how to harness his personal powers and those of the universe. The attainment of power requires humility in the face of death and constant awareness of the impermanence of life, for Don Juan holds that it is only when man realizes the fact of his death that he can fully experience life, which is both a wonderful and terrifying process. Man's role in life is to achieve a balance between the wonders and terrors of living, which can only be accomplished by his becoming fully aware. Such awareness has no place for abstraction and intellection, only for experiencing in the immediate present. Awareness of the here-and-now also emphasizes the unity and wholeness of the universe. Not only are life and death linked in a perpetual cycle, but so also are the lives of all things, everything being part of an inter-related whole, which is dynamic and everchanging. When a person realizes this they have achieved a different level of consciousness, a visionary consciousness; perceiving the universe and all things within it as inter-connected luminous orbs. This 'enlightened' state of awareness can be achieved by exercises and meditation, or through ritual practices, and can be facilitated in its early stages by the use of certain drugs.

The question of choice is also of paramount importance in Don Juan's teaching, for man frees himself by an act of will from the constraints of conventional being. In choosing this path he chooses himself, his identities, his personalities and his complete mode of being. The cultivation of will and intent is therefore necessary for the attainment of freedom. However, such freedom demands a lack of attachment to the persons and things of conventional life. Don Juan insists that this is a way of feeling — 'a path with heart' — rather than reason. It is a way of intuition.

Indeed, the whole of his teaching aims to debunk reason and remove attachment to the intellect, mind or ego. Mind is represented as a trickster, or illusionist, which deceives man into certain ways of seeing, thinking and acting. From this perspective, therefore, the world of conventional reality and the intellect's attachment to it, constitute a huge cosmic joke, the most appropriate response to which is uproarious laughter. Hence there is considerable levity, hilarity and humour in Don Juan's system, and in this, as in so many other respects, one finds close parallels with other traditions, especially the Indian notion that the Buddha, or enlightened one, laughs.

Yet again one encounters in the writings of Castaneda the familiar themes of expanded consciousness; the illusory nature of mundane reality and the possibility of its transcendence; the harnessing of human potential; emphasis on the will; the pre-eminence of the subjective; the need for balance in human affairs; and, above all, the attainment of enlightenment. However, as Castaneda discovered for himself, and makes clear to others, understanding such advanced human capabilities, much less realizing them, presents very real difficulties for those educated in the rational, intellectual tradition of Western culture. Therefore, many students of the esoteric, believing that greater understanding could be gained by absorbing traditional wisdom at its source, sought authentic spiritual teachers, and to this end journeyed, not only into the Mexican desert in search of Don Juan and his cohorts, but to other cultures, particularly India.

The magical mystery tour

The spiritual pilgrimage to the East was popularized by the Beatles' highly publicized trip to India during the late 1960s, and their subsequent adoption of a guru, the Maharishi Mahesh Yogi, and his Transcendental Meditation techniques. It was not only pop stars and disaffected 'hippies' who made the trip east but also a number of scientists, among them Richard Alpert, the former co-researcher, at Harvard, of Timothy Leary, who later returned to the West as Baba Ram Dass to promote yoga, meditation and other techniques for expanding consciousness (see Dass, 1978). Nevertheless, for many pilgrims the trip proved unrewarding, for as Mehta (1981) recounts, the spiritual seekers all too often found 'Guru Industries Ltd' — pre-packaged and commercialized mysticism. As she observes (p. 199), 'The whims of the West were so easily translated into revelation by India. But revelation comes expensive in the East.' Moreover, commercial exploitation was not the only discovery:

> The American poet Wallace Stevens reminded the West that the last illusion is disillusion. The Indian guru reminds the Westerner what lies beyond the last illusion.
> "But you're saying I'm God" say the disciples, "That I'm responsible."
> "That's right" answers the guru.
> "No. That's not fair. You're the guru. You're supposed to tell me what to do. I'm sorry but I can't handle the Law."
> The guru clears his throat and points out: "But, nonetheless, you are the Law. You cannot receive mercy. So it's no good being sorry."
> The guru has revealed the last move in the Hindu end game. He beams with the pleasure of a man who has fulfilled his karma as a Teacher. He waits to be showered with rose petals by grateful ashram graduates. But the distressed devotees are dashing for the exit.
> "What's happening?" asks the guru.
> "We have a headache," say the disillusioned disciples.
> "Maybe its the climate or the food or something. We think we'll go home for a while. How do we leave?"
> "That's an interesting question," says the guru, with a smile, "You're the tourists. You find out."   (pp. 194–195)

And they did. With their disillusionment, and that of the Beatles, the exodus to the East receded, although it continued throughout the 1970s, with thousands seeking enlightenment in ashrams and Zen monasteries, and, much reduced, continues to the present.

There was also a complementary East–West movement, albeit on a far smaller scale; first evident in the increased flow of literature from the East in the 1960s, and followed during the 1970s by the migration to the West of several gurus, most notably Maharaj Ji and Maharishi Mahesh Yogi, and most recently, in 1980, Bhagwan Shree Rajneesh, whose Orange Movement continues to flourish within the United States and Europe, thereby disseminating techniques of meditation and awareness.

The infiltration of Eastern influence into Western culture during the 1960s and subsequently, gave impetus to the development of what Ornstein (1976) has termed 'trademarked, franchised mystic cults', which offered, at a price, special techniques, or synthetic amalgams of techniques for expanding consciousness, and which according to Ornstein, thrived because in the cultivation of intellectual skills in the West, there has been an almost total neglect of teaching regarding the person, personal experience and self-knowledge. He argues that the popularity of these pop cults and movements offers a penetrating critique of contemporary education in the West, claiming that 'many have turned to the showman/salesman and to the recycled Indian drop-out to make up for the basic shortcomings of our education' (pp. 86–87).

Experiment and innovation in education

Naranjo (1974, p. 25) points out that education is not 'only one' more domain of culture but a microcosm of them all: 'Education is culture being passed on — and is inseparable from culture's very nature.' It is not surprising, therefore, that as traditional forms of authority in Western culture were abandoned, Western culture should find itself on the brink of deformalization of education, and a reconsideration of its aims and methods.

Nevertheless, recognition of the spiritual aridity of Western culture and education did not originate in the counter culture. Several innovators such as A. S. Neill and August Aichorn had attempted to pioneer more progressive education during the early decades of the twentieth century. In experimental British schools such as Summerhill, education focussed on the development of the whole person, rather than merely the intellect, and emphasis was laid on self-integration or actualization; the active/interactive nature of the learning process; the fostering of creativity and individuality; personal responsibility and potential. In so doing, these innovators were advocating a form of education which, by comparison with traditional methods, was regarded as permissive inasmuch that it promoted freedom from constraint and direction, freedom of thought, action and choice, and freedom to grow and develop.

The traditional emphasis on the student's trust in the teacher and the bodies of knowledge transmitted was replaced by the teacher's trust in the integrity of the learner and their facility for self-determination. Therefore, a fundamental requirement of progressive education, and perhaps to traditionalist reactionaries its greatest impediment, is that the learning situation, and power and authority within it, are transferred from the teacher — and indeed from the school and the system — to the individual. In this sense, progressive education requires a total and radical reconstruction of schooling within Western society; a 'deschooling' not in the sense of an abolition of education, but in the integration of intellectual concerns with other areas of human experience.

During the 1960s American education was subjected to a new and different barrage of criticism from Holt (1964), Herndon (1965), Kohl (1967), Kozol (1967), Leonard (1968) and Silberman (1970). As Patterson (1974, p. 4) explains: 'In short, the critics are saying that American schools — or at least most of them — are not fit places for human beings. The schools are inhumane, they do not treat children as persons.' He suggests that the mechanization of current processes and the application of technology are likely to compound what is wrong with American education — 'the failure to develop sensitive, autonomous, thinking, humane individuals'. He cites Silberman (1970, p. 196) as insisting that 'our most pressing educational problem is not how to increase the efficiency of our schools; it is how to create and maintain a humane society'.

Goodman (1960), Rogers (1969b), Postman and Weingartner (1969) and Illich (1970) were among others who, during this period, offered a forceful and influential critique of traditional American education, and in advocating a more progressive position pointed to the dangers in sustaining an educational system that lagged behind social change, and promoted a model of knowledge increasingly inappropriate to a rapidly changing world. Rogers (1969b, p. 59) states the case thus:

> for the general public and most educators the goal of learning to be free is not an aim they would select, nor towards which they are actually moving, yet if a civilised culture is to survive and the individuals within that culture are to be worth saving, it appears to be the essential goal of education.

Nevertheless, progressive education was viewed by its detractors as yet another cultic manifestation of the times, and as Hudson (1978) has pointed out, its advocates were accused of creating a state of permissiveness bordering on neglect and contrary to the best interests of children. Notwithstanding, there was a gradual deformalization of education in both America and Europe during the 1960s and early 1970s which led to an expansion of educational opportunities, broadening of curriculum and much innovation. There remained, however, deep-seated conflict between the progressive and traditionalist extremes. Hudson, in pointing to the dangers of either extreme and at the same time acknowledging the difficulties in achieving a balance between them, argued for the attainment of a middle path, an ideal which amounts to an educational Golden Mean or Tao.

This Utopian vision of education was portrayed by Huxley in his novel *Island* (1962, reprinted 1976). He had long been an outspoken critic of Western education, deploring a system which emphasized the development of the intellect and the transmission of knowledge to the neglect of feelings, personal experience, free expression, individuality and creativity. He was committed to the notion of educating the whole person, and perceived the aim of education to be the facilitation of a qualitative change in being. He identified a number of techniques for the development of the senses and emotions and urged that these be incorporated into the educational system. Huxley's dream, whilst not actualized in state education programmes, was realized in 1962, the year before his death, in the foundation of the Esalen Institute at Big Sur, California.

Esalen's founders, Michael Murphy and Richard Price, aimed at establishing an educational centre which encompassed the spiritual and intellectual, and in which those trends in education, religion, philosophy, art and science that emphasize the potentialities and values of human existence could be explored. To this end, exponents of many disciplines from Eastern and Western cultures, including Yoga, meditation, altered states of consciousness, the martial arts, dance, as well as religious leaders, philosophers, artists, scientists and psychologists, were invited to exchange views in seminars, workshops, and residential programmes, the first of which was offered to the general public in 1966. This interchange yielded many different approaches to, and techniques for the development of human potential; those derived from oriental philosophies and religions, or esoteric traditions, frequently being grafted on to the more familiar psychological approaches of the West, particularly those employed in psychotherapy.

By the late 1960s Esalen was offering year-round programmes that attracted vast numbers of students in search of self-development and growth. It became the prototype for many so-called 'growth centres' that subsequently flourished throughout the United States and Europe during the 1960s and 1970s, promoting the development of human potential and thereby disseminating a vast array of eclectic psychotherapeutic and quasi-therapeutic techniques. Indeed, Esalen spawned what was to become perhaps the most pervasive and influential of all the cults to emerge during the 1960s and subsequently—the cult of psychotherapy—which invaded mainstream culture and had a profound impact upon American culture and upon its psychology.

Chapter 5

THE CULT OF PSYCHOTHERAPY

psychotherapy as religion

Psychology is an indispensable handmaid to theology, but, I think, a very poor housekeeper.

T. S. Eliot[4]

Theologian and philosopher Paul Tillich (1952) considers the decisive event underlying the search for meaning in twentieth century Western culture to be the loss of God during the nineteenth century. Prior to that time values and meanings were provided by the Church, the family and the school, but organized religion, the rock upon which these authorities were based, was progressively eroded during the nineteenth century as a result of scientific progress, and with the secularization of society ready-made meanings were no longer provided. As Evans (1974, p. 9) indicates:

> In the past hundred years in particular what we might call 'the religious answer' has progressively lost its punch, with more and more people turning to the textbooks of science in an attempt at understanding the strange physical and mental environment we live in . . . unfortunately where the answers provided by religion fail to satisfy, science frequently has no suitable alternative.

The subsequent search for meaning during the twentieth century led to the emergence of numerous cults and quasi-religious movements which prompted many commentators to declare the counter culture an era of religious revival and faith. Lasch (1978, p. 7) insists, however, that the climate of the times was therapeutic rather than religious:

> People today hunger not for personal salvation, let alone the restoration of an earlier golden age, but for the feeling, the momentary illusion, of personal

[4]The search for moral sanction. In: *The Listener* 1932. Vol. **VII**, No. 108 (30), p. 446.

wellbeing, health and psychic security. Even the radicalism of the sixties served
. . . not as a substitute religion but as a form of therapy. Radical politics
filled empty lives, provided a sense of meaning and purpose.

Indeed, during the 1960s and subsequently there was a dramatic increase in
both the number of psychotherapies available and those who sought them. Even
so, Lasch's distinction between religion and therapy remains somewhat arbitrary,
and superficial inasmuch as it fails to consider that therapies of whatever
denomination may in many cases be treating the very same condition, or disease,
to which religion traditionally responds.

Laing (in Evans, 1981b) observes that the term 'therapist' originally derived from
a Greek word meaning 'attendant' and as such a therapist should be a specialist
in attentiveness and awareness. This is the object of Eastern meditative traditions:
to cultivate equal awareness of mental, emotional, social and physical experience,
the four foundations of mindfulness, wholeness and health. (It is interesting to
note in this connection that health and holiness derive from the same etymological
root, meaning whole.)

PSYCHOTHERAPY—THE CURE OF SOULS

In the ancient world human nature was viewed as a manifestation of the soul
or psyche. Human problems were therefore seen as fundamentally spiritual in
nature, being thought of as psychopathology—literally 'disease of the soul', and
its diagnosis and cure, or psychotherapy, were matters for ministers of religion
who dealt not only in healing souls but also in fighting the sin to which the human
soul was prey.

With the displacement of religion by science, the soul was replaced by mind,
which in turn gave way to brain function; psychopathology came to be seen as
'mental' illness, and psychotherapy, its treatment, within the province of the
'brain' sciences. Accordingly, doctors, psychologists and psychiatrists were heir
to what Frankl (1969a) has termed a 'medical ministry'; a role for which they
have no specialized expertise, and the arrogation of which has been the subject
of forceful criticism, most notably from within the psychiatric profession itself.

Indeed, with certain exceptions such as alcoholic psychosis and senile dementia
in which some organic pathology can be established, psychiatric taxonomy is not
based on biology or medicine. The criteria for mental illness are most usually
some deviation from social, ethical or legal norms. Thus, Szasz (1979) argues,
the concept of mental illness and the all-embracing taxonomies of psychiatry are
merely convenient metaphors that enable human problems to be treated as part
of objective medical science. In other words, persons are deemed to be mentally
ill, and are treated as such, not because of any physical malady, but because they
have sinned by not conforming to the canons of society. Szasz asserts therefore,

that psychotherapeutic interventions are moral in character and not medical, and its treatments metaphorical rather than literal. This being the case, psychiatry and its satellite, clinical psychology, constitute moral philosophy rather than medical science, and 'psychotherapy constitutes secular ethics' (Szasz, 1979, p. 9).

Szasz also asserts that the concept of mental illness, in enabling human problems to be treated as if objective, scientific 'facts', draws attention away from their fundamental cause, which he attributes to 'problems in living'. Schofield (1964) takes a similar view:

> The psychiatrist has expanded the domain of mental illness to include all degrees and kinds of psychological distress, failing to appreciate that the human suffers pain not because he is sick but because he is human.

From this perspective, therefore, psychotherapy may be thought of as the application of psychological methods to the treatment of the human condition. This, however, prompts the question 'What *is* the human condition?'

DIAGNOSIS OF THE HUMAN CONDITION

As noted previously (see Chapter 2) the Buddha's analysis of the human condition was that human existence is intrinsically problematic because human beings, apparently unlike animals, are aware of the inevitability of their death and the consequent tenuousness of their existence or being. Man thus experiences insecurity or uncertainty because he knows that his life can be terminated at any time by death.

Nineteenth century philosophers, Kierkegaard, Heidegger and Husserl, and the twentieth century philosophers Jaspers and Sartre, reached similar conclusions about the nature of human existence. These so-called 'existentialists' recognized that human beings, faced with the ever-present and unavoidable fact of their mortality, live in a constant state of uncertainty about their being which generates what Kierkegaard termed 'existential anxiety'. Moreover, like Buddha, they recognized that it is not only the prospect of death that generates anxiety or dread, but also other aspects of existence such as the individual's fundamental aloneness and isolation in the world, and the lack of any given purpose or meaning in life.

For many people, the fact of being born into the world, living in it and leaving it, quite alone and for no apparent reason generates not only anxiety but also frustration and a sense of emptiness. Frequently, these are the symptoms of the 'soul-sickness' or psychopathology which causes many people in contemporary society to seek professional, psychiatric help, where formerly they might have sought clerical guidance. Thus it is, as Schofield (1964, p. 150) indicates, that

> Psychotherapists . . . are increasingly confronted by would-be patients who do not manifest any of the more objective hallmarks of a neurotic problem,

who do not complain of failures of productivity or achievement, who do not suffer from serious interpersonal conflicts, who are free of functional somatic complaints, who are not incapacitated by anxiety, or tormented by obsessions, whose objective life circumstances they confess are close to optimal. These seekers for help suffer a freedom from complaint. The absence of conflicts, frustrations and symptoms brings a painful awareness of absence — the absence of faith, of commitment, of meaning, of the need to search out personal, ultimate values, or of the need to live comfortably and meaningfully each day in the face of final uncertainty. For increasing numbers of rational, educated and thoughtful men the central struggle becomes one of finding and keeping an emotional and psychological balance between the pain of doubt and the luxury of faith.

Therefore, as Lasch suggests, therapists become man's principal allies in the struggle for composure and peace of mind, and it is to them that he turns in the hope of achieving the modern equivalent of salvation — 'mental health'.

SALVATION AS SCIENCE

Recognition of the contemporary role of psychotherapy has prompted Szasz (1979, p. 9) to define psychotherapy as 'the religion of the formally irreligious'. However, as he points out, the view that psychotherapy is in many cases ersatz religion is inconsistent with the institution of medical psychiatry and was recognized to be such by the pioneers of modern psychotherapy, Jung and Freud, both of whom vacillated between claiming it for medicine or religion, before Freud, recognizing that science was the great legitimizer of the times, finally insisted, unlike Jung, that psychotherapy is science. Subsequently, therefore, psycotherapeutic approaches proceeded from various theories of man, and the kinds of treatment deemed to be appropriate to any disorder determined by the scientific outlook and beliefs of the therapist.

Psychologists and psychiatrists thus came to employ many different methods which depend on quite different assumptions about human nature, and imply altogether different philosophies of life. Therefore, 'Objective psychiatry is an unobjective attempt to control the largely non-objective events by objective means' (Laing, 1983, p. 41), for as Rogers observes (1969a, p. 85):

Our devotion to rigorous hard-headedness in psychology, to reductionist theories, to operational decisions, to experimental procedures, leads us to understand psychotherapy in purely objective rather than subjective terms.

That this is so is clear from an examination of the therapeutic approaches that correspond to psychology's dominant theoretical traditions, the psychodynamic and the behavioural. The former comprises all those therapies inspired by Freudian and neo-Freudian theories which employ notions about the structure and working of the mind; whilst the latter are based on learning theories and concerned with the dynamics of behaviour.

Superficially these therapies appear dissimilar in both theory and practice but closer examination reveals in both a deterministic and mechanistic model of man. Both conceive of man in terms of dynamics, either what Koestler has termed the 'slot machine' mechanics of behaviourism, or the id-ego-superego formulations of psychoanalysis; and both approach the person in terms of a number of techniques such as behaviour modification, desensitization and hypnosis. In so doing these therapies commit what Frankl (1969a, p. 6) regards to be the 'original sin of psychotherapy', namely reification:

> Approaching human beings merely in terms of techniques necessarily implies manipulating them; and approaching them merely in terms of dynamics implies reifying them, making human beings into mere things.

Moreover, as Laing (1983, p. 44) suggests, there are critical issues of deep power here, for both therapeutic approaches are concerned with the treatment of disorder through the control or elimination of socially undesired experience and conduct, whether thought, feeling or behaviour. Freudians conceive of the structure of personality as a power struggle between the libidinous and potentially destructive id impulses and the correcting superego, which represents internalized social forces or conventional reality. The therapeutic aim of psychoanalysis is the development of a strong ego which will control the id:

> The whole superego, ego, id scheme is a hierarchical structure which excludes the possibility that the association of free ie. non-exploited human beings can live harmoniously and without the necessity of controlling sinister forces.
> (Fromm, 1980, p. 7)

This insistence on control is evident in the practice of psychoanalysis as well as at the theoretical level. The client abdicates all personal responsibility in favour of the therapist, or analyst, who remains in control at all times, determining the goals of therapy and its entire course. All personal meaning is denied the client, whose language, dreams and reported experience are interpreted by the analyst in terms of Freudian symbolism. In this way the validity of the client's subjective experience is invalidated in favour of the therapist's interpretation; the therapist and Freudian dogma constituting the authority on the client's experience rather than the person himself. Moreover, the implicit assumption of the client's passivity is symbolized in the traditionally recumbent posture on the analyst's couch.

In behaviourism control is more explicit, Skinner having insisted that the application of scientific method crucially depends on the notion that man is not free, and evident in the therapeutic concern with the modification of observable behaviours, or their eradication through substitution with incompatible socially acceptable responses.

It can be argued, as does Lasch (1978, p. 13) that

> Having displaced religion as the organising framework of American culture, the therapeutic outlook threatens to displace politics as well, the last refuge of ideology.

THE POLITICS OF PSYCHOTHERAPY (Kurt Lewin)

During the 1960s the view of man implicit in the traditional forms of psychotherapy came under attack. One of its most forceful opponents was Carl Rogers:

> Man does not simply have the characteristics of a machine; he is not simply a being in the grip of unconscious motives; he is a person in the process of creating himself, a person who creates meaning in life, a person who embodies a dimension of subjective freedom. He is a figure who, though he may be alone in a vastly complex universe, and though he may be part of that universe and its destiny, is also able to live dimensions of his life which are not fully or adequately contained in a description of his conditioning or his unconscious.
>
> (1964, p. 129)

Such a perspective, which may be termed 'humanistic' in contradistinction to the traditional mechanistic view of man, has as its defining characteristic the assumption of a dimension of subjective freedom. This is not only antithetical to the deterministic assumptions of behaviourism and psychoanalysis, but like them, impossible to either prove or refute empirically, and being fundamentally untestable, constitutes ideology rather than theory. Nevertheless, it does have the advantage of according with both common sense and experience. Indeed, Frankl (1973) argues that the only two classes of person claiming not to have free will are so-called schizophrenics and deterministic philosophers.

During the 1960s a number of therapies emerged which focussed attention on subjective experience, personal responsibility and meaning. However, in their return to what might be regarded as spiritual human concerns they were reflecting currents within Western culture as a whole, and most notably the consciousness movement or counter culture, rather than any explicit opposition to positivistic, deterministic psychology as such. What these therapies shared in common, apart from their origins in the counter culture and similar philosophical and ideological underpinnings, is that most of them involved some planned intensive group experience. Whereas previously, psychotherapy had been considered to be essentially a one-to-one interaction between a therapist and client, emphasis now rested on a group of persons and one or more leaders.

The group idea was inspired by psychologist Kurt Lewin who, whilst at the Massachusetts Institute of Technology during the 1940s, recognized that training in human relationship skills was greatly neglected. He advocated the establishment of groups for training such skills, the first of which met in Maine in 1947 shortly after Lewin's death. Social scientists, made aware of the lack of knowledge about group behaviour by the horrific events of the Second World War, subsequently saw such groups as potential microcosmic laboratories in which to study aspects of group behaviour, particularly leadership functions, identity formation and decision making processes. Therefore, shortly after the first training, or T-group, met, the National Training Laboratories were established, and during the 1950s many of their contracts came from business schools and employment commissions which sent students to these groups in order to develop their managerial skills and interpersonal sensitivity. Initially groups of up to twelve persons came together once or more per week over a period of weeks in order to observe the nature of the group process, social interaction and human relations, and gradually this experience became known as sensitivity training.

During the 1950s the nature of the groups underwent a marked change as it became recognized that participation in T-group or sensitivity training often led to powerful personal experiences — dramatic and startling confessions and disclosures, cathartic emotional expression, heightened sense of well-being, and personal change. What occurred in many cases appeared remarkably similar to the effects claimed for psychotherapy, the aim of which, as Frankl (1969a) observes, has traditionally been that of secular confession.

These groups came to be viewed as a means whereby inidividuals could become more authentic and spontaneous and thereby lead more productive and effective lives. As a result, group leaders were drawn increasingly from the ranks of psychiatry and clinical psychology rather than from education, industry and social psychology as formerly was the case, and the T-group became transformed into the therapeutic group. Subsequently a plethora of 'group' therapies emerged, each offering different techniques for the promotion of self-development, growth and personal fulfilment, and by the 1960s Americans in their thousands were flocking to these and their spin-offs.

Lasch (1978) views the popularity of the confessional mode evident in such group therapies as testimony to the new narcissism pervading American culture. Such undisguised self-interest was in no small measure inspired, reinforced and legitimized in a growing body of theoretical writings by a number of psychologists, who, like Carl Rogers, refused to view man as a slave to environmental contingencies and his past, and attempted a fully human alternative to the mechanistic view of man prevalent in Western thought. Their concerns, focussing as they did on the individual as a perceiver and interpreter of himself and their world, and a determiner of their own behaviour, represented a return to the fundamental questions regarding the nature of the human self, soul or psyche and its development, and reinstated self concept, self esteem, agency, personal responsibility, choice and intentionality as legitimate issues for psychology. At the forefront of this shift in emphasis toward a 'psychology of being' was Abraham Maslow.

A psychology of being (Abraham Maslow)

Maslow took Western psychology to task for its emphasis on determinism and its concomitant neglect of the human. He was especially opposed to the generalization of findings derived from studies of the 'mentally ill' to man as a whole, arguing that psychology should be concerned with the study of mental health which he viewed as the fulfilment of a five-level motivational hierarchy of need culminating in the need for self-actualization.

He based his motivational theory on the optimistic assumption of man's intrinsic good nature, which he viewed as an essentially biological feature, partly general to the species as a whole and in part individual and unique. He conceived of this inner nature or self as possessing a dynamic for growth and actualization, but being weak rather than strong, easily frustrated, denied and suppressed thus giving rise to sickness and neurosis. Like Freud, Maslow regarded self-denial as the major cause of psychological illness and distress:

> From our point of view, Freud's greatest discovery is that *the* great cause of much psychological illness is the fear of knowledge of oneself—of the emotions, impulses, memories, capacities, potentialities, of one's destiny.
> (1968, p. 60)

He held this kind of fear generally to be a defensive protection of man's self esteem, self love or self respect, observing that man tends to be afraid of any knowledge that could cause self dislike or give rise to feelings of inferiority, weakness or shame, and that in order to avoid such unpleasant truths he employs repression and similar defences. He also claimed that man evades yet another kind of truth, that of personal growth and the change it implies because it too generates fear and anxiety:

> And so we find another kind of resistance, a denying of our best side, of our talents, of our finest impulses, of our highest potentialities, of our creativeness. In brief this is the struggle against our own greatness, the fear of hubris.
> (1968, p. 61)

Maslow argued that because of these fears the normal adjustment of the average common-sense person implies a continued successful rejection of himself and the depths of his human nature. The person effectively turns his back on much of himself because he fears the consequences of doing otherwise, with the result that most people are constrained into outmoded and ineffective ways of acting thus generating a state of being which Maslow termed 'the psychopathology of the average'.

By comparison, Maslow viewed health as equivalent to self-actualization, the characteristic features of which he identified through the study of persons in public life whom he deemed to be self-actualized. These features include:

superior perception of reality;

increased acceptance of self, others and nature;

increased spontaneity and greatly increased creativity;

increased autonomy and resistance to enculturation;

richness of emotional reaction;

increased identification with the human species;

changed interpersonal relationships;

change in values and a more democratic value structure;

an ability for mystical/spiritual experiences (so-called 'peak' experiences).

Maslow's particular focus on peak experience reflected his concern with the spiritual aspects of humanity. He regarded these as evidence of man's ability to transcend present personal experience to some ultimate experience or reality. There are in Maslow's writings, therefore, echoes of William James (1902) and Jung (1946) and their concern for expanded consciousness, religious experience and spiritual need in man.

Indeed, although Maslow is regarded as the founding father of humanistic psychology he can also be seen as spearheading what has become known as Transpersonal Psychology. Its relationship to humanistic psychology is clearly stated by Maslow (1968, pp. iii–iv):

> . . . I consider Humanistic, Third Force Psychology to be transitional, a preparation for a still 'higher' Fourth Psychology, transpersonal, transhuman, centred in the cosmos rather than in human needs and interest, going beyond humanness, identity, self-actualization, and the like . . . These new developments may very well offer a tangible, usable, effective satisfaction of the 'frustrated idealism' of many quietly desperate people, especially young people. These psychologies give promise of developing into the life-philosophy, the religion-surrogate, the value-system, the life-program that these people have been missing.

Maslow's views, particularly those relating to the capacity for peak experience, found resonance within the counter culture of the 1960s, and he was hailed as a major prophet of the consciousness movement. During the 1960s and 1970s transpersonal psychology developed alongside research into altered states of consciousness, drug-induced experience, Eastern religions and culminated in the publication of the *Journal of Transpersonal Psychology* in 1969.

Although as Cosgrove (1982) indicates, only at first a 'backroom' version of humanistic psychology, and still regarded by some as remaining so, transpersonal psychology developed into a fully-fledged movement during the 1970s. Its particular emphasis, however, is upon empirical, scientific study of spiritual experience and altered states of consciousness, because as Tart (1975, p. 58) explains, 'The realm of the spiritual and the connected realm of altered states of consciousness is one of the most powerful forces that shape man's life and destiny.' A more detailed treatment of the concerns of transpersonal psychology and its major contributors is provided by Boucouvalas (1980).

Nevertheless, Maslow's view of the human condition and his model of health, whilst breaking new ground in psychology, were neither new nor original. His concept of man and his emphasis on change are similar to that found in oriental psychologies, and his concept of health bears a striking resemblance to that of Dr Samuel Hahnemann, the pioneer of modern homeopathic medicine.

The homeopathic model

Reibel (1984) points to numerous parallels between homeopathy and the humanistic tradition, suggesting that the homeopathic approach forms a major paradigm of modern psychotherapy. Certainly in humanistic therapies the therapist, rather than opposing a problem facilitates confrontation with the problem as its solution and thus reinforces the homeopathic maxim that 'like cures like'. Moreover, humanistic theories of human functioning which underpin various therapeutic approaches closely resemble those of Hahnemann.

In his *Organon der Rationallen Heilkunde* (1810) Hahnemann used the term 'vital force' to describe the balancing mechanism in every living body which promotes, or at least protects health. He wrote that this vital force is stimulated by internal and external disorders to build up a counteractive reaction. The result of the interaction between the vital force and the conditions which set it in motion produces various symptoms in the body revealing that an imbalance has occurred. Disease is thus a product of stress and the failure of the body's own attempt to heal it, whereas health is the maintenance and development of the vital force or inner nature of the organism itself. Any treatment or healing must therefore deal with the whole organism in both its objective and subjective aspects, taking into account the individual's perception and interpretation of their symptoms and their individual features. Hahnemann therefore insisted that the vital force and its effects should be studied objectively and scientifically and subjectively. Similarly, Maslow urged that man's inner nature could and should be studied objectively through the application of the methods of science, and subjectively, by way of psychotherapy. It remained for Carl Rogers and Frederick Perls to facilitate this process, for as will be seen Perls' homeostatic, gestalt approach to human functioning is similar to homeopathy in both theory and practice, and Rogers therapeutic approach shares much with Hahnemann's, not only in trying to promote those conditions in which the vital force could flourish, but also in attempting to study these conditions empirically.

The psychology of becoming (Carl Rogers)

A danger inherent in any psychology of being such as that proposed by Maslow is that it has the tendency to be static and not account for movement, change, direction and growth, with the result that self-actualization or self-discovery comes to be viewed as an end in itself rather than as a process.

Carl Rogers, although taking a broadly similar view to that of Maslow, draws particular attention to the person in the process of becoming in his theory of personality, sometimes referred to as 'Self Theory' which he first put forward in 1947.

> . . . the individual has within him the capacity and tendency, latent if not evident, to move forward to maturity. In a suitable psychological climate this tendency is realised, and becomes actual rather than potential. It is evident in the capacity of the individual to understand those aspects of his life and of himself which are causing pain and dissatisfaction, an understanding which probes beneath his conscious knowledge of himself into those experiences which he has hidden from himself because of their threatening nature. It shows itself in the tendency to reorganise his personality and his relationship to life in ways which are regarded as more mature. Whether one calls it a growth tendency, a drive toward self-actualisation, or a forward-moving directional tendency, it is the mainspring of life, and is, in the last analysis, the tendency upon which all psychotherapy depends. It is the urge which is evident in all organic and human life—to expand, extend, become autonomous, develop, mature—the tendency to express and activate all the capacities of the organism, to the extent that such activation enhances the organism or the self. This tendency may become deeply buried under layer after layer of encrusted psychological defences; it may be hidden behind elaborate façades which deny its existence; but it is my belief that it exists in every individual, and awaits only the proper conditions to be released and expressed.   (Rogers, 1961, p. 35)

Rogers and Maslow clearly share common emphases in their psychological approach. They both recognize the fundamental pre-eminence of the subjective and the tendency toward self-actualization, which is synonymous with psychological health and represents the realization of the person's inherent capacities for growth and development; potentials which are deemed to be good or neutral. Essentially they are holistic in their approach rather than reductionist, in the sense that the person is viewed as a unique totality, no aspect of which can be studied in isolation. However, whilst Maslow was fundamentally concerned with human motivation and the effects of goals and purposes on behaviour, Rogers was essentially concerned with perception. For him the primary object for psychological study is the person and the world as viewed by that person. According to Rogers, therefore, the internal phenomenological frame of reference of the individual constitutes the proper field of psychology, which should be concerned primarily with the laws governing perception.

Rogers views the person as characterized in terms of his self concept and experience on the one hand, and his interpretations of environmental stimuli on the other. It is the degree of congruence between these factors which influences the extent to which self-actualization can occur. Rogers argues that changes in self perception and in the perception of reality produce concomitant changes in behaviour and that given certain psychological conditions the individual has the capacity to reorganize their perceptual field, including the way they perceive theirself. Of particular importance is any perceived threat to the self concept, as the self usually resists incorporating experiences which are inconsistent with its functioning. However, Rogers suggests that when the self is perceived to be free from any threat of attack then it may acknowledge rejected perceptions and reintegrate the self in such a way as to include them.

He considered therapy to be a process wherein the individual has the opportunity to reorganize his subjective world, and to integrate and actualize the self. Therefore, he viewed the central process of therapy as facilitation of the individual's experience of becoming a more autonomous, spontaneous, confident person.

Nevertheless, whilst insisting that the potential for self-actualization resides within the person, Rogers claims that the conditions for facilitating its development reside in the relationship between the person and the therapist, and comes about through a close, emotionally warm and understanding relationship in which the individual is free from threat and has the freedom to be 'the self that he really is'.

> I can state the overall hypothesis in one sentence, as follows. If I can provide a certain type of relationship, the other person will discover within himself the capacity to use that relationship for growth, and change and personal development will occur. (Rogers, 1961, p. 33)

The type of relationship Rogers seeks to provide has three particularly significant qualities, the first of which is the authenticity or genuineness of the therapist. For this to be achieved the therapist must be aware of his or her own feelings, in so far as possible, and rather than present any façade, be able to express the various attitudes and feelings if appropriate. The second condition of the therapeutic relationship is that of unconditional positive regard for the client; the prizing or valueing of the person as an individual irrespective of his condition, behaviour or feelings; the respect for, and acceptance of the person in his own right. The third condition of such a relationship is empathic understanding or genuine listening—a continuing desire to understand the feelings and personal meanings which the person is experiencing.

> Thus the relationship which I have found helpful is characterised by a sort of transparency on my part, in which my real feelings are evident; by an acceptance of this other person as a separate person with value in his own right; and by a deep empathic understanding which enables me to see his private world through his eyes. When these conditions are achieved, I become a companion to my client, accompanying him in the frightening search for himself, which he now feels free to undertake. (Rogers, 1961, p. 33)

Rogers argues that within such a relationship there is an implicit freedom to explore oneself at both conscious and unconscious levels, and also a complete freedom from moral or diagnostic evaluation, which he believes are always threatening. He claims that within such conditions the person moves from fear of inner feelings and defence of them to an encouragement and acceptance of them; from being out of touch with their feelings to greater awareness of them; from living life by the introjected values of others to those experienced by themself in the present; from distrust of the spontaneous aspects of themself to trust in them; towards greater freedom and more responsible choices.

Essentially, therefore, therapy in Rogerian terms ideally affords a situation in which the individual learns to be free. As such it is an educational process, and one Rogers believes can be as effective within the classroom as in the clinic. Rogers subsequently focussed attention on the implementation of a person-centred approach within schools, setting forth his educational principles in *Freedom to Learn* (1969).

Indeed the impact of Rogers' client or person-centred approach proved to be as influential within education as it had been in psychotherapy. Of particular importance in disseminating Rogers' theories, especially within Great Britain, was the emergence of the 'counselling' movement; a hybrid resulting from the interplay between Rogers' involvement in both psychotherapy and education.

The counselling movement

Daws (1976) defines counselling as 'a particular kind of expertise requiring certain insights and skills and practised within a framework of professional principles governing the nature of the outcome sought and the nature of the relationship which obtains between the counsellor and client' (p. 4), and as he points out, no educational innovation has ever appeared in Great Britain with quite such startling suddenness.

Daws attributes the phenomenal rise of counselling in English secondary schools during the mid-1960s to the dramatic social and cultural changes occurring at that time:

> As always at times of rapid social change when inter-generational communication is threatened, new forms of relationship and new ways of conversing need to be found. The appearance of counselling was therefore timely but in one sense predictable. It was a novel and acceptable means whereby the dialogue between the old and the young, so essential for the preservation of cultural continuity and so important in the end for the appropriate maturation of the young, could effectively be continued. The preservation and perpetuation of culture is by no means the sole function of counselling, but it was an important reason for its appearance in the 1960s and for its robust spread and persistence since.   (1976, p. 8)

As depicted thus, counselling appears as a conservative reaction against the counter culture, a gentle approach to the restoration and preservation of the *status quo* more appropriate to the times than the use of the rod. Indeed, it has to be said that as implemented within the framework of traditional education this was generally the case, and that counselling frequently represented the hand in the velvet glove behind which the strong arm of law and order remained flexed, particularly as the body of educators were out of sympathy with the movement.

The radical implications of Rogers' person-centred approach were glimpsed by relatively few, and welcomed by even fewer. Yet, as Farson (in Evans, 1981) observes, Rogers was, and is, a political figure whose cumulative effect on society has made him one of the most important social revolutionaries of our time. Some indication of the radical implications of the counselling movement is evidenced by the fact that as the socio/political pendulum has swung back towards the reactionary and conservative since the late 1970s and during the 1980s, counselling in British schools has declined dramatically. In the first of the economic cuts in education in the late 1970s counsellors were axed in most schools and counsellor training courses discontinued. Daws' assessment of the educational gains from the spread of Rogerian counselling therefore has a somewhat hollow ring:

> First, the non-directive method has brought an appreciation of the facilitative and catalytic power of the personal relationship that is established between teacher and pupil, and an awareness that more than one kind of relationship is possible . . . Secondly, many have learned to look more fully and more sensitively at children's behaviour, particularly in its non-verbal and emotional aspects, in order to achieve a deeper understanding of what is going on in the experience of their pupils. This has given to many an unanticipated bonus in greater ability to control classes of children constructively. Thirdly, in grasping the full meaning of empathy and client-centredness, they have come to realise just how institution-centred or society-centred they have usually been when they believed themselves to be considering the child's interests. They have learned the difference between an external evaluation of children in the perspectives of the school's purposes and an internal comprehending of an empathic kind that results from entering into the life of the child, sharing his confusions, his longings, his anxieties and his pain. The advent of counselling in schools, means, if it means nothing else, that children and the world of children will be better understood in future by teachers.
>
> (1976, p. 43)

In broader terms, however, Rogers' contribution has been immeasurable, for he has, as Daws indicates, reminded us of what it means to be a complete human being and of the value of authentic human relationships. He has also contributed more to the theory and practice of psychotherapy than any other psychologists, and greatly advanced scientific research in this field. 'Perhaps more than anyone he made psychology the business of normal people and normal people the business of psychology' (Farson, in Evans, 1981a).

THE HUMAN POTENTIAL MOVEMENT

During the 1960s Maslow and Rogers found a particularly receptive setting for their ideas on California's West Coast.

> The West Coast, it has been said often enough, is a state of mind located on the edges of culture, and many of the pop sociological observations about life in that zone, even on special scrutiny, seem to be perfectly true; the severance from history, the disowning of ethnic background, the preoccupation with the body, the receptivity to Eastern religion, the obsession with the apocalypse. And of course, money. There on the Pacific coast between Los Angeles and San Francisco the celebrated Esalen Institute was established, the T-group was wedded to the 'new culture', and the Encounter was born.
> (Mintz, 1973, p. 3)

At Esalen, as Mintz makes clear, all pretence of groups as the focus of scientific research or for dealing with social problems was abandoned. Instead, the development of human potential and the promotion of qualitative change in being were emphasized. Those aspects of the group that tended to produce the most dramatic changes—confrontations, confessions and catharsis—were explored more fully; techniques for generating more powerful expression of emotion were sought; and, with characteristic West Coast excess, encounters developed into 'marathons' extending for hours or even days.

Maslow and Rogers were both invited to give workshops at Esalen, and did so, alongside the popularizers of Eastern religions, notably Alan Watts and Ram Dass, and the body builders Bernard Gunther and Ida Rolf. Out of this curious synthesis there emerged numerous new-style therapies in which the influence of Eastern traditions was clearly evident, and emphasis on talking gave way to touch, gesture and other non-verbal forms of communication. These therapies, all of which were proclaimed under the banner of the Human Potential Movement, included among others, Rolf's Structural Integration, Assaglioli's Psychosynthesis, Lowen's Bioenergetics and various kinds of touch therapy. However, these disparate influences all came together most effectively in the form of Gestalt Therapy, the brain-child of Fritz Perls.

PATTERNS OF BEING (Frederick Perls)

Whilst the attribution of the term 'gestalt' to a form of therapy might be questionable to many psychologists, the Gestalt Therapy of Frederick (Fritz) Perls can rightly be regarded as a direct application of Gestalt principles to human functioning. *Gestalt* is a German word which has no exact equivalent in the English language, its closest approximation being configuration or pattern. More precisely, however, a gestalt is a whole which cannot be described merely as the sum of its parts. As such a gestalt is irreducible and is destroyed if divided into components.

The term gestalt was applied to a system of thought, derived from early twentieth century experiments in perception by a number of German psychologists, notably Kohler, Kofka and Wertheimer, in which all mental phenomena are regarded as being arranged in gestalts or gestalten. Accordingly an individual perceives any situation as a unified pattern which constitutes a meaningful gestalt. Hence the diffuse impressions received by looking through a window may have meaning in their totality as 'a country view'. However, by focussing attention on certain aspects of the visual field the individual may impose meaningful patterns such that these emerge as unified figures against the diffuse background. Therefore, the focus of attention at one time may be a group of trees, at another the linear flight of passing geese, or at still another, a solitary white horse in the distance. The formation of gestalten is thus a continuous process of emerging figures and receding backgrounds, all of which are nevertheless interdependent parts of a whole perceptual field.

Essentially, Perls viewed the individual organism as existing within an environmental field in which all parts are interdependent, so that change in any one part affects all other parts.

> No individual is self-sufficient; the individual can exist only in an environmental field. The individual is inevitably at every moment a part of some field which includes both him and his environment. The nature of the relationship between him and his environment determines the human being's behaviour. With this new outlook the environment and the organism stand in a relationship of mutuality to one another. (Perls, 1976, p. 16)

Stated thus, Perls' ideas share much in common with the Field Theory of Lewin (1952) and the Organismic Theory of Goldstein (1940), both of which are also derived from the insights of Gestalt Psychology. Whilst the theory of Lewin was applied to social systems and social change, Perls, like Goldstein, was concerned with the individual system—the organism or self—and its growth and change, but he nevertheless recognized that the human environment is essentially social, and thus his model may be viewed as psychosocial.

Like that of Rogers, Perls' view is essentially holistic and integrative. Moreover, it shares a common emphasis on self-actualization. Perls viewed the actualization of self—the becoming of 'what one is'—as an inborn goal in all human beings, plants and animals, and as such a fundamental need of all living things. He argued that self-actualization can only occur through the integration of the various parts of the self because it is in this way that the self emerges as a unified figure against its environmental field. Only then, when the self is located in relation to others and the world, does it become possible for the individual to act, and more importantly, take responsibility for such action, for this integrated self, like any unified field, is more able to utilize its potential. Such a process requires the constant monitoring of the self and redefinition of its contact boundaries, because the gestalten of the environmental field, rather than being static and fixed, are dynamic and everchanging, as the demands of self, others and the external world alter. The satisfaction of these various needs, which is equivalent to psychological health, is something of a balancing act, maintained by a kind of psychological homeostasis, the fundamental requirement of which is awareness of the immediate situation. Hence the aware individual is able to perceive changes in existing gestalten and act accordingly to create new patterns, thereby restoring the equilibrium between the self and its surroundings.

Like Maslow, Perls attributed much of the difficulty in achieving the figure/ground discrimination necessary for gestalt formation to society. He saw the problem as residing largely in the prescription of one central, enduring social role to the individual who consequently is obliged to suppress, disown or project on to others and his environment all those of themself that are inconsistent with the maintenance of that role. This denial of self invariably results in a progressive fragmentation of the person, and a difficulty in establishing boundaries between the self, others and the external world. The person experiences confusion as to where they end and others begin, and they cannot satisfy their needs as they are not aware of what they are. Such confusion can ultimately lead to complete disintegration or breakdown.

Perls viewed neurosis as this inability to perceive boundaries clearly, with the result that the person experiences the world as encroaching upon them. Not surprisingly, therefore, the neurotic is characterized by fear, anxiety, avoidance tendencies and elaborate systems of defence, all aimed at avoiding this intrusion. Moreover, being unable to define personal boundaries, the neurotic manipulates the environment for support in numerous ways rather than utilizing his personal potential. The individual is therefore unable to satisfy his needs and remains in a state of psychological disequilibrium that might justifiably be thought of as 'unbalanced'.

The emphasis implicit in Perls' Gestalt approach, as in Zen and other oriental traditions, is that all things are changing, and consistent with this Gestalt Therapy is not concerned with explanations or interpretations of past history, or with future behaviour. As Perls (1976, p. 44) explains:

> It's like a koan—those Zen questions which seem to be insoluble. The koan is: Nothing exists except the here and now. The now is the present, is the phenomenon, is what you are aware of, is that moment in which you carry your so-called memories, and your so-called anticipations with you. Whether you remember or anticipate, you do it now. The past is no more. The future is not yet. When I say 'I was', that's not now, that's the past. When I say, 'I want to', that's the future, it's not yet. Nothing can possibly exist except the now.

He continues:

> These are the two legs upon which Gestalt Therapy walks: now and how. The essence of the theory of Gestalt Therapy is in the understanding of these two words. 'Now' covers all that exists. The past is no more, the future is not yet. 'Now' includes the balance of being here, is experiencing, involvement, phenomenon, awareness. 'How' covers everything that is structure, behaviour, all that is actually going on—the ongoing process. All the rest is irrelevant—computing, apprehending and so on. Everything is grounded in awareness. (pp. 47–48)

Gestalt Therapy, like Zen, by focussing attention on this koan, aims to promote insight into the various modes of one's being and the integration of formerly disowned aspects of the self. Perls believed that individuals can assimilate the projected parts of themself by role playing and so he employed many techniques of an essentially theatrical nature that were intended to enhance perception, to heighten emotion and awareness of the immediate moment.

Largely as a result of the charismatic nature of Perls and the Gestalt approach's appeal to the counter culture, Gestalt Therapy emerged as one of the most powerful therapies to be developed this century, and it was also to prove one of the most influential forces in the development of the human potential movement, and its best known feature, the encounter.

ENCOUNTER

The encounter group was primarily developed by Rogers as a means whereby persons can break through the barriers erected by themselves and others in order that they can react openly and freely with one another. Its focus is therefore on the process and dynamics of immediate personal interactions. Such groups, comprising between eight and eighteen people, are relatively structured, the members choosing its goals and direction, but with some cognitive input provided by a leader or leaders whose responsibility is the facilitation of both thought and feeling in group members.

Rogers (1973, p. 14) formulated several practical hypotheses common to such groups:

> A facilitator can develop in a group which meets intensively, a psychological climate of safety in which freedom of expression and reduction of defensiveness gradually occur. In such a psychological climate many of the immediate feeling reactions of each member towards others, and of each member towards himself, tend to be expressed. A climate of mutual trust develops out of this mutual freedom to express real feelings, positive and negative. Each member moves towards greater acceptance of his total being—emotional, intellectual and physical—as it *is*, including its potential.

He suggests that change in personal attitudes and behaviour is more likely to occur in individuals who are less inhibited by defensive rigidity, and that encounter groups thus facilitate personal growth and development.

Rogers recognized that style of leadership greatly influences the conduct and experience of groups and that accordingly his description of such is less applicable to Gestalt and other groups in which leaders are typically more forceful and manipulative. The style of these groups is frequently more confrontative, with the leader taking responsibility for setting basic group norms, playing a more active role, and employing various techniques in order to effect the most speedy and dramatic breakthroughs. In addition many of these groups have a greater emphasis on physical behaviour and interaction than on verbal expression.

Esalen became identified with these more intensive and 'gimmicky' groups largely as a result of the contributions of Will Schutz (1967, 1973) who promoted the 'open' encounter in which nudity, for him the symbol of openness and honesty, was virtually mandatory. As a result, encounter came to be seen as characterizing radical approaches to living, rebellion against the traditional mores and values of society—a microcosm of the counter culture—and as offering a 'short-cut' to enlightenment.

Whereas psychotherapy had traditionally operated on a one-to-one basis and within a medical setting with all the overtones of 'mental illness' and social undesirability thus implied, encounter groups came to be seen as divorced from any therapeutic objective. They held the promise of self-discovery and the development of personal potential, which in addition to being highly fashionable also exerted a strong emotional appeal for many people, especially the young, within Western culture. They presented the possibility of answers to fundamental human questions of the spirit; the kind of answers that traditional religions had signally failed to provide for many. Moreover, they were a means of developing close and intimate interpersonal relationships of a kind often denied in the modern world. They were frequently also a lot of fun. Indeed, Schutz (1967) insisted that these groups could lead not only to self-understanding but also to ecstasy and joy.

Mintz (1973) suggests that the encounter movement,

> quite apart from its therapeutic aims, must obviously be seen as part of a universal effort in the modern world to restore the gratifications of community and to reinvent serviceable social mythologies.

He claims that encounter is just another way in which man seeks to fill the meaningless void of modern existence. In this sense it can be thought of as a modern religious movement. Certainly Rogers had set out the pastoral qualities of the therapist, and in identifying those conditions wherein the person is most likely to disclose themselves, pointed to the confessional role of the therapeutic relationship. Mintz (p. 7) has also pointed to other elements of encounter which share features in common with organized religion:

> The games and exercises, initially experimental ways of preparing people for changing lives, eventually became the rituals and sacraments, fixed cultic

performances. Catharsis became the obligatory sacrament, expected eventually to be taken by all; the group's progress from fear, to hate to catharsis to love, became the fixed order of service.

Hamilton (1973) has also pointed to the 'religious-like fervour' with which some of the newer forms of therapy have been developed and proclaimed. Certainly many have more than a little evangelical flavouring, and one can discern in them evidence of a revival of various forms of asceticism. Indeed in many of the newer approaches the deliberate infliction of psychological and physical pain and discomfort is fairly commonplace. Moreover, as Hamilton observes, the validity of these therapies, rather like belief in the existence of God, is an article of faith, to be taken on trust.

In addition to the faith demanded of acolytes, elevation of leaders into gurus is also evident; an identification all too readily made by some. If, as Mintz has suggested, Maslow represents the fathering theoretician of the human potential movement, and Rogers its chief clinician, then Perls must be regarded as its chief guru or high priest, for not only did he take up residence at Esalen, the shrine of the movement, but he also penned its credo, the Gestalt Prayer:

I do my thing, and you do your thing.
I am not in this world to live up to your expectations.
And you are not in this world to live up to mine.
You are you, and I am I,
And if by chance we find each other, it's beautiful.
If not, it can't be helped.   (1976, p. 4)

During the two years that Perls was in residence at Esalen his reputation and that of the workshops he ran attracted greatly increased numbers of people, many of them 'hippies', whose lifestyle, attitudes and dress were readily adopted by the Esalen community. Indeed, Esalen's idyllic setting on the Pacific shoreline against the backdrop of the Santa Lucia mountain range, its incomparable climate and natural sulphur baths proved to be wonderfully liberating. In time Esalen came to be viewed as something of a hedonist's paradise; a west coast Garden of Eden; a view encouraged by the much publicized nude bathing and nude encountering promoted by Schutz. Thus many of the developments at Esalen during the late 1960s and 1970s did much to obscure its fundamental commitment to the exploration of human potential and the values of human existence.

Disenchanted with what he termed the 'turner-onners', Perls left Esalen to set up the Gestalt Institute in Canada, and subsequently voiced reservations and grave concern about the direction that Esalen and the human potential movement was taking. He insisted (1976, p. 4) that 'the wild hedonistic, unrealistic, jazz-it-up, turner-onners have nothing to do with humanism'. He indicated that they were merely 'quacks and con-men' and that their emphasis on instant cure, instant joy, instant sensory awareness and instant enlightenment was a faddism which was dangerous to psychology.

Nevertheless, as Shaffer (1978, p. 5) indicates, it was thus that Esalen came to spearhead and epitomize the human potential movement:

> Esalen helped forge what had until then been a somewhat diffuse set of techniques and practitioners, some of whom had hardly been aware of one another, into a coherent movement — a movement that began to develop, in turn, an increasingly acute sense of its own identity and significance. Without Esalen, the human potential movement would not exist in the form that it does today, and without the human potential movement Esalen would have no raison d'être. *As with other factors related to the popular emergence of humanistic psychology, we can see cause and effect interacting in a reciprocal, mutually enhancing fashion, to a point where it is hard to determine just where one ends and the other begins.*

Chapter 6

THE PHILOSOPHY OF BEING HUMAN

towards a psychology of freedom

If experience is possible in practice it must be possible in theory.
R. D. Laing[5]

In its emphasis on human experience and subjectivity, and issues such as consciousness, emotion, values, personal freedom and responsibility, the human potential movement, like progressive education, Eastern religions, and various cults, had captured the mood of the counter culture, and could be said to reflect the popular psychology of that era. Its concerns were precisely those that orthodox Western psychology had so successfully avoided for the greater part of the twentieth century, but the cultural maelstrom of the 1960s was such that its reverberations were inevitably felt within the mainstream of traditional psychology.

THIRD FORCE PSYCHOLOGY

By the late 1960s psychology could be viewed as three distinct psychologies, or groups of psychology; the behavioural psychologies in the tradition of Watson, Skinner, Tolman and Hull; the psychoanalytic or 'depth' psychologies originating in the theories of Freud and psychoanalysis; and a number of heterogeneous approaches sharing a common focus on the person, and issues relevant and appropriate to human existence. Whilst the first two groups had a positivistic, objectivistic and reductionist orientation, conceiving of man in 'subpersonal mechanical terms' (MacQuarrie 1973, p. 258) that of the latter group was 'humanistic' in the sense that its concerns lay with what it is to be human, and with the everyday

[5]*The Voice of Experience: experience, science and psychiatry*, 1983, p. 65. London: Allen Lane.

functioning and subjective experience of the total human being. Whilst these concerns had been present within psychology for some time, most notably in the writings of William James (1892, 1902), the term 'humanistic psychology' was first coined in 1958, when John Cohen, a British professor of psychology, published a book under that title which represented an unashamedly hostile reaction against what he termed 'ratomorphic robotic psychology'. Subsequently humanistic psychology came to refer, not only to those approaches promoting self-actualization and personal growth as fundamental objectives, but also to those currents within psychology and on its fringes which viewed man as a person rather than a machine or giant rat, and which were concerned with topics such as emotion, intentionality, creativity, spontaneity, higher values and transcendental experience, which had little or no place in the predominant psychological approaches.

Maslow gave wide currency to the term humanistic psychology, claiming that it represented a third force in psychology—thereby employing to good effect the Cabbalistic concept of the third force or middle pillar, that healthy force, similar to kundalini in yoga, which results from a balancing of all the other forces within the body. Indeed, Maslow conceived of the humanistic approach as a unifying force which would synthesize the disparate fields of behaviourism and psychoanalysis and in so doing integrate the subjective and objective, private and public aspects of man into a complete holistic psychology. He insisted that a truly scientific psychology must embrace a humanistic perspective, treating its subject matter as fully human and accommodating within its realm experience and subjectivity as well as objective behaviour.

The growth of humanistic psychology in North America was rapid during the 1960s, where it was closely identified with the flourishing human potential movement. Landmarks in its development as a formal movement within psychology include the establishment of the *Journal of Humanistic Psychology* in 1961; the formation of the American Association for Humanistic Psychology in 1962; and the creation of the American Psychological Association's Division of Humanistic Psychology in 1970.

However, humanistic psychology was slower in gaining a foothold in countries other than the United States of America. Nevertheless, throughout the 1960s the influence of Carl Rogers spread rapidly in Britain with the proliferation of counselling and the establishment of counsellor training courses at the universities of Keele and Reading in 1965, and at Exeter, Swansea and Aston shortly afterwards. Meanwhile, Maslow's theories, which had been channelled into industrial and organizational psychology via the National Training Laboratories' programmes, became familiar throughout Britain and Europe with the expansion of courses in management and business studies. As a result of these initiatives the humanistic approach was widely disseminated and in 1969 the Association for Humanistic Psychology was established in Britain, and was followed in 1970 by the first international conference of the AHP in Amsterdam.

Notwithstanding these developments, the most dramatic impetus was provided by the human potential movement, and Esalen in particular, which became the prototype for over two hundred growth centres throughout the Western world and thereby proceeded in making humanistic psychology more visible and identifiable. By the end of the 1960s, humanistic psychology, as Rogers (1969a) observed, appeared to be 'the wave of the future'. Yet the rapidly rising tide of humanistic psychology was a product of far deeper and stronger currents within Western thought than its fashionable upsurge during the 1960s would suggest, and reflected influences which had existed within psychology and philosophy for several decades.

PHILOSOPHICAL AND PSYCHOLOGICAL SOURCES OF HUMANISTIC PSYCHOLOGY

It might be expected that humanistic psychology has philosophical origins in humanism, and to a certain extent this is the case. However, humanism is less a philosophy than an attitude which has been discernible in literature throughout history since it emerged during the Renaissance allied to developments in printing and the arts, or 'humanities'. Humanism, whilst recognizing the tragic dimensions of human existence, emphasized man's ability to go beyond himself—to transcend mundane reality—and realize his true nature. To this end humanism advocated education, and the development of awareness and human potential; themes reflected in humanistic psychology, together with its other characteristic concerns with human and personal values, responsibility and the unique experience of the individual.

However, despite remote historical roots in humanism, humanistic psychology derives its main inspiration from a more recent source—existentialism—which, although originating with Pascal in the seventeenth century, is largely a product of nineteenth and twentieth century thought.

EXISTENTIALISM

The particular focus of existentialism, as the name suggests, is existence, a term that derives from the Latin verb *existere*, which means to stand out from, emerge or become. Existence is therefore emergent; it is a *process* of coming into being, or becoming, rather than a *state* of being.

In existential thought man is responsible for his becoming in the sense that by choosing among different alternatives for behaviour he becomes authentically himself—that self which he really is—and it is this exercise of freedom that distinguishes man from all other creatures. Such a view challenges the doctrine, held by Western psychology for over a century, that man is determined by hereditary or environmental factors and early childhood experiences, and as Barnes (1959, p. II) indicates, asserts quite the opposite.

> A person does not possess a ready-made character, formed by hereditary and environmental pressures and developing in accordance with strict psychological laws. Man is not determined by passions which sweep over him like external forces. His emotions, like every one of his attitudes, are the result of the way he has decided to relate himself to the world around him. He is free at any time to make a new choice of himself; to choose a fresh way of living out his existence and to remake his so-called 'nature'.

The common interest which unites all existentialists is therefore a commitment to human freedom, and a rejection of all forms of determinism characterizes the existential approach.

The existentialists' concern with freedom, as Warnock (1970, p. 2) indicates, is not merely abstract but practical inasmuch as their primary aim is not merely to consider the nature of freedom but to experience it, and to show people that they are free to choose 'not only what to do on a specific occasion, but what to value and how to live'. Nevertheless, existentialists recognize that man's quest for authentic being meets resistance. As Sartre explains:

> What is universal . . . is not nature but the situations in which man finds himself: that is, not the sum total of his psychological traits but the limits which enclose him on all sides.   (quoted in Barnes, 1959, p. 12)

These limits or ultimate concerns, as recognized by all existentialists, are the intrinsic, and therefore inescapable features or 'givens' of what Heidegger termed *dasein*—man's 'being there' in the world. They include freedom, death, isolation and meaninglessness. However, existentialists differ in the emphasis that they place on each.

Freedom

The freedom of which existentialists speak is absolute. It is the state of total randomness or entropy—what the Ancient Greeks would have termed *khaos*—into which the individual is thrown at birth, and from which he has to create his own structure. Accordingly, life may be thought of as a game for which there is no set of rules and which has to be invented as it is played. The individual is therefore responsible for constructing his own experience and reality, his choices and actions. Every person is in the position of having to realize that they are the creator of their own world; that all life's experiences are there because they have drawn them thus, and that they can do with them as they choose; that one *is* one's choices. Tillich (1952) observes that from this perspective man is essentially finite-freedom inasmuch that he is free within the limits imposed by his 'being in the world' to make himself what he wants to be. For Tillich, therefore, the primary task of the individual is attaining the courage to be.

Creating oneself, or becoming, requires courage because most people fear the consequences and responsibilities of freedom and therefore refuse to acknowledge it in themselves and frequently attempt to deny it in others; they cannot acknowledge that their values, purposes, projects, are sustained by their own free choice, because to do so is to accept sole responsibility for their life. It is the burden of responsibility implied by human freedom that most people shun. Paradoxically, therefore, they desire to be free of freedom, hence Gibran's observation (1978, p. 56): 'I have seen the freest among you wear their freedom as a yoke and a handcuff.' However, frequently this is accompanied by guilt, as the person recognizes that as a result of failing to fulfil their authentic possibilities—their personal potential—they have become less than they could have.

The acceptance of death

Death also presents man with a paradox because in striving to create his own being he is at all times confronted with the inevitability of his non-being. As Sartre has observed, 'nothingness lies coiled at the heart of being', and awareness of this is reflected not only in the human fear of death, or loss of existence, but also in fears relating to loss of the sense of self or essence; loss of identity or face. Thus the sense *that* one is, and of *what* and *who* one is, is very tenuous and a matter of great concern in existence.

Death therefore features prominently in the writings of existentialists, and is frequently taken as evidence of a morbid or nihilistic outlook. However, existentialists do not see death merely as an end but as an intrinsic part of life. Death is thus considered in terms of how it impinges on life. Indeed, from an existential perspective it is the acceptance of death which makes it possible for man to live in an authentic manner. This insight was essentially that of Heidegger who conceived of two modes of existence; a state of mindfulness of being or authenticity in which the individual is constantly aware of the fragility of his being and his responsibility for it; and a state of forgetfulness of being or inauthenticity in which the individual is seduced by the way things appear to be in the world and abdicates responsibility for his life. Whereas in the former state the individual is fully self-aware, recognizing himself as the author of his being and embracing his potentials and his limits, in the latter the individual is 'benighted' or asleep, unawake to his authorship or creativity, his potential and the true nature of his being. This corresponds to the Indian concept of *avidja* or ignorance, when the mind is directed outwards to the world of appearances, illusion or *maya*. Similarly the concept of authenticity relates to the Indian concept of mindfulness, the path to transcendence which looks inwards to the nature of being; and in both Indian and existential philosophy it is the awareness of personal death which acts as a spur to shift man from the ordinary, soporific state of forgetfulness to the transcendent, awakened state of mindfulness.

Echoes of the role of death in man's awakening are found in the contemporary writings of Castaneda (1975, p. 56). Don Juan maintains that the first step towards seeing the world as it really is, or enlightenment, is to recognize the imminence of death; to see death as a hunter who may strike at any moment and to be prepared for that event: 'In a world where death is the hunter, my friend, there is no time for regrets and doubts. There is only time for decisions.' Death, rather than mere disintegration, is thus an integrating factor, awareness of which prompts decision, choice and action, and promotes authentic being. However, as Yalom (1980, p. 357) observes, 'Deep loneliness is inherent in the act of self-creation', and it is this which ensures the ultimate isolation of man.

Isolation

'Existential' isolation, which arises from the individual's lone responsibility for creating themself and their world, is distinct from interpersonal or intrapersonal isolation.

Interpersonal isolation, which is generally experienced as loneliness, involves isolation from other persons and it arises as a result of many different factors such as geographic distance, confinement, personality, or inadequate social skills, whereas intrapersonal isolation can be thought of as the distancing of parts of the self such that feelings and emotions, desires or wishes become remote and out of touch. Maslow (1968) suggested that in failing to acknowledge their personal potential many individuals effectively turn their back on a great part of themself, thereby becoming split, and not being 'together' they are unable to lead effective lives. Much energy is channelled into maintaining these separate parts or 'selves', until inevitably, as in juggling, the performance can no longer be sustained, and falls apart. The person literally 'cracks up' or 'breaks down'. For this reason many of the therapies allied to the Human Potential Movement focus on the person's recognition, acceptance and actualization of their full potential with the aim of integrating their 'split parts', hence the contemporary emphasis on 'getting it together'. Both forms of isolation can be dealt with by putting people in touch with themselves, or others through therapy, skills training, community programmes, encounter, or simply, through improved communication.

However, from the existential perspective man's aloneness, like his freedom, is absolute. Indeed, man's isolation arises because of his freedom because he alone creates his experience which is unique and untransferable. Accordingly,

> I see you, and you see me.
> I experience you, and you experience me.
> I see your behaviour.
> You see my behaviour.
> But I do not and never have and never will see your experience of me.
>
> (Laing, 1973, p. 15)

All togetherness is therefore illusory because no matter how close a person is to another, ultimately there remains between them a great divide, the unbridgeable gap of their individual experience, and defences inevitably arise as a person becomes aware of this isolation and loneliness. One response to such loneliness is to plunge oneself into relationships. Nevertheless, much human relating fails to satisfy the need for togetherness, because the relationship itself is illusory, arising from what Buber (1970) identified as an I–it relationship; a functional relationship between a person and an object, or equipment, wholly lacking in mutuality. Fromm (1979) distinguishes this form of relationship from need-free, mutual or reciprocal relating which involves a full experiencing and acceptance of the other—what Buber termed an I–Thou relationship in which the self is transcended. Such a relationship is a dialogue in the true sense of the word, as it involves the turning toward another with one's whole being.

Frankl observes that such dialogue is rare in the everyday world, because what passes as dialogue is frequently no more than monologue in tandem, where two or more people use the 'relationship' as an opportunity for self-expression and little else. Similarly, he argues that much so-called 'encounter' is equally vacuous. Lacking authentic relationships, therefore, people experience more acutely their existential isolation, and for this reason many existentialists regard isolation as human beings' most fundamental concern. As Yalom (1980, p. 368) observes, 'Our existence begins with a solitary, lonely cry, anxiously awaiting a response.' Similarly, Fromm (1979) views awareness of separation, or isolation, as the source of all anxiety, and considers overcoming separation to be man's major task. Accordingly, like Buber, he sees the basic mode of existence as relational.

Meaninglessness

The existentialist conceives of man having to create his own world in an otherwise unstructured universe, yet remain entirely alone within it then die. Such a process appears to be quite pointless, and herein lies the absurdity or meaninglessness of existence. Man, an apparently meaning-seeking creature, is unable to explain his own being, and this often gives rise to despair. However, despite viewing death as final proof of the absurdity of human existence, writers such as Camus and Sartre, saw death as something against which man can rebel, investing life with personal meaning and purpose and becoming committed to it. Their literary characters thus frequently find something to live for.

The problem of contemporary man is that the meanings formerly provided by religion, education and family life have been eroded, and as Yalom (1980, p. 448) observes:

> Work, what there is of it, no longer supplies meaning. Not even an extra-
> ordinarily fertile imagination could imbue many common forms of modern
> work with creative potential. The assembly line worker, for example, begins

to consider himself or herself as a mindless cog in the factory machinery. Furthermore, much work lacks intrinsic value. How can the members of clerical armies performing 'busy' work in vast, wasteful bureaucratic systems believe that their activities are worthwhile?

For this reason Frankl (1969b) considers that many people in contemporary society live in an existential vacuum which arises because of the gulf between their need for meaning in life on the one hand, and the lack of any perceived meanings on the other. He claims that as a result of this frustration of their will to meaning, which he views as the fundamental existential dynamic, many people suffer from what he terms 'noogenic neurosis', the remedy for which is his logotherapy which aims at helping the individual to discover or rediscover meaning in life. Nevertheless, although persuasively argued, Frankl's claim that logotherapy constitutes a true, and effective, existential therapy, is undermined by the lack of any clear indication of the actual process involved.

Themes such as freedom, choice, intentionality and responsibility are all prominent in existentialism, together with issues such as death, alienation, despair and guilt. However, as conceived by its modern founders Kierkegaard and Nietzche, and subsequently developed by Heidegger, Jaspers, Marcel, Merleau-Ponty and Sartre, and writers such as Camus, Becket and de Beauvoir, existentialism has come to embrace many different assumptions. Like humanism therefore, existentialism is not a philosophy in the strict sense of having a common body of knowledge to which all thinkers subscribe, but rather, a common label for several widely different revolts against traditional philosophy. It is, MacQuarrie (1973, p. 14) suggests, more a 'style of philosophising'.

Nevertheless, Warnock (1970) claims that it can be regarded as a kind of philosophy, and that it is therefore possible to differentiate between existentialist philosophers and non-philosophical existentialist playwrights, novelists and essayists. She distinguishes in existentialism not only common themes, but a common ancestry which comprises two different traditions; the ethical, which arises with Kierkegaard and Nietzche; and the phenomenological, established by Husserl, and insists that both are essential to philosophical existentialism.

The ethical tradition emphasizes man as a voluntary agent and a possessor of will, whereas the phenomenological tradition emphasizes a particular way of observing and describing man's connection with the world. In attempting to provide a systematic account of man's experience it represents a definite method rather than merely a literary style of form. Warnock claims that 'the non-philosophical existentialist will share the common interests of his philosophical cousin, but he will not share a method' (p. 3). This distinction, as will be seen, has important implications for humanistic psychology, and therefore requires fuller consideration.

The ethical tradition of existentialism

Kierkegaard and Nietzche, who are regarded as the founding fathers of modern existentialism, whilst not in agreement on all essentials, shared a common distaste for traditional Western philosophy with its insistence on objective knowledge, external reality and rationality, and the belief that they were a means to enlightenment and progress. Kierkegaard was opposed to the wisdom of the Greeks, attacking Greek heritage in both philosophy and theology. For him, enlightenment meant seeing beyond illusion and he committed himself with almost missionary zeal to showing people the light and freeing them from what he regarded as the fundamental illusions of Western science, namely objectivity or the stance of the observer, and causal determinism. He held the view that man is free because he is able to think and choose for himself without recourse to laws, rules and standards; that he is self-governing and creative, and his morality lies in his discovering himself. Kierkegaard thus rejected all scientism and positivism, and encouraged man to rediscover and value his subjectivity. As Kaufman (1956) observes, Kierkegaard was a man in revolt against reason.

Nietzche also regarded objectivity as the fundamental obstacle to understanding. He recognized that any apparently objective and scientific description of phenomena implicitly involves a subjective selection, categorization and interpretation and is ultimately a matter of choice, and that as the concepts thus selected are chosen to suit personal purposes, values necessarily enter into even the most mundane descriptions. He therefore viewed the notion of absolute objective truth and 'hard' identifiable facts 'out there' in the world as illusory and the human mind as leading to abstraction and falsification rather than truth. In his schema the phenomena of experience could not be separated from the experiencer and accordingly he rejected the Cartesian subject–object dichotomy in favour of a unified concept of man. He regarded the scientific search for absolute truth as a reflection of a desperate need for certainty in an uncertain world, and the outcome of fear. This anti-Cartesian, anti-rational characteristic of existentialism's ethical tradition is, as Warnock indicates, also shared by existentialism's other 'parent', the phenomenology of Husserl.

The phenomenological tradition encompasses various doctrines all of which share a common assumption that philosophical enquiry must commence with the phenomena of consciousness since this is all that is available to man, and that the only means of accessing this knowledge is through the exploration of consciousness by way of inner perception or insight. Husserl was committed to the clarification of experience and its objects, and he conceived of phenomenology as a scientific and exact method for mounting this examination.

The term phenomenology derives from two Greek words, *phenomenon* meaning appearance, or that which shows itself; and *logos* meaning study. Phenomenology is literally, therefore, the study of the appearance of things as they appear in consciousness, rather than the study of things in themself. It is a subjective approach inasmuch as reality is seen to reside in the person's perception of an object rather than in the object itself. In developing his phenomenology Husserl was influenced by Brentano, particularly his notion that psychological acts are directed to objects and thus intentional in the literal sense (from the Latin *intendere*—to stretch forth) that consciousness 'stretches forth' towards them. For Husserl consciousness is always consciousness 'of' something, and he perceived the task of phenomenology to be to identify the 'intentional lines' that connect man to the world.

The means by which this is achieved, the phenomenological method, relies solely upon the immanent object under investigation and the particular mode through which it is received. It therefore requires the suspension of all belief in reality beyond intentionality, that is, beyond the object wilfully extended toward, and follows the nature of the things to be investigated and not the person's prejudices and preconceptions. These must be neither introduced into the enquiry, nor dismissed, but suspended or 'bracketed' so that no use is made of them. The method involves three main phases: intuition, or focus upon the phenomena of consciousness, whether thoughts, fantasies, ideas or images; analysis or discovery of the various constituents of such phenomena and their relationships; and description or communication of these perceptions.

The influence of phenomenology is discernible in the work of many psychologists, notably those of the Gestalt school, including Kofka, Kohler and Wertheimer, and in the writings of James (1902), Goldstein (1940), Allport (1963), Snygg and Combs (1959), Kelly (1955, 1963), and Gibson (1950), but it is most clearly evident in the therapeutic approaches of Rogers and Perls. Perls (1969) claimed that phenomenology is the primary and indispensable step towards all knowledge, and that for this reason awareness is at the very centre of his approach.

Nevertheless, Husserl's phenomenology was most readily adopted by other existential thinkers such as Heidegger and Scheler. Indeed, as Warnock has pointed out, all existential philosophers are phenomenologists inasmuch as they adopt phenomenology as their basic method. This is not necessarily true of all existentialist writers whose main concern is to depict fictional characters who act in accordance with a psychology of freedom. The only existentialist to fulfil the criteria of both philosopher and writer was Jean-Paul Sartre—perhaps the most influential existential thinker of recent times, whose particular contribution was his attempt to provide a philosophical and methodological basis for a psychology of freedom.

Existential psychology

Sartre (1946, reprinted 1984) claimed existentialism as a humanism in the sense that it is concerned with human and personal values and with the realization of authentic human being. He viewed the life of every person as a pursuit of authentic self and insisted that the only way for a person to realize his true self is by recognizing that his being is his individual freedom; that he is responsible for all his acts and determined by nothing; and despite his attempts to escape responsibility for himself, which Sartre termed 'bad faith', cannot completely escape from the burden of lone individuality.

He also pointed to the inadequacies of conventional psychology, in particular its determinism and reductionism, but also its neglect of social factors. He claimed that psychology is too abstract and that the study of man is only meaningful when explored within its full social context. In so doing Sartre was not merely attempting to replace psychology with sociology but attacking the very definition of psychology by pointing out that the self or psyche cannot be studied, much less understood, in isolation from others and the environment in the widest sense. Its focus on the individual is thus partial and inadequate. Nevertheless, as he pointed out, he was not seeking to reject psychology, merely to integrate life. That this was the case is clear from his proposals for a full existential psychology; an applied psychology of freedom or humanistic psychology which he termed existential psychoanalysis, the aim of which would be to establish the person's existential mode—that is, the individual's choice of being and the relations thus established between their self, others and the external world. Such a psychology rests on three basic assumptions: that man is wholly conscious, and functions as a total unit whose actions can be fully explained only as an expression of a basic choice of existence or being, which is a free decision. Man thus chooses himself and is free to change himself as he wishes. Existential psychoanalysis, as framed by Sartre, is therefore a holistic psychology in which the person is viewed, not in terms of bits, pieces, reflexes and habitual responses, nor as a being in a vacuum, but as a total entity or gestalt; a social being whose total situation must be taken fully into account.

The term psychoanalysis, although confusing because of its Freudian connotations, is not, according to Sartre's translator Hazel Barnes, ill-chosen, for whilst Sartre attacked Freud on numerous grounds including his determinism, and his reductionist id, super-ego, ego model, his psychology owes much to Freudian insights. As Yalom (1980) indicates, the model of human functioning Sartre implies is similar in basic structure to that of Freud, although it is radically different in content. Whilst Freud viewed drives and instinctive mechanisms as bringing the individual into conflict with internalized social forces and the environment, necessitating the development of defence mechanisms as a protection against the anxiety thus generated, in existential psychodynamics, anxiety and the resulting defences are deemed to be a response to the individual's confrontation with the givens of existence. The conflict exphasized by Sartre is that man is unable to face the truth of his existence and seeks various forms of escape. Both his and the Freudian model emphasizes conflict, albeit of a different kind; both assume that this conflict generates anxiety; and both hold that certain psychic operations evolve to deal with this anxiety.

Nevertheless, Sartre did not claim existential psychoanalysis as therapy. It is, Barnes suggests, essentially an outline methodological theory rather than a theory of man and as such was not intended to pass for either a fully developed method or theory. Sartre himself declared that existential psychoanalysis had yet to find its Freud, and indicated that the skeletal theoretical structure he had provided needed padding with empirical evidence. He was content to have demonstrated that such an analysis is possible, and to have laid the groundwork.

Existential psychoanalysis remains incompletely systematized. Several European psychiatrists subsequently developed various forms of existential analysis, some of which were claimed as therapy. Leading European analysts have included Gebsattel and Zutt (Germany), Minkowski (France), Binswanger, Boss and Kuhn (Switzerland), Van den Berg (Netherlands), and Frankl and Caruso (Austria). However, their work remained largely unknown outside Europe until it was introduced to America by Rollo May in 1958. This is partly because the existential analysts do not represent a cohesive school, sharing little in common apart from their reaction against the mechanistic determinism of the Freudian approach and a commitment to phenomenological methods. Of greater significance, however, is that, Frankl apart, their works have seldom been translated. Yalom suggests that this is partly a result of 'the abstruse nature of their writing: they are steeped in a Continental philosophical Weltanschauung far out of synchrony with the American pragmatic tradition in therapy' (1980, p. 17), with the result that almost thirty years after the introduction of their approach to America, they exert little influence on its psychotherapeutic practice.

British existentialism (R. D. Laing)

During the 1950s and 1960s several British psychiatrists, notably R. D. Laing, David Cooper and Aaron Esterson, who were united in their opposition to existing conditions in state mental hospitals, enthusiastically embraced European existentialism, and especially that of Sartre. At this time conditions in British psychiatric hospitals were particularly bad. According to Holland (1977, p. 192), 'the only practicable methods of treatment were quick surgical, electrical, or drug therapies which were "empirical" rather than theoretically grounded and served more to bring patients under control than cure them'.

The British existentialists rejected the disease model of mental illness and were hostile to exclusively organic or genetic explanations of schizophrenia, which like Szasz (1972, 1973), they viewed as a metaphor for dealing with people whose behaviour and experience fails to conform to the dominant model of social reality; and to the literal medical and psychiatric treatments of these metaphorical diseases which ignore the social context of the person. As Shaffer (1978, p. 59) indicates, in Laing's hands 'Schizophrenia is transformed from a clinical entity into a metaphor for modern alienation and despair'. In his first book (1959) Laing offered an existential analysis of schizophrenia in terms of the developing schism within the self in response to intolerable social pressures, and he argued that so-called mental illness is the person's attempt at reintegration of this divided, fragmented self. It is therefore a journey to find the self in a hostile world.

Sartre's distinctive synthesis of existentialism and Marxist socialism held a strong appeal for British existentialists as Holland (1977, pp. 197–199) explains:

> The Marxian critique of society gives them a weapon for attack on the institutions which obstruct and offend them; this in the double sense of the psychiatric institutions themselves and again the institutionalised structure of society. It is the latter which controls the mental hospitals, giving controlling power to the medical profession, a profession of high status and with such studied seriousness and propriety in its practice that it might be a model of the bourgeois values Sartre attacks so scathingly.
>
> Sartre's sensitivity to the nuances of human feeling and experience, together with a confident phenomenological stance which enables him to explore these areas not as side issue or epiphenomena of some more objective biomedical reality, but as central subject matter of a human science, gives the British existentialists a sense that they are going to the heart of the matter of human relationships, rather than moving to a lunatic fringe of human experience and to the margins of their discipline.
>
> Sartre's aim of synthesising knowledge over several disciplines taking into account self, role, and group membership promises to clarify the relation between psychic and personality structures and the formative influence of the family, social groups and institutions.
>
> Possibly above all else Sartre, from his roots in European phenomenology, offers them a rigorous science, in Husserl's sense, to set against the institutionalised form of British science which is not only unsuitable to their purposes, but to the extent that it segregates and regulates medicopsychiatric knowledge, psychology and other disciplines, is integral to the oppressive practice they want to get rid of . . . They could with this philosophy, challenge existing definitions of scientific method, subject matter and disciplinary boundaries.

As a result of their stance against institutionalized science in general, and psychiatry in particular, the British existentialists were viewed as spearheading what came to be known as the 'anti-psychiatry' movement. In spite of the significant contributions of Cooper, Esterson and Berke, the movement is largely identified with the work of R. D. Laing, whose critique of conventional therapeutics also extended to so-called 'existential' therapies, including Ludwig Binswanger's (1958) *daseinanalysis* of Ellen West which is generally taken to be the standard work in this field and an exemplary model of its kind. Nevertheless, Laing (1983, p. 54) argues that it reveals Binswanger's inability to practice what he preached:

> In this attempt at existential analysis, we see psychiatric diagnostics carried to the extreme, and to the extremity of absurdity. To keep up the absurdity, one can diagnose in it all the familiar traits of the psychiatric syndrome of

distancing, cutting-off, objectification, reification, splitting, decomposition etc. It is a tragi-comical paradox that Binswanger's account is, in many ways, a perfect example of just what he is striving, not desperately enough, not self-reflectively and self-ironically enough, to eschew and leave behind.

Binswanger's study therefore exemplifies exactly what he attacks:

> His 'existential' look turns out to be a further sophistication of the very institutionalized depersonalized — depersonalizing objectivizing psychiatric diagnostic look, from which he is trying to disencumber himself.
>
> (Laing, 1983, pp.61–62)

The anti-psychiatrists took the view that approaching a condition in this way reinforces, maintains, and typically, contains it within a hospital framework. In attempting a more authentic existential approach to therapy they sought to remove all labels and diagnostic categories, together with all role distinctions between therapist and patient, and to provide an informal and unstructured environment in which so-called schizophrenics could discover themselves through genuine encounters with others. This approach, which Ruitenbeek (1972) termed 'radical therapy', was first attempted by Cooper, who in reporting on it (1967, p. 82) explains:

> The small but important minority of people entering mental hospitals who actually go mad (disintegrate) need psychiatrists and nurses who have sufficiently outgrown their fear, who have been at least relatively honest about their own madness, who have become capable of sanity by preferring it to normality. What was needed, I felt, in initiating a new type of psychiatric situation, was not techniques, or a programme, but the right people.

His Villa 21, introduced in January 1962, was an experimental therapeutic ward within a conventional hospital, specifically orientated to the problem of young people who had recently acquired the label of schizophrenia. It proved to be short-lived as its ethos was in conflict with that of the 'parent' institution. The counter culture it represented within psycho-medical practice and the opposition it attracted within that domain are well-documented in Loach's film *Family Life*. However, the experiment was not without gain, as Cooper acknowledges. It had shown clearly the limits of institutional change, and suggested that if such a unit were to develop further it should be located outside the larger institution, and ultimately become a place to which people choose to go. It should be a safe refuge; an asylum in the true sense of the word.

Subsequently Cooper joined Laing and Esterson in forming the Philadelphia Association, which as a registered charity took over Kingsley Hall, a disused workhouse in the East End of London, and converted it into a therapeutic community in which they, as therapists, lived alongside those seeking help. Until its closure in 1970 this provided asylum for those journeying through madness in search of themself. One of those who did so, Mary Barnes, wrote an account of her experience at Kingsley Hall in conjunction with her resident therapist Joseph Berke. This was published in 1973 and served to draw widespread attention to anti-psychiatry, which had gained momentum throughout the 1960s, and particularly to the work of Laing, whose radicalism found resonance in the counter culture. Indeed Laing was hailed as a major prophet of the counter culture. As Heather (1976, p. 93) observes, 'his influence has extended far beyond the confines of psychiatry and it is little exaggeration to say that he has affected the outlook of a whole generation of critical minds'. Shaffer (1978, p. 49) explains Laing's particular appeal for the counter culture in terms of the similar position he adopts *vis-à-vis* Western society, namely questioning its most basic assumption that the self or ego is an indivisible core element in all experience; being sceptical of almost all social institutions, including the family; and implying that the only means of salvation lies in the attainment of altered states of consciousness, whether through drugs, religious ecstasy or madness.

Certainly Laing's qualifications for the role of cult figure during the 1960s were second to none. He had experimented with the legal use of hallucinogens such as LSD and had befriended Timothy Leary; been involved in the radical 'underground' movement in Britain; lent his support to the movement to legalize marijuana; toured the East; studied Yoga and Zen; resided in a Buddhist monastery; become a media personality, appearing in both films and television; and gained something of a reputation as a jazz pianist. Given such credentials Laing's popularity was perhaps not surprising. However, as Barnes (1959, p. 155) points out:

> All existential writers offer—each in his own way—a challenge to conventional moral codes, a sense of urgency in matters of conscience, an interest in the private introspections of the individual. In addition, there are certain emotionally charged psychological concepts which are forever recurring, ideas scarcely found in other philosophies—anguish, dread, nausea, despair, the compulsive demand for passionate choice and commitment.

New World existentialism

During the 1960s the United States of America embraced existentialism, although few therapists were committed to any one system of therapy or theoretical approach, merely extracting certain elements from the varieties of existential thought and synthesizing these with other approaches. May (1967) likened existentialism in the USA to 'a tower of Babel, a confusion of tongues'; a confusion which owed much to existentialism being held in a casual half-embrace by humanistic psychology.

Rogers (1969a, p. 130) enthusiastically welcomed what he termed 'the phenomenological–existential movement', claiming it as a new philosophical emphasis:

Here is the voice of subjective man speaking up loudly for himself. Man has long felt himself to be a puppet in life — molded by economic forces, by unconscious forces, by environmental forces. He has been enslaved by persons, by institutions, by the theories of psychological science. But he is firmly setting forth a new declaration of independence. He is discarding the alibis of *un*freedom. He is *choosing* himself, endeavouring, in a most difficult and often tragic world, to *become* himself — not a puppet, not a slave, not a machine, but his own unique individual self. The view I have been describing in psychology has room for this philosophy of man.

He went on to state the consequences for psychology of this 'fresh new current in modern culture':

It will make confident use of subjective, intuitive hypotheses formulated by the scientist who has immersed himself in his field of study and senses a pattern, an order, which he can perhaps only partially articulate.

It leads, I believe, to a naturalistic, empathic, sensitive observation of the world of inner meanings as they exist in the individual. The whole range and scope of the human situation as it exists in each individual is thus opened for consideration.

It leads to the formulation of heuristic concepts based upon such observation. In my judgement these concepts will tend to have more of a process-quality than do the psychological concepts of the past. It requires careful definition of observable behaviours which are indexes of these subjective variables. It is recognised that variables of inner experience cannot be measured directly, but it is also realised that the fact that they are inner variables does not preclude their scientific study.

It is leading and will, I believe, increasingly lead to the imaginative development of clearly operational steps and operational tools for the measurement of the behaviours which represent these inner variables.

It seems quite evident that it will lead to a diminishing of the dichotomy between subject and object as it studies the relationships between the internal variables and such external variables as environmental stimuli, outward behaviour and the like . . .

It will lead to theoretical formulations which will be as shocking to conventional psychologists as theories of non-Euclidian space were for conventional physicists. We shall be attempting to discover the functional process-relationships which hold for the inner world of personal meanings and to formulate these with sufficient precision that they may be put to empirical test.

It contains within it the seeds of a newer philosophy of science which will not be fearful of finding room for the person — both the observer and the observed — in his subjective as well as his objective mode. It will carry within it a view of man as a subjectively free, choosing, responsible, architect of self.

(pp. 130–131)

Maslow also drew attention to existentialism, claiming that it might supply psychology with the philosophical underpinning it lacks and thereby effect 'an overdue revolution in the theory of science' (1968, p. 15).

Nevertheless, despite the claims of Rogers, Maslow, May and others that an existential perspective would enrich not only psychology but science in general, there was outright hostility to existentialism in the USA where it was associated with 'drop outs' such as Kerouac and other writers of the 1950s 'beat' era. As Allport (1969, p.96) observed, 'The beatnik aspect of existentialism is European, not American, in flavour.' Certainly, much existentialism is not to American taste, and despite its many attractions even some humanistic psychologists found it to be rather too preoccupied with dread, anguish, despair and nausea for their liking. Trends in American thought tend to be rather more optimistic and expansive as befits America's pioneering and youthful spirit, and the existential emphasis on resignation and acceptance, and even the 'courage to be' advocated by American theologian and existentialist Paul Tillich were unattractive. The result is that the American field of humanistic psychology is by no means synonymous with the European existential tradition. There is a fundamental difference in accent, which Yalom (1980, p. 19) explains:

> The existential tradition in Europe has always emphasised human limitations and the tragic dimensions of existence. Perhaps it has done so because Europeans have had a greater familiarity with geographic and ethnic confinement, with war, death and uncertain existence. The United States (and the humanistic psychology it spawned) bathed in a Zeitgeist of expansiveness, optimism, limitless horizons, and pragmatism. Accordingly, the imported form of existential thought has been systematically altered. Each of the basic tenets has a distinct New World accent. The European focus is on limits, on facing and taking into oneself the anxiety of uncertainty and non-being. The humanistic psychologists, on the other hand, speak less of limits and contingency than of development of potential, less of acceptance than of awareness, less of anxiety than of peak experiences and oceanic oneness, less of life meaning than of self-realization, less of apartness and basic isolation than I-thou and encounter.

Moreover, in addition to its New World accent and West Coast jargon, American existentialism is, as Child (1973) observes, dispensed in a characteristically sentimental style which carries with it a simple religious optimism about man's capacity for good. His propensity for evil, exploitation, and even failure, is subtly avoided. Inevitably therefore the value judgements as to the nature of human life are rather different than in European existentialism. In the American format love, sense of self, becoming and self-actualization are the key concepts. Holland (1977) attributes the contrast between American and British existentialism to the different experience of those such as Allport, Rogers, Kelly and Maslow to that of Laing, Cooper and Esterson. He suggests that whereas the former dealt primarily with middle-class and not extremely disturbed counselling clients, many of whom were students, the British group were dealing with largely working-class, hospitalized patients with the full range of disturbances in institutions already overflowing with the most deteriorated and hopeless cases. Thus

> Whereas the American theorists filter out the more radical elements of existentialist theory, the British existentialists can hardly find a theory radical enough to make sense of their experience. So the British existentialists' reaction takes them from the safe centre to the very edge: instead of a retreat into positive generality it is a full scale attack on the boundaries of social knowledge and social norms. (p. 192)

Holland therefore criticizes the Americans for importing great sources of European knowledge, phenomenology and existentialism, but in such a selective way that much of their force and originality is 'left somewhere in mid-Atlantic or in the customs post' (p. 59). Moreover, he claims that in developing their own specialized interpretation of these sources they created an American variant of existentialism which is not rooted in its predecessors, lacks their substance and as a result is not capable of dealing with human experience and action.

Holland's claim is essentially that humanistic psychology is an American kind of existentialism which lacks a method for dealing adequately with its subject matter, human beings. In Warnock's terms such an existentialism is little more than a literary form. Holland suggests that 'Having lost is earthy grip, it cannot, as a science, ascend to heaven: it remains in the limbo of fantasy' (p. 59). In order to test these claims it is necessary to determine to what extent humanistic psychology has methods, and how adequate, or otherwise, any such methods are.

Chapter 7

TECHNOLOGY OR TAO?

methods in psychotherapy

The way to do is to be.   Lao Tsu

Barnes (1959, p. 324) states that 'in the literature of humanistic existentialism the psychology of freedom is everywhere implied. In many instances . . . the fictionalised characters are presented almost as case studies illustrative of a new view of human personality. Yet since these beings are imaginary they cannot of course serve as conclusive evidence for a psychological theory.' She explains that it is for this reason that Sartre sought to demonstrate his psychological method by compiling biographies of real literary figures such as Baudelaire and Genet. However, as Barnes indicates, whilst these are fully consistent with Sartre's existential analysis, neither resembling case histories in the more usual sense nor literary studies, there is nonetheless, no absolute means for establishing their truth.

It can also be argued that the psychology of freedom is everywhere implied in the literature of humanistic psychology inasmuch as the principles of self-actualization, self-determination, autonomy, authenticity, personal choice and responsibility are constantly reiterated and eulogized, and illustrated by reference to case studies. Maslow's portrayal of self-actualized persons (1954) amounts to little more than a biographical analysis of various figures in public life, and as such has no greater claim to truth than the biographies compiled by Sartre. Furthermore, it can be argued that Maslow's accounts, relying as they do rather too exclusively on unsystematic observation and conjecture, are considerably less rigorous than those of Sartre and more akin to literary caricatures.

It is not immediately clear therefore how the humanistic psychologist differs from the playwright, novelist or essayist. For this reason Murphy (1971), quoted in Westland (1978, p. 124) lays down the challenge:

> If by humanistic psychology you mean you're going to do more than the playwright and the novelist and the historian do, if you are going to attempt the discipline of psychology, a scientific study, then meet the standards of science.

Thus, given that science is largely defined by its method, it seems appropriate to distinguish literary humanism from psychological humanism in terms of method, in much the way that Warnock (1970) distinguishes literary and philosophical existentialism. However, on posing the question 'What are the methods of humanistic psychology?', or simply, 'What do humanistic psychologists do to justify their claims to psychological science?', one runs headlong into a fundamental problem.

THE NON-METHOD OF BEING

In embracing existentialism, humanistic psychology is implicitly committed to a philosophy of being, not doing; a philosophy which promotes qualities of being rather than specific actions. As such it is anti-method. The Indian scholar Rajneesh (1979, pp. 98–99) employs a parable to illustrate this attitude:

> A king wanted to pick the wisest man among his subjects to be his prime minister. When the search finally narrowed down three men, he decided to put them to the supreme test. Accordingly, he placed them in a room in his palace and installed a lock which was the last word in mechanical ingenuity. The candidates were informed that whoever was able to open the door first would be appointed to the post of honour. The three men immediately set themselves to the task. Two of them at once began to work out complicated mathematical formulae to discover the proper lock combination. The third man, however, just sat in his chair doing nothing. Finally, without putting pen to paper, he got up, walked to the door, turned the knob and the door opened. It had been unlocked all the time.

Similarly, one cannot unlock the problem of man by discovering his combinations through mathematical and scientific laws, but only through awareness. From this perspective, therefore, what is important is not method, or doing certain things, but the attitude that is brought to a situation. This concept of non-doing is fundamental to Eastern culture and emphasized in various rituals such as the Japanese tea ceremony which draws attention, not to *what* is done, but the manner in which it is accomplished. Eastern philosophy aims to frustrate the individual in his search for specific methods by which to gain understanding. It may be thought of as the philosophy of the ordinary, as is illustrated in the following example from Zen literature included in a collection by Reps (1978, p. 101):

> A monk told Joshu: 'I have just entered the monastery. Please teach me.'
> Joshu asked: 'Have you eaten your rice porridge?'
> The monk replied: 'I have eaten.'
> Joshu said: 'Then you had better wash your bowl.'
> At that moment the monk was enlightened.

As Rajneesh (1979, p. 108) points out, wisdom is not a matter of doing anything special but of being as one is:

Enjoy your food, enjoy your bath, enjoy the sun, enjoy the wind and the rains, and enjoy everything that is available to you. And just remain whosoever you are—true to yourself, creating no hypocrisy, creating no pretension, creating no façade, no face.

It is this quality of being themselves that humanistic psychologists bring to all the usual pursuits of psychology, whether in clinical practice, education, industry, counselling or research, rather than any special methodology, together with a genuine concern for persons. Therefore it is an attitude which defines humanistic psychology rather than any particular method. Carl Rogers' main contribution has been to introduce this attitude to psychology by way of counselling and psychotherapy, and to emphasize that it is the non-doing of the counsellor, psychotherapist or educator which is all important.

Rogers insists that personal change is facilitated when the counsellor or therapist is what he is; when in the relationship with his client he is genuine, and without front or façade, openly being the feelings and attitudes that are flowing in him at the moment. He coined the term 'congruence' to describe this condition whereby the feelings of the therapist are available to him such that there is harmony between what he is at any point in time and what he appears to be. He explains:

> Congruence is the opposite of presenting a façade, a defensive front, to the patient or client. If the therapist is experiencing one thing in the relationship, but is endeavouring to be something else, then the condition (of congruence) is not met . . . To be transparent to the client, to have nothing of one's experience in the relationship which is hidden . . . this is, I believe, basic to effective psychotherapy. (quoted in Jourard, 1971, p. 147)

Rogers claims that the less the therapist presents a façade and is congruent, the more he can listen accurately to what another person is attempting to communicate and the more likely it is that the other person will feel empathically understood. In so doing the therapist is offering the opportunity for a genuine encounter between two persons, because in being himself he allows the client to be himself also. He is essentially therefore a facilitator. As Lao Tsu observed, 'Such listening as his enfolds us in a silence in which at last we begin to hear what we are meant to be.'

This ability to 'be and let be' is essentially an existential attitude, and as Hora (1960) points out, the existential therapist does not 'do' therapy, he lives it;

> He does not seek to make interpretations, he does not evaluate and judge; he allows what is to be, so that it can reveal itself in the essence of its being, and then proceeds to elucidate what he understands.
> (quoted by Jourard, 1971, pp. 144-145)

Being and letting be means that the therapist accepts the client unconditionally, just as he is. Shaffer (1978, p. 74) poses the question of whether this means that the client is in no way subject to the therapist's influence. His answer is that 'of course the therapist has potential influence; otherwise there would be no point to the therapy. Somewhat paradoxically the therapist's catalytic role is to remind the patient of his freedom; the patient (freely) decides whether or not he will allow himself to be so influenced.'

This, however, seems to miss the point of an existential encounter, in two ways. Firstly, the very term 'patient' employed by Shaffer, (and also by Hora), implies a certain role or status relationship between the individual and the therapist that is not fully consistent with the notion of an open existential encounter, and also connotes a person who passively waits for something to be done to or for him. The use of this term also reinforces what appears to be a failure to recognize that it is not what the therapist does that is important, but what he is.

The effective therapist can be likened to a magnet, a metallic substance within which there is a characteristic organization of domains or regions in which all the atoms have their magnetic moments aligned in the same direction, as a result of which it attracts and magnetizes other metals. A magnet, therefore, does not *do* magnetism, but *is* magnetic: the very nature of its being effects changes in other substances. Rogers' notion of congruence can thus be compared with magnetism inasmuch as it implies an internal organization or harmony. The greater the degree of harmony within the individual the greater is their ability to facilitate this in others. Effective therapists therefore elicit and reinforce authentic behaviour in others by manifesting it themselves.

Jupp (1976) suggests that support for the existence of these interpersonal force fields comes from unified field theory and quantum physics which recognize that the more integrated and unified a physical field the more force it exerts. He observes (p. 48) that 'it appears quite incontrovertible that in any interaction between two persons, especially when one is more congruent and the other is less congruent, that some "directive" influence will occur, however unconscious or unintentional'. This being the case, Rogers' claim that his approach to counselling and psychotherapy is non-directive is misleading. It is possible that the phenomenon of congruence, in addition to the interpersonal influence it exerts, is also responsible for the undoubted charisma of certain individuals, and that it may have other effects. In this connection Jupp finds Rogers' emphasis on congruence and empathy of particular interest, indicating that they have both been found to be decisive factors in research on altered states of consciousness and paranormal phenomena. He concludes that they may have far greater influence in interpersonal relationships than has been realized.

THE METHOD OF DOING

Irrespective of the possible psychic significance of such an approach, the existential attitude of non-doing in which the therapist neither takes over the client's problems nor tries to solve them for him but merely is and lets be, is quite alien to the Western world, with its obsessive concern for means, ends, objectives, outcomes, processes, performance and achievement. For the males of Western culture, who are particularly conditioned to the idea of 'doing', a more active approach has greater appeal.

> Indeed it can be discerned among beginning therapists that there is often a considerable dread of passivity because it constitutes a threat to masculine identity. Beginning therapists seem to be most fascinated by 'manly' active techniques such as hypnosis, reflection, interpretation etc; the kinds which will be difficult to master but which will make them feel they are doing something to the patient which will get him well. These techniques however leave the self of the therapist hidden behind the mask of his professional role and has limited effectiveness. (Jourard, 1971, p. 38)

The Western emphasis on doing leads therapists to employ a number of techniques despite the claims of Rogers and Jourard that it is not the technique or theoretical orientation of the therapist which fosters growth. Farson (in Evans, 1981) claims, quite justifiably, that Rogers' work has been corrupted by practitioners who have discovered the technique but not the underlying philosophy. They have become impatient and have turned to gimmicks to get people to express themselves, often, he claims, where there is nothing to express. He insists that this gimmickry and its implicit lack of concern for persons has been irresistably satisfying even to humanistic psychologists, with the result that performance is winning out over safety, aggressiveness over acceptance, and emotionality over dignity.

Jourard claims that the 'technical therapist' is striving to manipulate both himself and the client rather than respond openly and spontaneously, and suggests that this technical behaviour almost certainly impresses the client. The authority, power and prestige conferred by such techniques, or gimmicks, all too frequently appeal to the therapist, and have the additional attraction that they can be learned. Yet, as Rajneesh (1978, p. 33) observes, therein lies their danger, because in becoming efficient in mechanical things they have become inefficient in human ones which cannot be learned or technically achieved. Awareness, unlike mechanics or techniques, cannot be trained.

Jourard (1971, p. 148) also claims that 'technique, including reflection, silence, interpretation, seems to function as a defense (sic) against immature being, and it is doubtless valuable for that reason'. Rowan's telling use of the term 'armoury' (1976, p. 60) to describe a variety of psychotherapeutic techniques is thus, unwittingly, appropriate. Jourard is in little doubt that investment in powerful techniques serves to enhance the therapist's professional role and so provide a more impenetrable defence of the therapist's immaturity and inauthenticity. It can also be argued that if such an armoury is used as a means of penetrating the client's defences it is perhaps more likely to provoke more vigorous defence, and at best prove unproductive. At worst it constitutes an act of alienation and hostility, for as Frankl (1969b) reminds us, to approach a person in terms of technique is to reify, and thus dehumanize them. In either event, the use of technique tends to distance the therapist and client, and reduce the likelihood of a genuine encounter taking place. It is ironic therefore that Rowan, an enthusiastic British advocate of humanistic psychology, should declare (1976, p. 70) Laing's existential approach to therapy 'non-humanistic' because it eschews technique and 'can be recognized by the fact that the therapists pretend to be just like the residents and refuse to *do* any therapy' (emphasis added); and also recommend open encounter because it affords a greater number of techniques.

Indeed, all too frequently humanistic psychology is identified and characterized in terms of its special techniques and their great diversity. Its programmes typically emphasize the number of different things that one can do, or have done to onself, in pursuit of growth or self-actualization, as is reflected in the widespread use of the term 'workshop' to describe many of its therapeutic sessions. Moreover, consistent with the Western work ethic, it seems that the more techniques that are on offer the better. Rowan indicates that a growth centre programme might typically involve a Gestalt workshop, a 48-hour marathon, co-counselling, open encounter, a psychodrama workshop, a movement group, and Reichian massage.

The one advantage of technique is that through the use of technology the process of therapy is converted into a number of facts, or objectively discernible features, which can be described and communicated to others. This allows for comparison of different approaches but necessarily leads to distortion and generalization because the essence of all therapy is experience, which is unique, individual and non-transferable, varying from person to person, and in any one person across time and situation. As the experience of therapy can never be conveyed or communicated adequately, many writers have resorted to case studies or to fictionalized accounts in an attempt to illustrate different therapeutic processes. The 'flavour' of various therapies may be obtained by consulting Morse and Watson (1977), Patterson (1980), Rhinehart (1976), Perls (1969, 1976).

However, humanistic therapies will be outlined here in terms of the different kinds of technique they employ in order to emphasize their ubiquity. In addition to the techniques already referred to, such as reflection, interpretation and the controlled use of silence, there is an almost endless number and variety of techniques employed in these therapies, including sensory isolation and sensory overload, humiliation, mimicry, biofeedback, improvisational theatre, hypnosis and self-hypnosis, relaxation, dance, various forms of physical exercise, hyper-ventilation, intense experiences and every conceivable kind of meditational practice. Accordingly it is more appropriate to conceive of contemporary psycho-therapy as 'psychotechnology'.

The activities of techniques favoured by humanistic therapists can be somewhat crudely differentiated into three categories—the psychosomatic, the dramatic and the mystic. The psychosomatic focus upon the unity of mind and body, whereas the dramatic explore the individual's relation to their social roles and those of others, and the mystic aim to integrate and transcend both.

PSYCHOSOMATIC TECHNIQUES (Wilhelm Reich)

These derive primarily from the theories and practices of Wilhelm Reich (1897–1957), an Austrian psychoanalyst and student of Freud, whose main contributions to psychoanalytic theory during the 1920s, namely orgasm theory and character analysis, were eventually to lead to his severance from the psychoanalytic movement.

Reich's orgasm theory is that sexual energy is constantly built up in the body and needs release through orgasm involving the whole body, and that if this natural 'bio-energy' is inhibited for any reason stasis of the energy sets in, giving rise to all kinds of neurotic response. Release of the blocked bio-energy through re-establishment of the function of the orgasm is the therapeutic goal since this is held to establish the natural flow of energy and eliminate neurosis. Reich claimed that a person's neurotic responses were indicated in his entire behaviour, including his characteristic muscular expressions and posture, which he termed 'muscular armouring'. His character analysis was directed toward identifying and eliminating the muscle armouring. Reich's ex-wife and collaborator, Ilse Ollendorff-Reich explains the contribution of the character analytic approach to psychotherapy as follows:

> It did away with the psychoanalytic taboo of never touching a patient, substituting physical attack by the therapist on the muscular attitudes (armouring) in the patient: thus the therapist treats the patient not only from the characterological point of view, but also physically by provoking in him a sharp contraction of the musculature in order to make the patient aware of those contractions which have become chronic. The relaxation of the bound-up energy in the musculature in whatever part of the body would often be accompanied by recall of the trauma which had led to the contraction or neurotic symptom in the first place. In this way neurotic symptoms could be attacked at the same time in their psychic and somatic manifestations.
>
> (1969, p. 36)

Through the development of character analysis Reich moved farther and farther away from the passive role of the therapist as the interpreter of material offered by the patient to the more active therapy of what was then called 'vegetotherapy', based on the functions of the vegetative nervous system, and which eventually became known as Orgone Therapy. In his search for the biological foundation of the Freudian concept of libido or sexual drive, Reich claimed to have discovered the life force, or orgone energy, and this he saw as fundamental to all bioenergetic functions.

The view that sickness, whether mental or physical, derives from inhibition of orgone energy or the life force, is also found in both Indian and Chinese philosophy, where the life force, which is synonymous with breath, is known as *prana* and *chi* respectively. The aim of traditional oriental practices such as Yoga and T'ai Chi is the performance of movements that stimulate the even flow of breath, blood and energy within the body, thereby nourishing it and bringing it to a state of harmonious balance. Similar notions are also encountered in acupuncture, herbalism, reflexology and methods of oriental medicine such as Japanese Shiatsu. In more recent years the term bioenergetics (derived from the Greek words for life and force) have been adopted for the somatic aspects of Reich's work.

Bioenergetics (Alexander Lowen)

Alexander Lowen, a pupil of Reich, developed bioenergetics as a systematic methodology for dealing with the relationship between somatic functioning and psychological trauma. He established the Institute for Bioenergetic Analysis in America in 1956 and since then it has been developed in Europe and elsewhere. Lowen (1975, pp. 43–44) describes the goal of bioenergetics as 'to help people regain their primary nature, which is the condition of being free, the state of being graceful and the quality of being beautiful'. It seeks to bring about the healthy integration of body and mind by working on three areas, breathing, character structure, and what is known as 'grounding'.

It can be argued that, literally and metaphorically, contact with reality is maintained by keeping both feet on the ground. Grounding is a method which teaches a particular stance whereby the energy in the body moves in a harmonious flow from the respiratory system, making positive contact with the ground, and in this way enables the individual to discover his or her sense of identity.

Defensive blocks in the body are held to be revealed in patterns of breathing which are unconsciously established by chronic muscular tensions which result from emotional trauma in earlier years. In bioenergetic therapy, breathing is developed by placing the body under stress, typically through the use of a breathing stool over which the person's body is positioned.

Character structure in bioenergetics is conceived in terms of five personality types, the schizoid, oral, psychopathic, masochistic and rigid, each of which is characterized by a typical muscular and psychological pattern. These are diagnosed by the therapist through touch and confronted in dynamic therapy.

Biodynamic therapy (Gerda Boyeson)

Gerda Boyeson, a Norwegian psychotherapist, derived Biodynamic Therapy from Reichian notions of bio-energy and armouring. As in all bioenergetic therapies it is an holistic approach in which the processes of mind and body are seen as interrelated aspects of the one biodynamic entity. In Boyeson's theory the primary personality is seen as becoming submerged during development in a secondary personality which corresponds to Reich's concept of armouring with which a person protects themself from the onslaughts of the environment and their own socially unacceptable emotions. Thus a child punished for expressing fear may suppress it by muscular effort so that this suppression in time becomes part of the muscular armouring, and hence the body structure, and no longer feels that emotion. Boyeson takes Reich's concept of armouring further than Lowen in terms of her concepts of visceral armour and tissue armour. Central to her approach is the concept of the emotional cycle which is both a physical and psychological process in the sense that emotional events cause physiological changes which cease when the emotional event has passed. This can only occur in conditions of relaxation when the organism is no longer tensed for action, but when people are under stress this self-regulating process is inhibited. The body loses its capacity to 'clear itself' with the result that the effects of the trauma are retained. This loss of homeostatic response constitutes visceral armouring and when this prevents bioenergy flowing freely in the body every cell is impaired resulting in tissue armouring.

Biodynamic therapy varies with each client but often involves special massage techniques to disperse the body armouring. In some persons this process occurs at an organic level only, whilst in others it is accompanied by profound psychological change.

Structural integration (Ida Rolf)

This therapy, which is also known as Rolfing after its originator Ida Rolf, was developed during the 1930s in America, but gained attention chiefly through its promotion by the Esalen Institute during the 1960s. Drawing heavily on the work of Reich, it is essentially a method of deep massage—some would claim brutal massage—in which the therapist manipulates the client's body in order to return it to a desired postural and structural position. It is claimed that this technique, at the same time as freeing people from the muscular imbalances of the armouring process, also discharges emotional and psychological blockages.

The concept of gravity is important to Rolfing inasmuch as gravity is seen as further accentuating distortions of posture. Therapy seeks to ensure that the person's posture is correctly aligned with the earth's gravitational field, and that they are correctly grounded. Hence there is a particular emphasis on the feet which are seen as the means by which the person keeps in touch with reality and gravity. In addition to massage and footwork the person is also encouraged to develop their breathing.

The Alexander technique

Related to the bioenergetic therapies is the technique developed by F. Matthias Alexander (1896–1955) for the improvement of posture and muscular activity. As in the other bioenergetic approaches it rests on the holistic assumption that there is no separation between body and mind. To this Alexander added the observation that every activity, whether physical, mental or spiritual, is translated into muscular tension which becomes habitual and distorts thinking, feeling and doing.

The technique is not a set of exercises as such, but the development of awareness by the individual as to how he performs certain activities. It is concerned, not with what is done, but how it is accomplished, and as such demands the same kind of awareness that is required in Zen and other oriental disciplines such as Akaido, T'ai Chi and Yoga. It presumes that by increasing personal awareness of physical attitudes the individual will perceive choices in the way they act, and will choose to act more naturally and spontaneously.

Whilst the Alexander Technique is not promoted as a psychotherapy, many of its enthusiastic supporters have made such claims for it (see Barlow, 1975), suggesting that it gives rise to profound psychological and emotional changes and feelings of well-being.

DRAMATIC TECHNIQUES

Psychodrama (Jacob Moreno)

Other action-oriented therapeutic approaches include those which employ dramatic or theatrical techniques. Most notable in this regard is Psychodrama which was developed by Jacob Moreno, a Viennese psychiatrist and contemporary of Freud, who like Reich sought alternatives to the predominantly verbal approach of orthodox psychoanalysis which would facilitate powerful emotional release or catharsis.

Taking Shakespeare's notion that 'All the world's a stage and all the men and women merely players' he suggested that most human problems arise from the need to create and maintain social roles which may be in conflict with each other and the essential self, and that this conflict is the source of anxiety. He therefore proposed that within the relative safety of psychodrama groups of individuals could explore not only these role conflicts but also those aspects of self not given expression through any existing role and thus effect integration and balance in themselves.

Such a psychodramatic enactment requires a setting or stage free from the constrictions and constraints of everyday life which provides, at the same time, security for self-expression and exploration. This is usually provided by the therapeutic group who also engage in scene setting in the sense that they also attempt to create or recreate the appropriate physical and emotional climate within which action takes place. The action which occurs therein is present-centred, taking place in the here and now, and as if happening for the first time.

The principal actor dramatizing his problems and conflicts is termed the protagonist, in addition to whom there are several auxiliaries who form the rest of the cast under the direction of the therapist who assumes overall responsibility for the drama, and who employs a number of techniques in facilitating the dramatic process. One such technique is soliloquy whereby the protagonist verbalizes aloud his feelings to the audience. In another technique known as mirroring members of the group mimic or exaggerate the protagonist's behaviour as a means of providing effective feedback of his actions. The technique of doubling, in which another person represents the alter-ego of the protagonist by moving in close proximity to him and speaking for him, is also employed as a means of facilitating the expression and clarification of feelings.

Gestalt therapy

Many of these psychodramatic techniques or modifications of them are employed by Gestalt therapists, although Perls (1969, p. 1) objected to anyone calling themself a Gestalt therapist and using techniques, which like Rogers and Jourard he viewed as 'gimmicks', useful in seminars on sensory awareness, but not therapy. As he explains '. . . the sad fact is that this jazzing-up more often becomes a dangerous substitute activity, another phony (*sic*) therapy that *prevents* growth'.

Working with his clients 'centre-stage', as it were, in front of an audience, Perls dispensed with most of the elements of psychodramatic enactment by requiring the client to play all of the parts of a drama themself, either by acting each role (including those of the props) in turn, or in the form of dialogues between these elements, whether animate or inanimate. For this latter purpose the famous empty chair technique was developed whereby the client projects into a vacant chair any element of the drama in order to confront it. The 'occupant' of the chair might be an aspect of the self typically unexpressed in a given situation—the repressed self, which Perls labelled the 'underdog'; or other aspects of the personality; real or imagined persons, creatures or objects—indeed anything that the client or therapist wishes it to be, the idea being that by bringing these into the open the client might be able to identify and integrate the diffuse parts of him/herself and achieve an individual gestalt. Perls worked on unresolved conflict situations, interpersonal relationships, thought and fantasies in this way, and also on dreams which he regarded as 'existential messengers' because of their potential importance to individual self-understanding.

The use of dramatic techniques in Gestalt Therapy has the advantage that sole responsibility for the creation of the drama lies with the client, and is less liable to misrepresentation by others than in psychodrama. Perls also used mirroring and doubling techniques, in which the therapist rather than auxiliaries provided feedback for the client.

Transactional analysis (Eric Berne)

Developed during the 1950s by American psychiatrist Eric Berne (1910–70) Transactional Analysis clearly owes much to psychoanalytic theory. It rests on the assumption that personality can be sub-divided into three ego states, namely the Parent, Ego and Child, each of which has a characteristic mode of functioning which approximates to that of the Super-ego, Ego and Id of orthodox Freudian theory.

The technique of TA, as it is commonly known, lies in identifying through role play the deployment of the various ego states being assumed by an individual in their personal transactions. This 'structural analysis' enables the individual to understand their behaviour and change it, thereby gaining more control over their life. It is usually conducted on an individual basis, after which the person is free to participate in group transactions, or 'transactional analysis' proper.

Participants in group transaction are encouraged to experiment by enacting more appropriate ego roles, and observing their effects on themselves and others. The aim of this transactional analysis is social control and it focusses on the individual's tendency to manipulate others in destructive and non-productive ways, and to respond to the similar manipulations of others. Berne (1968) identified a number of distinctive games which are typically employed in social relationships and which serve to prevent intimate and authentic relationships taking place, and TA involves analysis of the various games or strategies that the individual engages in.

Script analysis is also a feature of TA; scripts being the overall strategies that an individual has developed, usually during childhood, for playing out their life. The aim of script analysis is to free the individual from the restrictive 'typecasting' achieved by compulsive adherence to a possibly long-outmoded strategy of adjustment, and to enable them to act spontaneously and appropriately.

In addition to the various stages of structural analysis, transactional analysis, game and script analysis, TA also includes a number of techniques which Berne has identified as interrogation, specification, confrontation, explanation, illustration, confirmation, interpretation, crystallization and regression analysis, and which have all been incorporated into the characteristic TA jargon.

Primal therapy (Arthur Janov)

The Primal Therapy of American psychiatrist Arthur Janov may also be included in the category of dramatic or theatrical techniques inasmuch as it encourages the individual's re-enactment of traumatic episodes in early life. The aim of Primal Therapy is to overcome defences built up against the intolerable pain associated with childhood traumas by experiencing the pain fully whilst reliving memories of the events that caused them. Janov (1973) holds that birth represents the primary trauma from which all others emanate and is therefore the source of all anxiety. The therapy therefore attempts to facilitate the re-enactment of the birth process through careful 'staging', such as the client assuming a foetal position, being covered in pillows thereby simulating the birth canal, and receiving physical contact from others. Janov suggests that this 'rebirthing' may symbolically represent the person's desire to make a new start in life and that the enactment is cathartic, releasing blocked emotions and the pain associated with the birth process. He claims that this cathartic release of emotion is achieved through the so-called 'primal scream' which the individual is encouraged to vent.

Elements of these different dramatic techniques are to be found in a number of psychotherapies that have been developed over the past twenty years, but nowhere are they more evident than in the theory known as est.

Est (Werner Erhard)

Est or Erhard Seminars Training was developed by Werner Erhard, a former car salesman and student of esoteric traditions, in the early 1970s, and during the remainder of the decade it became the fastest growing and most controversial enlightenment programme in the USA.

Some idea of its popular and commercial success is provided by Yalom (1980) who indicates that by 1978 it had over 170,000 'graduates', and grossed over nine million dollars. It had a full-time paid staff of 300, and a part-time voluntary staff of 7000, and included on its advisory board business executives, attorneys, university presidents, the former Chancellor of the University of California Medical School, eminent psychiatrists, government officials and popular entertainers.

Like its advisory board est is highly eclectic, borrowing techniques from many different religions and therapeutic disciplines, including Gestalt, psychodrama, encounter, and sensitivity training among others. Its aim, quite simply, is to transform lives by encouraging people to take responsibility for themselves. Paradoxically, however, whilst ostensibly representing 'the mass merchandising of responsibility assumption' (Yalom), this is achieved by means of manipulative techniques which include various forms of deprivation, sensory overload and shock tactics.

Its one highly original features lies in its being the first therapy to work with crowds, for est brings together in two weekend sessions lasting over sixty hours some 250 people who are shouted at, ordered around, humiliated, lectured, and coerced into a heavily structured programme of exercises and procedures (described by Rhinehart, 1976), as a result of which they disclose and share experiences, discover hidden aspects of self, and, it is claimed, ultimately attain enlightenment—which in the est format is realizing what life is and accepting it just as it is: 'taking what you get when you get it and not taking what you don't get when you don't get it'.

Rhinehart points out that many est techniques, such as the use of a raised platform from which the trainer addresses the audience, the stylized behaviour of the trainers and their comic/dramatic monologues, are clearly theatrical, and that as the members of the audience are the principal performers it can be regarded as a form of participatory theatre.

Co-counselling (Harvey Jackins)

Co-counselling is a form of mutual counselling and support which was developed in America during the 1950s by Harvey Jackins under the name of Re-evaluation Counselling with the aim of promoting emotional discharge and catharsis. It gains its name because two persons working as a pair each take turns to be counsellor and client. The client and counsellor hold hands and maintain eye contact throughout the process which involves the client 'acting out' those emotions which are to be released. Heron (1979, p. 12) explains:

> . . . the client uncovers memories of early painful experiences and releases the pain through emotional discharge: grief at being unloved is released through tears and sobbing, anger at arbitrary interference through loud sound and storming movements, threats to personal identity through trembling, embarrassment and false imposed guilt through laughter.

In addition, techniques derived from other sources such as guided fantasy, regressive techniques similar to those employed in Primal Therapy, and elements of TA and Gestalt have been introduced.

MYSTIC TECHNIQUES

During the 1960s the influence of Eastern approaches to self-awareness and enlightenment became evident in a number of psychotherapeutic approaches. Typically, meditational techniques were incorporated into some form of encounter resulting in approaches that tend to be more gentle and passive in the sense that they don't involve physical exertion and activity or dramatic performance. The two best-known mystical approaches are the Enlightenment Intensive and Psychosynthesis.

Enlightenment intensive (Charles Berner)

The Enlightenment Intensive was developed in California during the 1960s by Charles Berner and is basically concerned with divesting persons of their social roles. It can thus be regarded as an exercise in disidentification. Its method derives from techniques of co-counselling and the Zen practice of meditating on *koans* or paradoxical questions, but encounter techniques are also clearly discernible. The process is based upon pairs that take turns in asking and answering a koan, but the progressive nature of the exercise enables up to ninety people to participate.

Pairs form for periods of forty minutes, initially taking turns to answer the question 'Who are you?'. The ensuing exchange may proceed something as follows:

Question: Who are you? Answer: Mary Jones.
Question: Who are you? Answer: I'm Fred Jones' wife; mother of Amanda and Paul. I'm a housewife.
Question: Who are you? Answer: I don't know what you're getting at.
Question: Who are you? Answer: I don't know.
Question: Who are you? Answer: I am me.

The questioning continues until an individual believes he has solved the koan, whereupon he is presented to the group facilitator for evaluation in much the same way that a Zen student confronts the master. When both of the individuals in a pair have reached a solution new pairs are formed and the process continues with a new koan such as 'What are you?'; 'What is life?'; 'What is another?'; 'What is death?'. The process can continue for variable periods of up to a week, theoretically providing insight and awareness and the possibility of integrating various aspects of the self.

Psychosynthesis (Roberto Assaglioli)

This approach draws heavily on the practices of oriental mysticism and aims at the integration of the physical, social and spiritual aspects of the self using basic meditational techniques and methods for the development of intuition. It emphasizes the harmonious interplay of two complementary modes of consciousness, intuition and intellect, which correspond to the predominant modes of consciousness of Eastern and Western cultures. Its originator, Italian psychiatrist Roberto Assaglioli (1975) points out that in most people the marriage of the two is stormy and difficult and frequently ends in divorce, whilst a significant number of people never contemplate such a marriage, remaining content to use either intellect or intuition alone. In Western culture intellect is favoured over intuition which accordingly tends to be suppressed, and it is for this reason that the development of intuition is encouraged in this approach. However, whichever mode of consciousness predominates the result is imbalance and fragmentation of the self. For Assaglioli humanistic psychology is ideally a synthesis of Eastern and Western approaches, and their respective modes of consciousness, and on this basis he claims Psychosynthesis as a truly humanistic psychology. Nevertheless, whilst its methods are all efforts to cooperate with the natural processes of growth in order to attain balance, many techniques are employed in the

the development of awareness, including guided imagery and fantasy, and symbolic art work.

DO THE TECHNIQUES WORK?

Whilst these techniques frequently satisfy the need of many therapists and counsellors to engage in activities which give the semblance of 'doing' something for the client it is nevertheless reasonable to ask whether in fact such techniques work. At a theoretical level it can be argued that such techniques cannot work— at least in the sense that their advocates intend, as they are incompatible with the declared aims and objectives of humanistic psychology, namely its holism and respect for persons.

Campbell (1984, p. 19) indicates that probably the most serious charge against humanistic psychology is that in its focus on the individual it has promoted a narcissistic, selfish and hedonistic trend, and people so involved with their personal development that they 'hide behind a false and pollyanna picture of the world as they would like it to be' and fail to look at the real issues in the world. In emphasizing the individual self and evading social realities, therapists are open to the accusation that they have unwittingly encouraged people only to think of themselves. However, as Adorno (1968) observes

> The individual is not simply individual, the substratum of psychology, but, as long as he behaves with any vestige of rationality, simultaneously the agent of the social determinants that shape him. His psychology points back to social moments.

Accordingly, any psychological approach which fails to account for social structures is incomplete. This is precisely the basis of Sartre's criticism of psychology: that it fails to integrate life.

It can be argued therefore that humanistic psychology, in largely ignoring social factors, provides only a partial and superficial account of human functioning and in this sense is anything but an holistic approach. Moreover, by operating in abstraction from the real social world it is unlikely to be effective in promoting change in being which is to a great extent contingent upon social constraints and influences. Adorno argues that such social and political naivety actually supports and maintains the *status quo* and the dehumanization of persons. He argues (p. 76) that the cult of psychotherapy

> is the necessary accompaniment to a process of dehumanization, the illusion of the helpless that their fate lies in their own hands. Thereby, ironically enough, precisely the science in which they hope to encounter themselves as subjects tends immanently to turn them back into objects.

Such an argument pivots on the issue of whether or not free will and the responsibility it implies are illusory. As such it is fundamentally irreconcilable. Even so, it can be countered with the argument that a person, in developing self-awareness, is likely to gain some insight into those features which shape them, becoming more socially aware; and in acknowledging their personal agency and its limits, also more socially responsible. Moreover, given that any social system is composed of individuals, any change in the individuals — particularly in the direction of greater autonomy — will change the system. Such a view has not only been advanced by social theorists and philosophers such as Sartre, but is the basis of one of the most influential theories of contemporary science, that of Prigogine, who in 1977 was awarded the Nobel Prize for Chemistry for his work on dissipative structures (see Chapter 9 for further discussion). In Prigogine's theory all systems contain sub-systems, a single or combined fluctuation of which may become so powerful, as a result of positive feedback, that it shatters the pre-existing organization. Given this perspective, any change in the human sub-system or individual is potentially threatening to the *status quo*. Accordingly, humanistic psychotherapies, in seeking to promote change, cannot be regarded as conservative in either the personal or political sense.

Nevertheless, such theorizing, however elegant, gets no nearer to answering the question of whether or not psychotherapeutic techniques actually work — whether they do change people and alter lives. Their effectiveness is somewhat hard to judge from the consumer response. Yalom (1980, p. 258) points out that an

> enthusiastic chorus of testimonials has surrounded every new personal growth technology from T-groups, encounter groups, nude encounters and marathons, to Esalen body awareness, Psychodrama, Rolfing, TA, Gestalt . . . Yet the natural history of so many approaches (which will most likely be the history of est as well) includes a period of bright pulsation; then a gradual dimming, and ultimate replacement by the next technology.

Clearly there is abundant enthusiasm for these approaches — but evidence? Hamilton (1973) complains that

> The retreat from science has become clearer in recent years with the development of Existential and so-called Humanistic psychology. Based on these systems new methods of therapy have been developed and proclaimed with religious fervour, and when outsiders like myself ask for proof of their efficacy, we are not given evidence. Instead we are faced with a complete rejection of science and with claims that proof and experiment are irrelevant.

The assertion, whilst perhaps not an unfair reflection of the consumer or lay person approach to these therapies, has to be regarded as something of a distortion of the attitudes of the majority of humanistic psychologists. A considerable body of research into the effects of these psychotherapies has been conducted over the past thirty years; much of it favourable (Truax, 1963, 1971; Truax and Carkhuff, 1967; Leiberman *et al.*, 1973). Nevertheless, Yalom claims that these attempts to produce empirical evidence have proved to be of limited value and have made little impact on therapeutic practice because despite their use of sophisticated psychological tests and instruments they failed to tap what was meaningful to the individuals undergoing the therapy. He proposes that the proper means of understanding these issues is the phenomenological method which goes directly to the phenomena themselves and which is eminently feasible in psychotherapy because every good therapist attempts to relate to the client in this manner. Phenomenological analysis, which focusses on what and how people experience, can be very precise and accommodate both human complexity and consciousness. However, as Yalom (1980, p. 23) points out 'this phenomenological approach raises staggering and as yet unresolved problems for the researcher who struggles to achieve high scientific standards in his or her work'; one of the consequences of which is that most clinicians in the United States stop conducting empirical research once they have met the academic requirements of tenure. Another is that there is a dearth of good phenomenological research, with, according to Hetherington (1983), less than two per cent of papers given as symposia and conferences since 1947 on topics even remotely phenomenological. The collective result is that research in this area is seen as non-scientific and of low academic status, and studies which appear to confirm the effectiveness of the newer psychotherapies are all too frequently dismissed. Thus, despite popular enthusiasm for these approaches, and claims made for them in the research literature, the prevalent view within mainstream academic psychology is that these therapies are largely ineffective, or at least less effective than behavioural therapies.

Davis (1972) and Shapiro and Shapiro (1977) argue that the prevalence of a double standard in the appraisal of psychotherapies lends spurious credence to this view. They indicate that behavioural therapies are compatible with the established methods of empirical science and therefore more likely to yield outcomes which can be demonstrated and evaluated by scientific means, whereas the procedures of humanistic psychology—by their very nature non-empirical—are not amenable to evaluation by empirical means and the established verification procedures of behavioural science.

Returning, therefore, to the question of whether or not humanistic psychology has method, it is clear that if method is synonymous with technique humanistic psychology suffers an embarrassment of riches. However, whilst it does not lack method *per se*, it lacks *the* method—scientific method, and in the eyes of its detractors is therefore ineligible for scientific recognition or status. This, in turn, poses the question, if humanistic psychology is not science, is it psychology?

Chapter 8

HARD AND SOFT PSYCHOLOGIES

the maddening problem of method in psychological research

A prophet is not without honour, save in his own country.
Matthew, 13, 5, 7.

There are many vociferous critics of humanistic psychology, mainly, although by no means exclusively, within the realm of academic psychology. Criticism is based partly on the conviction that questions about ultimate concerns, meaning and purpose are those for which science has no answer, and as such are illegitimate questions for psychology and more appropriate to literature, philosophy and theology. For their part, humanistic psychologists strenuously assert that these questions are not only legitimately within the scope of psychology but are central to it and not merely peripheral as implied by the dismissive 'trendy West Coast' label frequently applied to humanistic psychology in America. They insist that the questions of humanistic psychology are of the utmost human significance and those that the layman expects psychology to address, if not actually answer. Nevertheless, it is not the human relevance of these concerns that its critics dispute, but their relevance to science.

HARD AND SOFT PSYCHOLOGIES

The argument as to whether or not psychology should be concerned with relevant human questions which may defy precise 'scientific' answers, polarizes psychology into two camps: the extremes of which contrast so sharply that they may be

101

regarded as two different psychologies, which Child (1973) characterizes as 'hard' and 'soft'. He highlights the contrast thus:

> The hard psychologies are founded on the rock of experimental method. Their great strength lies in the establishment of knowledge about small circumstantial aspects of behaviour and experience. Examples of their achievements would be a precisely defined curve relating the apparent brightness of a very dim light to the number of minutes the eyes have been in darkness or a graph showing how the number of errors made in learning a list of nonsense syllables is related to the length of the list or the time between successive rehearsals.
>
> The soft psychologies are warm and sensate, faithful to and aware of the immediately felt reality of human experience and human personality. They take as their starting point the multi-faceted reality of conscious experience, the dynamic diversity of the integrated person as he knows himself and is known to others. From this starting point it is not easy to move on to scientific investigation; to framing limited questions testable by systematic observation. The soft psychologist may not see this as a great inadequacy. He wants first of all to be faithful to human reality as he knows it. He hopes a psychology that takes the conscious experience of the organised person as its subject matter will eventually lead to understanding man better than can a psychology that denies these obvious realities or clings to precise methods even at the possible expense of irrelevance.

The hard–soft dichotomy, as depicted above, is between the empirical research tradition in which 'certainty is required to the point where broader significance is forsaken', and the extreme humanistic position which demands relevance 'so immediately that verification is not sought'. It pivots on the thorny issue of method; the balance of psychological opinion being very heavily weighted in favour of the empirical 'scientific' approach, and it is from the vantage point of this down-to-earth position that the lightweight 'airy-fairy' humanistic approach is evaluated, and to which it is compared and inevitably found wanting. Yet it is clearly inappropriate to measure humanistic psychology by the same yardstick as objective behavioural science, and against standards of objectivity, replicability, consistency, quantifiability, and laboratory verification. Evaluation which focusses solely on method, and fails to take into account the difference in the subject matter, aims and objectives of humanistic psychology, is literally a means test. Humanistic psychology aims at transformation; promoting a qualitative change in being through the development of awareness. It focusses on experience and feeling rather than fact; subjectivity rather than objectivity; and its concerns are precisely those excluded from scientific method. Therefore, to evaluate humanistic psychology in terms of the extent to which it meets the standards of science is invidious.

Ferguson (1978) observes that there are many people who have not had transformative experiences and do not believe they exist, and to such people the only verification that these experiences are possible is 'data'. However, the scientific requirements for the collection of data under controlled conditions, their objectivity and replicability, all pose problems in the study of man because they preclude anecdotal evidence, introspective data and rare or one-off events.

Much of the endeavour of humanistic psychology has been within the sphere of psychotherapy, but there are numerous problems in any empirical study of the psychotherapeutic process, which by its nature is experiential and subjective. Yalom indicates that one of the problems frequently encountered in empirical research in this area is that the more methods used to assess the outcome the less certain is the researcher of his results. He suggests that researchers typically deal with the problem by relying upon a single source of data in an attempt to increase reliability or only measuring objective factors in an attempt to avoid 'soft' subjective criteria, but 'again and again one encounters a basic fact of life in psychotherapy research: the precision of the result is directly proportional to the triviality of the variables studied. A strange type of science!' (1980, p. 24). Consequently many humanistic psychologists, seeing little point in being precise about issues which have little relevance, and in quantifying the trivial, have preferred to study significant issues with qualitative methods which fall short of the precision demanded by science. Nevertheless, humanistic psychologists recognize that their approach demands the development of an awareness or empirical attitude towards the self—an inner empiricism—which is as rigorous as that which empirical science provides in respect of outer data. Needleman (1978) observes that inner data must be examined with as much care, tough-mindedness, experimental method and verification possible, whilst acknowledging that public verification cannot be achieved in the way possible with scientific hypotheses.

The basic tenets of existentialism are such that empirical research methods are often inapplicable or inappropriate, and its fundamental holistic principle is negated by a reductionist, analytic approach. Nevertheless, Yalom (1980) cites numerous examples of empirical work in this area, but it has not silenced the critics. Westland (1978, pp. 126–127) suggests that many exponents of the humanistic approach are so convinced they are asking the right questions that they have not concerned themselves with obtaining answers, but have embraced ready-made answers afforded by existential philosophy and its variants, providing them by fiat without reference to any testing procedures. This reliance on insight unsupported by any kind of evidence—what Koch (1964) termed 'an escape to an answer rather than a problem'—is unacceptable to science, for as Rychlak (1977, p. 201) indicates:

> Science means a stand on evidence not a stand on the human image. If science dictates the human image it is no longer science.

Certainly to the extent that humanistic psychologists are content to make prescriptions about human nature rather than attempting any actual study of it, they can be accused of promoting ideology rather than psychology. Equally it can be argued, as has Heather (1976), that in maintaining and legitimizing a mechanistic view of man, positivistic psychology is also promoting ideology. Westland (1978, p. 122) dismisses this argument, insisting that

> Whereas science in general has sometimes been described as an ideology, in a philosophical sense, traditional science has never expressed its conclusions *as* ideology. This trend then seems (to the tough-minded observer) to seek to make psychology not even a rational philosophy, and certainly not science under any accepted definition.

It is precisely the accepted definition of science that most humanistic psychologists challenge, regarding it as too narrow and restrictive to accommodate an adequate study of man, and arguing that a fully human science goes beyond science in the ordinary sense. This is not to say, however, that humanistic psychology is hostile to science, as May (1967, p. 32) indicates:

> The existential position is, in my judgement, not at all anti-science. But it does insist that it would be ironic indeed if our dedication to certain methodologies in psychology should blind us to our understanding of human beings.

He urged that recognition of the limits of traditional scientific endeavour should lead to effort in finding new scientific methods more adequate in revealing the nature of man. Similarly Maslow (1968) insisted that it is not necessary to choose between experience and abstraction; that humanistic psychology, in attempting to integrate them, aims at complementing traditional approaches in psychology rather than supplanting them, thereby enlarging science not destroying it.

Certainly Rogers at no time rejected the rigour and conceptual clarity of empirical methods, but he also drew attention to the need to include experience in any attempt to understand man and the universe, insisting that there can be no scientific knowledge without reference to experiential knowledge. Capra (1978), like Rogers, considers that a scientific approach to understanding reality has to be based on experience, and therefore must be an empirical approach, but suggests that the experience can be of various kinds and not merely that conducted in laboratories. Needleman (1978) suggests that the individual is a laboratory and that there are all kinds of instruments for perception in this laboratory of the self. Nevertheless, it is true that some students of humanistic psychology, in their enthusiasm for experience, are frequently hostile to empirical research, and adopt anti-scientific and anti-rational stances which are more harmful than helpful to the aims of third force psychology.

This opposition to science on the one hand, and the claims on the other that humanistic psychology constitutes, variously, a science of the person, a science of being, or a science of consciousness, has given rise to both confusion and hostility within psychology. It does appear that humanistic psychologists want both to have their cake and eat it. Westland (1978, p. 123) pinpoints the issue as being 'precisely that many who explicitly or implicitly refuse to abide by these principles (of science) even in their very general formulation equally refuse to give up or even amend their claim to be operating as scientists. This is what makes accommodation within the profession almost impossible and sceptical derision from outside perhaps inevitable.'

Westland's comment about accommodation within the profession clearly implies that there is no place for humanistic psychology within contemporary psychology. However, scrutiny of the inroads made by humanistic psychology over recent years proves this claim to be false. The insights provided by humanistic psychology have informed conventional empirical research in a number of different areas. Child (1973) indicates that much of what is now termed 'cognitive psychology' has come from adapting the methods of the empirical research tradition to the study of more complex aspects of the human mind, and accepting its useful standards of objectivity and verifiability but rejecting the assumption that only simple relationships can be studied by a discipline holding these standards. He claims that as a result of this modified stance cognitive psychology promises to develop a mechanistic psychology sufficiently complex to have a place in a more general humanistic psychology. Whilst it can be argued as to whether humanistic issues are being handled adequately by cognitive psychology, the theoretical constructs under test simply not being adequate to the task, the shift in a more 'humanistic' direction is clear, especially in the work of Neisser (1976).

Child also points to areas in psychology's recent past where there has been fruitful interplay between humanistic speculation and empirical research. He cites as examples the work on creativity by MacKinnon (1965), to which can be added that of Roe (1953) and Hudson (1966); and to research on aesthetic sensitivity (Child and Iwao, 1968). He also points to a humanistic tradition in experimental social psychology which derives from the work of Lewin, and includes Festinger's work on cognitive dissonance (1957), Zimbardo's work on motivation (1969), and that of Schacter and Singer (1962) on emotion. He suggests that the model of man emerging from studies in social psychology appears to be that applied in a naive or common sense point of view.

The common sense approach

Something of a concern with the common sense or naive psychology of the person in the street is evident in studies of the ways in which people in everyday life interpret their behaviour and that of others. This area of research owes much to the development of attribution theory (Heider, 1958; Kelley, 1967; Jones and Davis, 1965; and Jones and Nisbett, 1971), which accounts for the ways in which people organize their interpersonal world.

During the 1970s in particular there emerged within psychology an increasing acknowledgement of, and respect for everyday common sense, largely as the result of the writings of two British psychologists, R. B. Joynson and John Shotter. Joynson (1974) pointed to the absurdity of a psychology of man which systematically ignores, and even denies common sense, and is not guided by it. Shotter (1975) suggests that it is not so much the person in the street who is naive but the psychologist in the laboratory, and like Harré and Secord (1972) has been concerned with providing a more realistic account of how everyday life is actually made to work by the human beings who conduct it. He insists that this interest in actual social practices in making and maintaining the social order is of crucial importance in serving to highlight 'particular concerns in, and constraints upon, people's actions not always present in laboratory experimentation', and emphasizes that it does not always mean forsaking the standards so vigorously fought for by empiricists and behaviourists. Nevertheless, he asserts that the major phenomenon in social psychology is meaning, and that meanings are generated through the agency of persons. He therefore seeks a return to the acceptance by psychology of human agency and responsibility. Shotter takes a broadly similar position to that of Harré (1983) who insists that psychological activities occur in a moral order and with respect to rights and that it is because of this moral order that psychology cannot be invested in the same mode as the physical world. The physical world, and therefore the physical sciences also, have nothing like a moral or social order in which psychology is embedded. The physical sciences are therefore divested of morality. Accordingly, Shotter advocates an alternative psychology which he defines as a moral science of action rather than a natural science of behaviour — a science in which man is viewed as an active agent able to make things happen and to construct events rather than an impotent reactor determined by his genes and environment. His emphasis on *action* rather than behaviour is an attempt to capture both the inner and outer aspects of human conduct in a single notion — that of behaviour formed by intention.

Reversal Theory (Apter, 1982) is also a kind of action theory inasmuch as it focusses on the concept of action rather than behaviour, and in so doing represents a return to a tradition in psychology far older than behaviourism. The theory, which is essentially a structural phenomenological account of certain aspects of motivation, is based on the view that 'behaviour cannot be completely understood without reference to the mental correlates of that behaviour, including the subjective meaning which the behaviour has for the person who performs it. Reversal Theory is concerned mainly with a particular aspect of subjective meaning, namely certain ways in which the individual interprets his own motivation' (Apter, 1982, p. 2). The primary aim of Reversal Theory is to show that various aspects of a wide variety of behaviours may be explained by reference to certain pairs of metamotivational states, such as negativism and conformity, and the reversals which occur between them. These states may be described as phenomenological states or frames of mind, and they represent the way in which the individual interprets his own motives. In posing a view of human beings as

synergistic systems shifting between two opposite but complementary states
Reversal Theory has similarities with the Taoist notion of opposing universal
principles and the flux between them. It also echoes Platonic views on the structure
of personality. Importantly, however, it challenges the view generally held within
the social and behavioural sciences that human psychological processes are simple
and consistent, and suggests that human complexity and inconsistency can be
approached through concepts such as reversal and bistability, and methods which
are phenomenological.

The hermeneutic approach

Interest has also been shown in the adoption of an hermeneutic method in
psychology (Shotter, 1981; Hetherington 1983). The term 'hermeneutic' derives
from the Greek *hermeneutikos* meaning expert in interpretation, and it relates
to the interpretation of biblical texts. Shotter (1981, pp. 166–167) explains the
method thus:

> One's understanding of the precise part played, or function served by a
> particular expression or piece of text is clarified by constructing (or
> reconstructing) the larger whole, its context, the wider scheme of things the
> author had in mind in expressing himself so; the construction being shaped
> and limited by having to accommodate the item of text in its every aspect.
> Thus the process does not begin with a pre-established order of things to
> which puzzling facts must be assimilated, with them being explained as
> particular instances of general rules or laws constituting the order, with their
> uniqueness thus lost. It begins with the puzzling facts in their full individuality
> . . . and then proceeds by degrees in a back and forth process from part to
> whole, and from whole to part again, to articulate an order adapted to the
> undistorted accommodation of the initial facts. Or, to put the matter another
> way, in the process, an initially global, superficial, and undifferentiated grasp
> of an action's meaning is transformed into a well articulated grasp of its actual
> meaning.

That such a method has a place in psychological explanation is suggested by the
increasing attention paid to what might be thought of as the sub-text of empirical
psychological research.

Empirical psychology is open to the charge that it is a 'science of totally artificial
behaviours in essentially unreal settings' (Westland, 1978, p. 19). Giorgi (1970)
points out that its unnaturalness lies in its being almost totally structured by
an experimenter who selects equipment, defines the variables under study, selects
stimuli, chooses subjects, directs procedures, collates and interprets results. The
whole situation is therefore the creation of the experimenter and is in no sense
independent of him. Notwithstanding, the conventions of empirical research
assume the experimenter's objectivity within this situation, and the 'objectness'
of the human 'subject', who is implicitly denied subjectivity, agency and

intentionality. However, as Orne (1959, 1962) has indicated, the human subject is not merely a passive object to be manipulated but a person who actively tries to make sense of the situation they find themself in. In speculating as to the purpose of the experiment the subject is also generating hypotheses which may then be tested by providing the experimenter with those results which are thought to be what the experimenter wants, or by withholding them, deliberately falsifying results or trying to confound the experimenter's hypothesis. Psychologists typically have overlooked such factors, despite the fact that most of them at some point of their student lives will have found themselves as 'naive' subjects in experiments which they have tried to 'fathom out'. However, since the studies of Orne, and Rosenthal (1966) it appears indisputable that the humanness of both the experimenter and the subject interest in numerous ways which are likely to have a profound effect on experimental outcomes. The experimenter's appearance, sex, age, mood, manner, race, social class, dialect and dress are all likely to influence the subject so that instead of the experimenter being an external 'objective' observer, he is, in effect, a participant who actively contributes to the behaviour that he wishes passively and objectively to observe and record. Westland (1978, p. 19) observes that awareness of such factors

> turns the standard defence of the laboratory method on its head—that defence being the argument that only by rigorously controlling variables can effective connections be established, and that control is almost impossible in natural settings. The counter argument is that in 'nature' variables never do interact on a one-to-one basis; there is always a variety of confounding variables which affect the outcome. Thus the stripped-down laboratory situation, far from achieving clarity or simplifying, merely obscures by creating a totally unrealistic analogue.

The net result is that psychological research characteristically reveals little about how human beings function in real life situations.

Awareness of the wider context in which psychological research is embedded has focussed attention on the moral dimensions of the experiment. Shaffer (1978) observes that the objectification of the human subject within the experimental situation gives rise to ethical questions, when, for example, the subject is coerced into involvement—where participation is an obligatory component of a course of studies, as is the case in many American universities and colleges; or when the person is manipulated or deceived. Ethical questions also attach to those situations in which the person is presented with experimental conditions damaging to their self-esteem, whose effects are long-lasting, or provide false information about the person. One such experiment is the controversial study on compliance with authority (Milgram, 1974) in which persons were deceived into believing that in administering electric shocks of increasingly high voltage to a subject with an alleged heart condition they were participating in a study of learning. In actual fact the 'subject' was a 'stooge' or collaborator who received no such shocks, a recording of his voice being used to relay his painful shouts, protests and appeals for help to the true subject of the experiment—the person applying the supposed shocks; the real aim of the experiment being to establish the extent to which a person would comply with authority in a situation demanding the deliberate infliction of an aversive, and potentially fatal, stimulus to another human being. Shaffer suggests that the de-briefing and reassurance which many social psychologists recommend takes place after such experiments does not necessarily negate the doubts and impressions thus implanted, either about the self or the confidentiality of the situation. Humanistic psychologist Sidney Jourard (1971) insisted that many of these, and related problems could be overcome by encouraging openness and dialogue between the experimenter and subject, and, in effect, treating subjects with full regard to their humanness and subjectivity. His research, which was effectively the application of Rogerian principles to the laboratory situation, suggested promising results inasmuch as the more the experimenter disclosed to the subject about the aims and purposes of the experiment the more honest was the subject, and Jourard claimed, the more reliable were the results obtained. Unfortunately Jourard's work in this area was not continued owing to his untimely death.

However, John Heron (1981, 1982) has taken this approach further, proposing a research model of cooperative enquiry in which both subject and experimenter actively contribute to research thinking, planning, action and experience. Heron (1982, pp. 19–20) explains:

> The way of cooperative enquiry is for the researcher to interact with the subjects so that they do contribute directly both to hypothesis-making, to formulating the final conclusions, and to what goes on in between. This contribution may be strong, in the sense that the subject is co-researcher and *contributes* to creative thinking at all stages. Or it may be weak in the sense that the subject is thoroughly *informed* of the research proposals at all stages and is invited to assent or dissent, and if there is dissent, then the researcher and subject negotiate until agreement is reached. In the complete form of this approach, not only will the subject be fully fledged co-researcher, but the researcher will also be co-subject, participating fully in the action and experience to be researched.

Examples of collaborative, participative research conducted by Heron and others are presented by Reason and Rowan (1981), who, recognizing the need to collate in a systematic manner principles, methods and examples of research being developed in a number of different fields have produced a sourcebook of new paradigm research.

New paradigm research

This represents an attempt to synthesize naive enquiry—the kind of ordinary day-to-day thinking people engage in—and orthodox research, and as such is considered by Reason and Rowan to be 'objectively subjective'. It opposes the positivistic, deterministic, reductionistic, mechanistic approach to research, testing and measurement, or what Reason and Rowan term 'quantophrenia', by way of which, they claim, research produces results that are statistically significant but humanly insignificant. They insist that in the field of human enquiry it is preferable to be deeply interesting than accurately boring.

New paradigm research is opposed to deception, debriefing, manipulation and mystification, but retains, and even expands upon certain aspects of orthodox methodology and procedure, particularly the earlier and later parts of the enquiry into the research process; 'writing up these parts of the procedure with as much care and attention as is usually given to the main part of the investigation'; and expanding literary searches to include not only multidisciplinary sources within the social and physical sciences but also plays, novels, works of philosophy, theology and history. Its reports are therefore a statement of where the researchers stand, not only theoretically, but politically, ideologically, spiritually and emotionally inasmuch that they discuss the many influences which have shaped the thinking and feeling which has led to the current investigation.

In promoting new paradigm research humanistic psychologists have anticipated Hetherington, who in his Presidential Address to the British Psychological Society (1983), emphasized the need for a paradigm shift in psychology and the development of its own methods. His thesis is that psychology is not adequately described as a bioligical science because the methods of the natural sciences can at best yield only partial knowledge about why people behave in the ways they do. He insists that there has to be a phenomenological approach if we are to make sense of human behaviour. Therefore, since psychology is part natural science and part interpretive science it needs to develop methods adequate for the study of human beings as organisms, as members of social organizations and as people with whom we engage in dialogue.

Hetherington's views echo those of Gale (1983) who identifies 'seven deadly sins' committed by psycho-physiologists: theoretical simplemindedness; obsession with correlation rather than process; poor psychometrics and physiology; trivial experimentation; procedural insensitivity; low-level data handling and interpretation. He suggests that if psychologists are to avoid eternal damnation they will have to achieve a paradigm shift which will include having a general theory of human behaviour; acknowledging the complexity of the subject matter; studying psychological processes; recognizing the possible relevance to behaviour of a person's phenomenological experience, and conducting experiments which sample real life rather than confined in a laboratory.

In urging for a paradigm shift in psychology Hetherington reminded psychologists of William James' observation (1892, p. 335) that 'the natural science assumptions are provisional and revisable things'. It is these assumptions which are currently being revised by humanistic psychology, thereby confirming the views of Maslow and Rogers that it contains within it the seeds of a newer philosophy of science—a science not based exclusively on measurement, but an understanding of reality that includes quality and experience; a science which includes consciousness.

That there is a place in psychology for the humanistic approach should not, however, be taken as implying that psychology can contain it. Humanistic psychology goes far beyond the scope of traditional psychology and its dominant paradigm. It is but one aspect of a paradigm shift in science that is revolutionizing the Western view of the universe and man's place in it (see Chapter 9). However, for the most part its 'parent' psychology fails to acknowledge not only humanistic influence on recent developments in psychology but also a number of important shifts within psychology and science as a whole which arise from serious criticisms of the mechanistic paradigm within which it has traditionally operated. Vine (1977) claims that most psychologists remain reluctant to accept human agency, and despite all the lip-service paid to Rogers there is little sign that conscious experience, subjective and inter-subjective construal of reality, and the essentially purposive nature of most human behaviour has permeated into the psychology taught in British universities. Vine argues that as a result 'psychology teaching still remains set in the behaviourist/mechanistic mould that ensures its basic irrelevance to major human concerns and everyday human experience'. Additionally it can be argued that it also guarantees its growing irrelevance to science because, ironically, science no longer meets the standards of psychology. It is appropriate therefore, to question the current 'scientific' status of psychology.

Chapter 9

PARADIGMS AND PARADOXES

science, psychology and the new physics

In my end is my beginning   T. S. Eliot[6]

If one were to accept the dominant view prevalent within academic psychology one might reasonably conclude that humanistic psychology is incompatible with contemporary science. Such a conclusion would be a fallacy. Rychlak (1977, p. 193) observes that 'if we survey the leading figures in science over this century—for example, Bridgman (1959), Bronowski (1958), Conant (1952), Eddington (1958), Einstein (1934), Oppenheimer (1956), Schrodinger (1957) and Whitehead (1958)—we find much more support for a humanistic theory of behaviour than for a mechanistic account . . . A liberal approach to scientific theorizing is more current and appropriate than is the staid and lifeless form of Newtonian science that is still dreamed of in too many psychology departments'. Indeed, the decline of the industrial age has forced an awareness of the limitations of a machine model of reality and a science based upon it. Thus, whilst it is undoubtedly the case that many respected psychologists are totally opposed to humanistic psychology, many eminent physical scientists recognize and welcome this approach as part of a new vision of reality, or paradigm.

The term 'paradigm', from the Greek *paradigma* meaning pattern, was coined by Thomas Kuhn (1962) to refer to the pattern of the universe perceived by scientists. Tart (1975) describes a paradigm as a major intellectual achievement that underlies normal science and attracts and guides the work of an enduring number of adherents in their scientific activity. It is a kind of super-theory: a theory about the nature of reality of such wide scope that it seems to account for all, or most of the major known phenomena in its field. The paradigm therefore becomes an implicit framework or perspective for most scientists.

[6]*East Coker*. London: Faber & Faber.

Tart insists that it also inevitably becomes a set of blinkers inasmuch as it defines certain kinds of endeavours and issues as trivial, impossible or meaningless. However, when the impossible becomes possible, or the apparently trivial yields results inconsistent with the dominant paradigm, a state of crisis arises in the fields so affected. Ferguson (1982) observes that in such a time of crisis most problems can be likened to Zen koans which cannot be solved at the level at which they are addressed; they have to be reframed in a wider context. This change of context represents a new paradigm, and such crises are therefore a precondition for the emergence of a new perspective. Kuhn introduced the concept of 'paradigm shift' to explain this change in the perceived pattern and indicated that the history of science is characterized by such shifts because it is only as a result of these changes in perspective that scientific understanding develops.

Kuhn suggests that a paradigm shift commences with the blurring of the existing pattern, and consequent loosening of the rules for normal research. This is ushered in by the proliferation of competing views, a willingness to experiment, the expression of explicit discontent and argument over fundamentals, but although scientists begin to lose faith in the existing paradigm, they do not renounce it. Part of the problem is that it is not possible to embrace a new paradigm until the old one has been relinquished. Kuhn points out that the perceptual shift involved, rather like the gestalt switch which operates in the perception of visual illusions, must occur all at once. Therefore, as Ferguson (1982, p. 28) observes, 'Real progress in understanding is rarely incremental. All important advances are sudden intuitions, new principles, new ways of seeing.'

Nevertheless, 'reformulations of reality, of the way things are, are wrenching' (Dossey, 1982, p. 15). Hence established scientists who are emotionally and habitually attached to the old paradigm are rarely able to make the switch, and tend to react towards its proponents with scorn, derision and hostility. Tart indicates, therefore, that where such paradigm clashes occur, so also does profound antagonism. Indeed, Schrodinger has suggested that this reluctance to accept the new perspective ensures that at least fifty years elapses before any major scientific discovery penetrates public consciousness. The implications of this time-lag are considerable, because in the meantime adherence to the old paradigm results in attempts to solve problems on an irrational basis, with the old concepts and methods, rather than those appropriate to the task.

Marilyn Ferguson, editor of *Brain/Mind Bulletin*, is among a number of commentators, including distinguished physicists such as David Bohm, Professor of Theoretical Physics at Birkbeck College, University of London, and Fritjof Capra, of the University of California at Berkeley; Karl Pribram, Professor of Neuropsychology at Stanford University, and the chemist and Nobel Laureate Ilya Prigogine, who are insisting that the world is currently facing just such a crisis; not merely an intellectual crisis but an existential one, that is manifested in, among other things, high unemployment, inflation, problems in health care, escalating drug and alcohol abuse, pollution, environmental disasters, overpopulation, famine, rising crime, violence and terrorism. They suggest that these problems are different facets of what is essentially a crisis in perception which derives from the fact that leading thinkers and academics subscribe to a narrow world-view and are trying to apply the concepts and methods of classical Newtonian science to a reality that can no longer be understood in these terms.

Prigogine and Stengers (1985) point out that the scientific vision of nature is undergoing a radical change toward the mutliple, the temporal, and the complex. Whereas in the classical view the processes of nature were considered to be deterministic and reversible, with processes involving randomness or irreversibility being considered to be exceptional, today the role of irreversible processes and fluctuations is to be seen everywhere. The result is a totally new understanding of the world. Prigogine and Stengers (p. xxviii) outline this conceptual revolution thus:

> This revolution is proceeding on all levels, on the level of elementary particles, in cosmology, and on the level of so-called macroscopic physics, which comprises the physics and chemistry of atoms and molecules either taken individually or considered globally as, for example, in the study of liquids and gases. It is perhaps particularly on this macroscopic level that the reconceptualization of science is most easy to follow. Classical dynamics and modern chemistry are going through a period of drastic change. If one asked a physicist a few years ago what physics permits us to explain and which problems remain open, he would have answered that we obviously do not have an adequate understanding of elementary particles or of cosmological evolution but that our knowledge of things in between was pretty satisfactory. Today a growing minority, to which we belong, would not share this optimism: we have only begun to understand the level of nature on which we live . . .

They point out that the reconceptualization of physics is far from being fully achieved, and only quite recent, and that if it is to be fully appreciated and understood it has to be placed in proper historical perspective; that is, within the history of twentieth century science.

THE UNCERTAIN UNIVERSE

Albert Einstein's Theory of Special Relativity (1905), together with his Photon Theory of Light which was published in the same year, dealt a major blow to classical Newtonian physics and shifted understanding of the universe from a mechanistic, deterministic paradigm to a relativistic, uncertain one. Subsequently the experimental investigation of the subatomic realm at the beginning of the twentieth century yielded 'sensational and totally unexpected results' (Capra, 1983, p. 67) that completely undermined the Cartesian/Newtonian notion of a clockwork universe. It was discovered during the 1920s that an electron makes a discontinuous jump—a quantum leap—from one orbit to another without leaving any trace of its path.

> This quantum leap, no matter how infinitesimal, always makes a sharp break with the past. More astonishing, this quantum leap is also the instantaneous collapse of a wave of probabilities into a single real event. And in an actual and metaphorical sense this quantum leap is also the link between two entirely separate locations, events or ideas—a shift in gestalt, an 'aha' experience, the moment when the previously intangible, inchoate and indefinite is suddenly made manifest. (Heutzer, 1984, p. 81)

Quantum theory holds, therefore, that a particle such as an electron does not have a meaningful trajectory but abrupt and unpredictable motion. Thus at the subatomic level, matter does not exist with certainty at definite places, nor do atomic events occur with certainty at definite times and in definite ways. Rather, matter shows 'tendencies to exist' and atomic events show 'tendencies to occur'. The mathematical formulation of quantum theory, or quantum mechanics, achieved by Scrodinger and Heisenberg subsequently imposed order on this entropy by giving the probabilities of when and where a particle might be. Accordingly atomic events cannot be predicted with certainty, only the likelihood of its happening.

Nevertheless, Einstein insisted on the commonsense view that an electron really exists in a definite place and with a definite trajectory—whether or not it is observed to do so—maintaining that observations merely uncover the reality of the atom and that any ambiguity or uncertainty encountered is the result of imprecision in the measuring instruments used. However, this view was invalidated by several developments in quantum theory, notably Godel's Incompleteness Theorem, Bohr's Principle of Complementarity, and Heisenberg's Uncertainty Principle.

GODEL'S INCOMPLETENESS THEOREM

Heutzer indicates that in its barest form Godel's achievement, which involves the translation of an ancient philosophical paradox—Epimenides paradox—into mathematical terms, was to demonstrate that every encompassing system of logic must have at least one premise that cannot be proved or verified without contradicting itself. The implications of this deduction are that objective verification of reality is impossible; 'For if all (including the verifier) is to be verified, how do you verify the verifier?' (Heutzer, 1984, p. 83). Godel's observation is reminiscent of the teaching of the mystic Sri Ramana: 'This world which you try to prove to be real, is all the time mocking at you for seeking to know it, without first knowing yourself. How can the knowledge of objects arising in relative existence to one who does not know the truth of himself, the knower, be true knowledge.'

BOHR'S PRINCIPLE OF COMPLEMENTARITY

Observations of the subatomic realm in the early years of this century had revealed that subatomic units of matter are very abstract entities which have a dual aspect, such that depending on how they are observed, they appear sometimes as particles and sometimes as waves. This duality is also exhibited by light, which can take the form of electromagnetic waves or particles. The curious nature of matter and light presented physicists with a paradox, because logically it seems impossible that something can be at one and the same time both a particle confined to a very small volume, and a wave spread over a large region of space. Bohr's contribution to the evolution of quantum physics was to resolve this paradox by suggesting that the particle and wave pictures are two complementary and mutually exclusive descriptions of the same reality, both of which are necessary. In so doing he pointed to the inadequacy of classical concepts, such as those of waves and particles, in describing atomic phenomena. Subsequently, it was recognized that an electron is neither a particle nor a wave, but can show aspects of either depending on how it is observed.

> While it acts like a particle, it is capable of developing its wave nature at the expense of the particle nature, and vice versa, thus undergoing continual transformations from particle to wave and from wave to particle. This means that neither the electron nor any other 'atomic' object has any intrinsic properties independent of its environment. The properties it shows — particle-like or wave-like — will depend on the experimental situation, that is, on the apparatus it is forced to interact with.   (Capra, 1983, pp. 67–68)

HEISENBERG'S UNCERTAINTY PRINCIPLE

Heisenberg's discovery established that there are limits beyond which the processes of nature cannot measure accurately, at the same time — limits beyond which there can be no certainty and which are not imposed by the inexactness of measuring devices or the extremely small size of the entities being measured, but by nature itself.

> The uncertainty principle reveals that as we penetrate deeper and deeper into the subatomic realm, we reach a certain point at which one part or another of our picture of nature becomes blurred, and that there is no way to reclarify that part without blurring another part of the picture! It is as though we are adjusting a moving picture that is slightly out of focus. As we make the final adjustments we are astonished to discover that when the right side of the picture clears, the left side of the picture becomes completely unfocused and nothing in it is recognizable. When we try to focus the left side of the picture, the right side starts to blur and soon the situation is reversed.

If we try to strike a balance between these two extremes, both sides of the picture return to a recognizable condition, but in no way can we remove the original fuzziness from them. The right side of the picture, in the original formulation of the uncertainty principle, corresponds to the position in space of a moving particle. The left side of the picture corresponds to its momentum. According to the uncertainty principle, we cannot measure accurately, at the same time, both the position *and* the momentum of a moving particle. The more precisely we determine one of these properties the less we know about the other. If we precisely determine the position of the particle, then, strange as it sounds, there is *nothing* that we can know about its momentum. If we precisely determine the momentum of the particle, there is no way to determine its position.   (Zukav, 1980, p. 133)

The primary significance of the uncertainty principle is that all attempts to observe the electron alter it. Thus at the subatomic level we cannot observe something without changing it. Therefore, the universe does not exist independently of the observer who measures it.

Quantum theory, as presently formulated, affords no consistent notion of the reality that underlies the universal constitution and structure of matter. Einstein, in the course of his life-long quest for a unified theory of physical reality, has contributed to quantum theory in a number of major ways. Nevertheless, he remained dissatisfied with the probabilistic world view it implied, declaring that 'God does not play dice'. Many of the discoveries of the new physics disturbed him, particularly those of Heisenberg, which suggested that reality is not only *not* independent of the observer, but also shaped by him. So, in 1935 with Boris Podolsky and Nathan Rosen, he devised an argument which he believed to be the *reductio ad absurdem* of quantum theory. This Einstein-Podolsky-Rosen theorem essentially proposed that if quantum theory is correct, then 'a change in the spin of a two particle system would affect its twin simultanaeously even if the two had been widely separated in the meantime' (Dossey, 1982, p. 99). This would imply the occurrence of some form of telepathic communication or psychokinesis—physical action at a distance—and as such represented an unthinkable proposition for most physicists conditioned to regard telepathy and psychokinesis as occultist nonsense, including Einstein who regarded the idea as 'ghostly and absurd'.

However, in 1964, J. S. Bell formulated a mathematical proof, subsequently known as Bell's Theorem, which suggested that Einstein's impossible proposition of action at a distance—instantaneous change in widely separated systems—could occur. This was confirmed experimentally by Clauser and Freedman in 1972 and the findings have been replicated on numerous occasions since. Nevertheless, these experiments were not precise enough to settle the crucial question and advocates of Relativity Theory believed that nothing ever would, but in 1983 a French team of scientists led by Alain Aspect added a crucial refinement to previous experiments which established beyond doubt that, as far as action-at-a-distance is concerned, Quantum Theory was right and Einstein was wrong.

The original experiments consisted of measuring the polarization of matched pairs of photons emitted by a common source to see whether the behaviour of one member of the pair was affected by a measurement of the other. Aspect's experiment, which was devised by David Bohm, improved on this by introducing a switch into the system which effectively blocked any signal passing from one photon to the other. There are several possible interpretations to the Aspect experiment, all of which have dramatic implications for physics. One possible explanation is that some kind of information can travel faster than the speed of light, which would mean that existing concepts of space and time require modification; or it may mean that everything in the universe is inter-related and inter-connected. Whichever explanation is favoured, the implications of Bell's Theorem are staggering, as Zukav (1980, p. 306) indicates:

> No matter how formulated, it projects the 'irrational' aspects of subatomic phenomena squarely into the macroscopic domain. It says that not only do events in the realm of the small behave in ways which are utterly different from our commonsense view of the world but also that events in the world at large, the world of freeways and sports cars, behave in ways which are utterly different from our commonsense view of them.

Bell's Theorem therefore appears to confirm Gurdjieff's prediction that 'in the infinitely small we shall find the same laws as in the infinitely great. As above, so below.' Bell's Theorem also resonates with the theories of Carl Gustav Jung who argued for the interconnectedness of all things in his essay *Synchronicity: An acausal connecting principle* (1972) written in collaboration with the physicist Wolfgang Pauli.

Synchronicity is the term Jung uses to describe the simultaneous occurrence of two meaningfully but not causally related events, or the timely coincidence of two or more unrelated events with the same or similar meaning. Heutzer (1984) suggests that the Jungian concept of synchronicity is a modern derivation of the archetypal belief in the fundamental unity of all things. As she points out, since antiquity influences, sympathies, and correspondences have been invoked as explanations for events that seem unaffected by causal laws. This doctrine of the 'sympathy of all things' can be traced back to Hippocrates and it is a recurrent theme in the teachings of Pythagoreans, Neo-Platonists and the philosophers of the Renaissance, until the eighteenth century, when following the Newtonian revolution 'causality was enthroned as the absolute ruler of matter and mind' (pp. 89–90). It was this reign that quantum theory brought to an abrupt end, for

> If all actions are in the form of discrete quanta, the interactions between different entities (eg: electrons) constitute a single structure of indivisible links, so that the entire universe has to be thought of as an unbroken whole. In this whole, each element that we can extract in thought shows basic properties (wave or particle etc.) that depend on its overall environment in a way that

is much more reminiscent of how the organs constituting living things are related, than it is of how parts of a machine interact. Further the non-local, non-causal nature of the relationships of elements distant from each other violates the requirements of separateness and independence of fundamental constituents that is basic to any mechanistic approach.

(Bohm, 1980, pp. 175-176)

A conclusion to be drawn from modern physics is therefore that at a deep and fundamental level the apparently separate parts of the universe are connected in an intimate and immediate way.

THE TAO OF PHYSICS

The organic, holistic, ecological world-view emerging from modern physics restates, albeit in the language of mathematics, occult and mystical descriptions of reality in evidence since antiquity, and still emphasized within Eastern cultures. Pribram (1978) asserts, therefore, that the current paradigm shift will bring about a blending of Eastern and Western traditions and a 'scientific-religious' experience.

The striking parallels between the discoveries of modern physics and Eastern mysticism has been identified by numerous commentators, including Le Shan (1969, 1974), and a thorough discussion of the correspondences between the theories of subatomic and atomic physics and Taoist thought, in particular, has been provided by Capra (1976) and Zukav (1980). Capra indicates that Bohr was well aware of this correspondence, and particularly that between his concept of complementarity and the Taoist notion of complementary opposites, Yin and Yang, the two great powers of the universe. Nevertheless, he observes (1983, pp.66-67) that initially many physicists reared in the classical Newtonian tradition which associated mysticism 'with things vague, mysterious and highly unscientific' were shocked at this comparison, but increasingly are aware that mystical thought provides a consistent and relevant philosophical background to the theories of contemporary science; 'a conception of the world in which scientific discoveries of men and women can be in perfect harmony with their spiritual aims and beliefs'. Yet, as Staal (1975, p. 114) observes, most contemporary psychologists have confined themselves to selecting data from mysticism in support of some view or other, or to comparing psychotherapy to mysticism in a general way; and 'in both respects, the light generated, though suggestive at times, has remained hazy'.

There are, however, rather more pragmatic implications to quantum theory, the key features of which clearly show the inadequacy of mechanistic notions of order; that is, the way in which the universe was thought by Newton to be arranged. Bohm explains that the mechanistic order may be described as explicate in that each of its elements lies only in its own regions of space and time and outside the regions appertaining to other things. It is in this sense that events are conceived as separate and independent, and understandable in terms of the regular arrangements of objects, as in rows, or of events in sequence.

The undivided wholeness implied by quantum theory, in which all parts of the universe, including the observer and all instruments, merge and unite in one interdependent totality demands a new order.

> To begin with undivided wholeness means, however, that we must drop the mechanistic order. But this order has been, for many centuries, basic to all thinking on physics . . . Evidently it is not easy to change this, because our notions of order are pervasive, for not only do they involve our thinking but also our sense, our feelings, our intuitions, our physical movement, our relationships with other people and with society as a whole and indeed every phase of our lives. It is thus difficult to 'step back' from our old notions of order sufficiently to be able seriously to consider new notions of order.
>
> (Bohm, 1980, p. 175)

Undaunted, however, Bohm has proposed a new notion of order appropriate to this undivided separateness.

THE HOLOGRAPHIC UNIVERSE

Bohm (1980) suggests that the universe is holographic, that is, like a gigantic hologram. He explains that a hologram is formed when a laser is passed through a half-silvered mirror on to a photographic plate. Part of this beam goes directly to the photographic plate whilst another part of the beam is reflected so that it illuminates a certain whole structure. The light reflected from this structure also reaches the photographic plate where it interferes with that arriving by the direct path. The resulting interference pattern which is recorded on the photographic plate is very complex and very fine yet it is relevant to the whole illuminated structure albeit only in a highly implicit way. This relevance of the interference pattern to the whole illuminated structure is revealed when the photographic plate is illuminated with laser light. A wavefront is then created which is very similar to that coming off the original structure, with the result that one sees in effect the whole of the original structure in three dimensions and from a range of possible viewpoints. Moreover, if only a small region of the plate is illuminated the whole structure is still visible but in somewhat less sharply defined detail and from a decreased range of possible viewpoints. It appears, therefore, that each part of the hologram contains information about the whole, and indeed, if the hologram is broken into pieces each piece will reconstruct the whole image. This means that the hologram cannot be understood in terms of the mechanistic order. It has to be understood in terms of a total order contained implicitly in each region of time and space. Here the term implicit (from the verb 'to implicate' meaning to fold inwards) is used in the sense that each region contains a total structure 'enfolded' within it. As such it conjures the image of the way in which mayonnaise is formed by folding drops of oil into raw eggs.

Bohm indicates that the implicate order can be demonstrated within the laboratory in a similar fashion by stirring an insoluble drop of black ink in a very viscous colourless fluid. It can be observed that the ink drop is gradually transformed into a thread that extends over the whole fluid and is distributed 'randomly' so that it is visible only as a shade of grey. The droplet thus loses its contours or boundaries and becomes diffuse and 'blurred'. When distributed in this kind of way it nevertheless has some kind of order; an order enfolded or implicated in the visible grey mass. Bohm suggests that what happens here is similar to what happens in a hologram. The value of the hologram is that it focusses attention on this new notion of order in a clearly perceptible manner. Nevertheless, the hologram is an instrument which makes a static record of this order, whereas the order itself is conveyed in a complex movement of electromagnetic fields in the form of light waves. Bohm therefore suggests that what carries the implicate order is what he terms the holomovement—an unbroken and undivided totality from which particular aspects such as light and sound or electrons can be abstracted but which are essentially inseparable. This holomovement, which in its totality cannot be limited in any specifiable way, nor bound by any particular measure, is undefinable and immeasurable.

Bohm's theory is essentially that *what is* is movement, and that the explicate order—the world of manifest reality—is a secondary derivation from this primary order of the universe. Hard reality is therefore an abstraction from the blur of basic reality; a notion long held by mystics and sages, and reflected in the teachings of Gibran's prophet:

> Life, and all that lives, is conceived in the mist and not in the crystal. And who knows but a crystal is a mist in decay.
>
> (Gibran, 1978 edn, *The Prophet*, pp. 108–109)

THE PHYSICS OF MAYA

Like the mystics of antiquity, Bohm, in describing a holographic universe, is depicting a world in which what appears to be stable, tangible and 'out there' is not really there at all, and thus an illusion, a magic show. In the terms of Indian philosophy it is *maya*. Such a view has also been advanced by neuroscientist Karl Pribram (1976). In addressing the problem of how memory could be distributed throughout the brain rather than localized in any one region, he proposed that the information is enfolded over the whole in much the same way as in a hologram. Having put forward this holographic model of the brain, he pursued the notion, formerly advanced by psychologists of the gestalt school, that the world perceived 'out there' is isomorphic with brain processes; that is, they both exhibit the same form, and thereby arrived at the inescapable conclusion that the world is a hologram, unaware that Bohm had done likewise. He went on to suggest that reality is not what is perceived by the eyes; that the brain may act as a lens, transforming mathematically the blur of primary reality into 'hard' reality, and that without these mathematics we would possibly only know a world organized in the frequency domain; a world without space or time, such as that described by poets and mystics throughout history. Hence, in the words of St Exupery (1974), 'what is essential is invisible to the eye'.

Nevertheless, the problem for the physicist and neuroscientist is to account for 'normal' perception of mundane, 'explicate' reality; that which the Indian sages term *avidja*—a not-seeing. Castaneda's tutor, Don Juan, claims that 'we train our eyes to look as we think about the things we look at';

> So in essence the world that your reason wants to sustain is the world created
> by a description and its dogmatic and inviolable rules which the reason learns
> to accept and defend.

He argues that true 'seeing' demands suspension of thought, reason, logic. Bohm suggests that we learn to see the world in certain ways. Therefore we do not necessarily notice the primary order because we are habituated to the explicate order which is emphasized in thought and language, both of which are predominantly linear and sequential. Indeed Western culture as a whole is habituated to the rational, the logical, the linear and sequential, and to a description of a manifest, explicate reality. As a result the ability to 'think straight' is highly valued and there is a tendency to feel that primary experience is of that order. Another possible reason, according to Bohm, is that the contents of memory, in the manner of a holograph, focusses attention on what is static and fragmented, with the result that the more subtle and transitory features of the unbroken flow 'tend to pale into such seeming insignificance that one is at best only dimly conscious of them' (1980, p. 206).

Mystical traditions emphasize that true seeing, or direct perception of reality, can be achieved by developing insight, literally a looking inwards, which might be thought of an enfoldment. This notion is consistent with the holographic notion that the world is enfolded within each of its parts. Accordingly, the truth of the universe, ultimate truth, resides within the person:

> The things we see . . . are the things which are already in us. There is no
> reality beyond what we have inside us.   (Herman Hesse, *Demian*)

Therefore, by looking inwards to the centre, or the heart of one's being, one encounters nothingness, variously referred to in the literature of mysticism as pure or 'cosmic' consciousness, Brahman, Atman, the universal Tao, accounts of which bear an uncanny resemblance to the descriptions of reality offered by quantum theory:

> Pure consciousness is indivisible, it is without parts. It has no form and shape, no within and without. There is no 'right' or 'left' for it. Pure consciousness, which is the heart, includes all, and nothing is outside apart from it. That is Ultimate Truth.   (Sri Ramana)

The contents of this experience are often said to be 'ineffable', incapable of being fully communicated in words, but Huxley (1977) indicates there are likenesses running through attempts to do so. The highest common factor is the experience of undifferentiated light; an uncoloured light, which in the Buddhist tradition is identified as the 'clear light of the void'. There is also the experience of light in differentiated forms, when it is embodied in shapes, landscapes and personages.

> And here again we find, curiously enough, a certain uniformity. We find likenesses running through the various descriptions of this. For example, the experience will very often begin with a vision of what may be called geometries, geometrical forms brilliantly lighted, continuously changing. These may modulate into some kind of geometrical objects such as carpets, mosaics, and so on. There may be visions of landscapes of an extraordinarily brilliant and glowing nature . . . And then there are sometimes visions of figures, strange faces, and there's a very interesting fact—which is recorded again and again . . . that when faces are seen, they are never the faces of people that the experiencer knows . . . And this is a very interesting fact— that at the sort of antipodes of our mind, in this remote area of our mind, it is so far beyond the personal consciousness that we don't see anything connected with our own private life, or even the general life of mankind. We see something quite different.   (Huxley, 1977, p. 279)

Huxley claims that this visionary world—the world seen with what he terms the 'inner eye'—is accessed through the deepest levels of hypnosis; various forms of meditation; total isolation such as practised by certain Hindu and Tibetan monks; breathing exercises; fasting, and by chemical means. Mescaline, Peyote, Opium and other substances have been used in mystical practices from the earliest times, and Huxley observes that within this century many scientists have used similar methods in order to explore the visionary realm, including the distinguished psychologist William James, who employed nitrous oxide, and more recently John Lilly (1973) who has reported on his combined use of sensory deprivation and drugs in his explorations of consciousness.

Many researchers, including Huxley himself, have advocated the use of psychedelic drugs as a means of accessing the visionary realm, none more stridently than former Harvard psychologist, Timothy Leary, whose first experience of psilocybin made a profound and lasting impression:

> I gave way to delight, as mystics have for centuries when they perceived
> through the curtains and discovered that this world — so manifestly real —
> was actually a tiny stage constructed by the mind. There was a sea of
> possibilities out there (in there?), other realities, an infinite array of programs
> for other futures.   (1983, p. 32)

Certain drugs, it seems, prevent one from 'thinking straight', and by-pass what
Huxley has termed the 'reducing valve' of ordinary consciousness, enabling direct
perception of reality; the undifferentiated frequency domain postulated by
Pribram. Indeed the eminent Czech psychiatrist Stanislav Grof (1979) argues
that psychedelic drugs, notably LSD, facilitate access to the holographic universe
described by Bohm and Pribram.

In the light of these speculations, focus upon altered states of consciousness,
mystical experience, psychic phenomena and psychedelic experience can no longer
be dismissed as trivial. They have to be admitted within any scientific framework
which purports to be a complete understanding of reality. According to Grof,
the essential conflict is no longer between science and mysticism;

> Rather it is between the emergent paradigm and a 'coalition' paradigm: the
> joining of the old mechanical model of science and ordinary 'pedestrian'
> consciousness. In other words, the problem is not so much contradictory data
> as contradictory states of consciousness — a conflict Grof feels is resolved by
> the holographic view.   (Ferguson, 1982, p. 413)

FAITHING THE FACTS

That science and mysticism are coming together is evidenced in a number of
ways. Burge (1985) indicates that recent experimental successes in physics have
combined with developments in mathematics in a way which makes some
physicists think they may be within sight of the goal that eluded Galileo, Newton
and Einstein — the single law which underlies all the phenomena of nature.
However, as they draw nearer to a single theoretical explanation of reality, or
ultimate truth, they have found it necessary to desert experiment and to accept
that there may be no way of proving what they know. Modern physics, therefore,
demands not evidence, but belief, faith and aesthetics. Nevertheless, as Burge
(p. 13) observes:

> Others, fearful of incipient mysticism, state that experimentation is the object
> of physics and that anything beyond it must be passed over in silence. Against
> this it is possible to point out that Einstein produced the General Theory
> of Relativity, his famous theory of gravity, with all but no experimental
> evidence and with only restricted prospects of testing it, yet he was so confident
> of its truth that he was able to declare it 'too beautiful to be false'.

Similarly, the most recent theories of physics are held because of their internal consistency, simplicity and elegance rather than supporting evidence. One such, the theory of super-symmetry, originally proposed by Kaluza in 1919 and recently resurrected, goes beyond Einsteinian threefold unification theory to a theory of fourfold unification, integrating gravity with the other apparently independent forces that govern the universe: the electromagnetic force, and those forces which operate only at the subatomic level—the 'strong' force, which binds the atomic nucleus, and the 'weak' force, involved in some kinds of radioactivity. It has, as Silcock (1985, p. 13) observes, 'mindboggling ramifications', because although it can be formulated in four dimensions—three of time and one of space—it is much simpler to formulate in eleven dimensions, just as the symmetry of a solid can be perceived more easily from a three-dimensional model than on paper.

Exactly how an eleven-dimensional, super-symmetrical universe appears only to have four dimensions is explained in terms of the now familiar concept of enfoldment; it being held that seven of the dimensions are 'curled in' upon themselves. The theory also predicts the existence of several as yet undiscovered particles. Nevertheless, many commentators feel that, however improbable this theory might appear, like Einstein's theory of relativity, it is too beautiful to be false and will ultimately be borne out by experiment. Indeed, Cern, the European nuclear research centre at Geneva, recently reported that mysterious events have occurred in showers of secondary particles produced by collisions in Cern's gigantic particle accelerator. In a few cases, the showers are 'lop-sided', with particles streaming from one side and not the other; a situation sufficiently reminiscent of the Zen koan which concerns the sound of one hand clapping to justify their being termed 'Zen events'. It seems clear that a particle which leaves no other traces is involved; particles such as those predicted by supersymmetry.

A CONSCIOUS UNIVERSE

The emergent paradigm afforded by quantum theory and the new physics admits consciousness in a previously unconceived way, implying, in contradistinction to commonsense views of reality, that it may not be the brain that produces consciousness, but rather consciousness that creates the appearance of the brain, matter, space, time and everything that is taken as constituting the physical universe. Given such a possibility consciousness must be considered in any attempt at understanding the universe and man's place in it. Indeed, as Polanyi (1958) has indicated, any science attempting a strictly detached, objective knowledge and to abolish all personal knowledge would be aiming, unwittingly, at the destruction of all knowledge. The ideal of exact science would thus turn out to be fundamentally misleading and possibly the source of devastating fallacies.

It is ironic, therefore, that at the very time scientists were awakening to the possibility that the universe is more akin to a cosmic consciousness than a machine, psychology, in its insistence on so-called 'objective' fact was rejecting all subjective phenomena as unscientific. The absurdity of such a situation is highlighted by Koestler (1976, p. 32):

> Materialism is 'vieux jeux', a century out of date. Only you psychologists still believe in it. It is a very funny situation. We know that the behaviour of an electron is not completely determined by the laws of physics. You believe that the behaviour of a human being is completely determined by the laws of physics. Electrons are unpredictable, people are predictable. And you call this psychology.

Clearly, any psychology that is going to be relevant to contemporary science has to be a psychology of consciousness. However, the problem for a psychology working within the framework of a materialistic, mechanistic paradigm has been in generating its original subject matter, consciousness, from an impersonal universe; a problem it had unsatisfactorily resolved during the first half of the twentieth century by ignoring, and even denying the existence of consciousness. Cosgrove (1982, p. 73) argues the case for materialism in psychology by insisting that a humanistic psychology, in attempting to justify the existence of consciousness when the material universe cannot produce it, is building its view of human nature on a presuppositional basis that will not support a lofty view of man. He insists that 'this is not just a biological problem that will some day be solved. Trying to draw more from nature than it has to give demands a suspension of logic that scientists make in no other part of their work.' In the light of the new physics this assertion is patently untrue. Moreover, it seems, Cosgrove has failed to take into account the recent contributions of the distinguished chemist, Ilya Prigogine.

A CREATIVE UNIVERSE

In 1977 Prigogine was awarded the Nobel Prize for his Transformation Theory which established the connectedness of living and non-living forms, and thus bridged the critical gap between living systems and the apparently lifeless universe in which they arose; a theory which Prigogine recognizes as consistent with the visions of poets, mystics and Eastern philosophers of an open, creative universe.

Prigogine's theory concerns dissipative structures—all living things and some non-living things such as certain chemical reactions—whose form is maintained by a continuing dissipation of energy. Ferguson (1982, p. 177) describes a dissipative structure as a flowing wholeness, which is highly complex and always in process. The greater its complexity the more energy the structure requires to maintain its coherence. This produces the paradoxical situation that the greater its coherence the greater its instability, and it is this instability which is the key to transformation because the dissipation of energy creates the potential for sudden reordering.

> The continuous movement of energy through the system results in fluctuations; if they are minor the system damps them and they do not alter its structural integrity. But if the fluctuations reach a critical size they 'perturb' the system. They increase the number of novel interactions within it. They shake it up. The elements of the old pattern come into contact with each other in new ways and make new connections. *The parts reorganise into a new whole. The system escapes into a higher order.*
>
> The more complex or coherent a structure, the greater the next level of complexity. Each new level is even more integrated and connected than the one before, requiring a greater flow of energy for maintenance, and is therefore still less stable. To put it another way, flexibility begets flexibility. As Prigogine said, at higher levels of complexity, 'the nature of the laws of nature changes'. It has the potential to create new forms by allowing a shake-up of old forms.   (Ferguson, 1982, p. 178)

Paradoxically, therefore, it is this instability, or the capacity for being 'shaken up' which is the key to growth. Structures that are insulated from disturbance are protected from change. They are stagnant and never evolve toward a more complex form.

Such a view resonates with that of the Buddha, who, in recognizing the possibility for transformation through acceptance of change, saw man's clinging to the habitual as a defence against impermanence and a barrier to growth. Similarly, the idea of creating new order by perturbation is paralleled in numerous ways in the traditional wisdom of the Orient, and reflected in certain practices such as the Zen master striking his pupil, thereby enabling him to 'see' the truth of a paradoxical koan.

The notion of entropy as the progenitor of order also finds a parallel in the views advanced by Laing (1959) that mental illness or 'dis-order' enables reintegration of the personal self. Indeed, Prigogine's theory that order and organization can arise spontaneously out of disorder and chaos through a process of self-organization helps to account for effects such as those claimed for meditation, hypnosis, guided imagery and psychotherapy:

> An individual reliving a traumatic incident in a state of highly-focused inward attention perturbs the pattern of that specific old memory. This triggers a reorganisation—a new dissipative structure. The old pattern is broken.
>   (Ferguson, 1982, p. 183)

Ferguson also indicates that long before the theory was experimentally confirmed, its significance had stunned the Israeli research chemist Aharon Katchalsky, who identified the brain as a perfect example of a dissipative structure. Unfortunately, his untimely death prevented further research on the theory of dissipative structures as it may apply to the human brain and consciousness; research which might explain the transformative power of psychotechnologies, altered states of consciousness and psychedelic experiences to alter learning that is resistant to change in ordinary states of conscious; and in so doing vindicate Leary in his insistence on the scientific value of psychedelic research.

Ferguson also indicates that the theory of dissipative structures relates well to holographic theory, Pribram having suggested that dissipative structures may represent the means of unfolding from the implicate order; the way it is manifested in time and space. She also cites Nazarea of the University of Texas at Austin as expressing 'quiet optimism' that theoretical work on dissipative structures may 'vindicate in its main outlines the so-called holographic theory . . . though from a different direction' (1982, p. 203).

Toffler (1985) claims that the Prigoginian paradigm is of particular interest because it shifts attention to those aspects of reality that characterize today's accelerated social change: disorder, instability, diversity, disequilibrium, non-linear relationships and temporality. He suggests that the work of Prigogine and his colleagues may well represent the next revolution in science, as it enters into a new dialogue not merely with nature, but with society itself.

FROM ANCIENT MYTHS TO MODERN MOVEMENTS

Capra (1983, p. x) suggests that 'the conceptual revolution in physics foreshadows an imminent revolution in all the sciences, and a profound transformation of our world views and values'. He argues that the beginnings of this transformation are evident in a number of different movements in various disciplines, all of which seem to be in the same direction and emphasizing different aspects of the new vision of reality, but most of which still operate separately, having not yet recognized the inter-relatedness of their aims. He identifies developments in economics, politics and the social sciences as part of this movement, together with certain trends in medicine and psychology. Campbell likewise regards these as 'threads in a broad cultural pattern, the shape of which we are just beginning to see' (1984, p. 16).

The so-called 'new biology' is consistent with the new understanding of reality. Rose et al. (1984) insist upon the unitary ontological nature of a material world in which the biological and the social are 'neither separable, nor antithetical, nor alternatives, but complementary'. Awareness of this inter-relatedness and complementarity—the universal Tao—means that organisms or the environment can no longer be conceived of in isolation from each other:

> Just as there is no organism without an environment, there is no environment without an organism. Neither organism nor environment is a closed system; each is open to the other. There is a variety of ways in which the organism is the determinant of its own milieu.   (Rose et al., 1984, pp. 273–274)

Hence, 'There is no universal physical fact of nature whose effect on, or even relevance to an organism is not in part a consequence of the nature of the organism itself' (p. 276).

This new biology calls for a radical reappraisal of our thinking about 'being in the world', and has important implications for medical science in particular. Dossey (1982, p. xii) argues for a new model of health and healing consistent with the new paradigm. He insists that

> We have built a model of health and illness, birth and death, around an outmoded conceptual model of how the universe behaves, one which was fundamentally flawed from the beginning. While the physicists have been painfully eliminating the flaws in their own models, we have in medicine ignored these revisions totally. We find ourselves thus with a set of guiding beliefs that are as antiquated as are body humors, leeching and bleeding.

The movement in medicine is away from the disease model in which the body and mind are viewed as separate; the body being viewed as a machine in good or bad working order, and the mind as a secondary factor in organic illness. It is also a movement away from treatment of individual symptoms by 'objective', emotionally uninvolved, authoritarian practitioners with drugs and surgery, towards an holistic perspective in which the mind and body are seen as a dynamic entity, integrated with each other and the wider environment, all of which are involved in disease and healing. Accordingly treatment is achieved by discovery of patterns of being (indeed diagnostic procedures can be likened to an encounter between psychotherapist and client); minimal technological intervention, caring, and emphasis on the autonomy and responsibility of the person in the healing process. This holistic model, which corresponds closely with the homeopathic approach, is being pursued in numerous alternative approaches to therapy, including the treatment of cancer (Simonton et al., 1978; Pelletier, 1978).

These developments in what might be thought of as 'humanistic' medicine correspond closely with certain trends in psychology, notably humanistic and transpersonal approaches. Welwood (1978) identifies this psychology as the nexus of a number of disciplines that our changing contemporary culture, and the one area where science, personal experience, mysticism and transformation come together in a patchwork. In so doing his views echo those of Maslow (1968, p. iii):

> I have come to think of this humanist trend in psychology as a revolution in the truest, oldest sense of the word, the sense in which Galileo, Darwin, Einstein, Freud and Marx made revolutions ie; new ways of perceiving and thinking, new images of man and of society, new conceptions of ethics and values, new directions in which to move. The third psychology is now one facet of a general Weltanschauung, a new philosophy of life.

In addition to promoting new paradigm research in many areas, humanistic psychology is forging links with other disciplines in a number of ways, and particularly in the field of consciousness research. Since the 1960s there has been an upsurge of interest in this area and numerous studies have been conducted. These include studies of altered states of consciousness (Lilly, 1973; Tart 1975; Grof 1979); bimodal consciousness (see Ornstein, 1975); hypnosis (Orne, 1959; Hildgard 1965; Chertok 19(81)); psychic phenomena (Taylor, 1975; Targ and Puthoff, 1977); meditative states (Hirai, 1975), and biofeedback (Pelletier, 1978). *The Journal of Humanistic Psychology* and *The Journal of Transpersonal Psychology* are both increasingly publishing papers that relate the new physics in particular, and new paradigm research in general to psychological concerns.

Esalen, in its commitment to expanding frontiers of human potential and promoting interdisciplinary exchange, remains at the forefront of this movement. Thus, whilst Hetherington (1983) had to urge members of the British Psychological Society to recognize that, however unwelcome, investigations of anomalous phenomena, properly witnessed and reliably reported, are potentially as important in contributing to a paradigm shift in psychology as were the results of early twentieth century experiments on light to Newtonian physics, it required no such prompting.

For nine years theoretical physicists Nick Herbert and Saul-Paul Sirag have brought together at Esalen a small number of scientists interested in quantum theory, and Bell's Theorem in particular. In 1983 Russell Targ and Harold Puthoff convened the third annual conference in parapsychology to be held at Esalen; the 1982 conference having contributed new ideas on psychic research, and specifically, experimenter bias in research. The first in this series of conferences, held in 1981, had examined data for precognition as it relates to new concepts in modern physics. In 1983 George Leonard convened a gathering of seven scientists who reported their investigations into 'subtle' energies, focussing on psychokinesis, intentional extraordinary control of bodily states, and synchronicity of physiological functions such as brain waves. During 1983 Fritjof Capra also held workshops at Esalen in which he examined current transformations in science, society and culture; a theme continued in 1984 when David Finkelstein, Professor of Physics at the Georgia Institute of Technology, convened a meeting to explore frontiers of thinking in physics.

With its holistic, integrative approach, humanistic psychology is fully consistent with the new paradigm. However, as Capra (1983, p. 406) observes, the new psychology is still far from being a complete theory of man, being developed so far only in the form of loosely connected models, ideas, and therapeutic techniques. The most comprehensive theory to date is that advanced by Wilber (1977), which unifies numerous approaches into a spectrum of psychological models and theories that reflects the range of human consciousness from the narrow focus of the individual ego or mind, to that of cosmic consciousness, which Wilber terms Mind.

Wilber's spectrum psychology traces the development of personal identity through several levels of consciousness, commencing with the *ego level* at which the personal self, ego or mind is identified, and progressing in fine gradations through stages of *social* awareness, in which social and cultural influences are identified; *existential* awareness, or self-awareness in which dualism of mind and body, self and other are resolved; *transpersonal* awareness of the connectedness of the cosmos as a whole; and finally, the level of *Mind*, the mystical state of transcendence, where all dualities are resolved and all individuality merges into universal, undifferentiated one-ness. As such it parallels both the spiritual development of man as depicted by mystics and Eastern sages, and the historical development of Western psychology. It draws together the traditional focus of concern of Western and Eastern cultures and their respective psychologies, mind, and Mind—of which the former is but a part—in such a way that what were previously thought of as polar opposites, can now be seen to be aspects of one consciousness.

It is this curious circularity which is clearly evident in man's attempts during the past two thousand years to impose meaning on the world in which he finds himself. The wisdom of the ancients once again informs man's attempts at a unified description of the universe, and the myths of antiquity recur in the form of a new cosmology, as, at the frontiers of modern knowledge, physics merge with mysticism, and psychological insight with scientific outlook. It would seem, as Rajneesh (1979) has observed, that at the extremes everything changes into its opposite; that, ultimately, everything comes full circle. Such an awareness reinforces the traditional wisdom of achieving the centre, or balance in all things; and of pursuing a middle path, for this centre is the still point or pivot around which all else turns. Attainment of this balance is the aim of third force, humanistic psychology, and to the extent that it is able to do so it is likely to endure. Shaffer (1978, p. 186) perceives an enduring space for humanistic psychology 'at the boundary between what is known and what is unknown about man, between the potential that has already been actualised and the potential which remains unfilfilled'. Nevertheless, in a world of dramatic and accelerating change it is difficult to anticipate future developments, or to avoid the feeling that the way forward lies in where we have already been. It could well be that

> We shall not cease from exploration
> And the end of all our exploring
> Will be to arrive where we started
> And know the place for the first time.[7]

---

[7]Choruses from the rock. In: *Selected Poems* 1961. London: Faber & Faber.

BIBLIOGRAPHY

Adorno, T. 1967. Sociology and psychology. *New Left Review* Nov/Dec Vol. **46**, pp. 67–81.

Adorno, T. 1968. Sociology and psychology (II). *New Left Review* Jan/Feb Vol. **47**, pp. 79–97.

Allport, G. W. 1955. *Becoming.* New Haven: Yale University Press.

Allport, G. W. 1963. *Pattern and Growth in Personality.* London: Holt, Rinehart and Winston.

Allport, G. W. 1969. Comment on earlier chapters. In: *Existential Psychology* (ed. R. May) pp. 93–99, New York: Random House.

Anderson, M. 1962. *The Unknowable Gurdjieff.* London: Routledge & Kegan Paul.

Anderson, M. 1969. *The Strange Necessity.* New York: Horizon Press.

Apter, M. J. 1982. *The Experience of Motivation: The theory of psychological reversals.* London: Academic Press.

Ashe, G. 1977. *The Ancient Wisdom.* London: Macmillan.

Assaglioli, R. 1975. *Psychosynthesis: a manual of principles and techniques.* New York: Hobbs Dorman.

Baigent, M., Leigh, R. & Lincoln, H. 1982. *The Holy Blood and the Holy Grail.* London. Cape.

Bancroft, A. 1978. *Modern Mystics and Sages.* London: Paladin (Granada).

Barlow, W. 1975. *The Alexander Principle: How to use your body.* London: Arrow.

Barnes, H. E. 1959. *Humanistic Existentialism: the literature of possibility.* Lincoln: University of Nebraska Press.

Barnes, H. E. 1967. *An Existential Ethics.* Chicago & London: University of Chicago Press. Reprinted 1978.

Barnes, M. & Berke, J. 1973. *Mary Barnes: two accounts of a journey through madness.* Harmondsworth: Penguin.

Berke, J. 1977. *I Haven't Had To Go Mad Here.* Harmondsworth: Penguin.

Berne, E. 1968. *Games People Play.* Harmondsworth: Penguin.

Binswanger, L. 1958. The case of Ellen West. In: (ed. R. May) *Existence: a new dimension in psychiatry and psychology.* New York: Basic Books.

Boucouvalas, M. 1980. Transpersonal psychology: a working outline. *Journal of Transpersonal Psychology* Vol. **12**, No. I. pp. 37–46.

Bohm, D. 1980. *Wholeness and the Implicate Order.* London: Routledge & Kegan Paul.

Bridgman, P. W. 1959. *The Way Things Are*. Cambridge, Mass: Harvard University Press.

Bronowski, J. 1958. *The Common Sense of Science*. Cambridge, Mass: Harvard University Press.

Buber, M. 1970. *I and Thou*. New York: Charles Schribner's Sons.

Burge, J. 1985. What Einstein never knew: in the beginning was the equation. *The Listener* March 8th, pp. 12–13.

Burt, C. 1962. The concept of consciousness. *British Journal of Psychology* Vol. **53**(3), pp. 229–242.

Campbell, E. 1984. The end of innocence. *The Journal of Humanistic Psychology* Vol. **24**, No. 2, pp. 6–29.

Camus, A. 1955. *The Myth of Sisyphus: and other essays*. New York: Knopf.

Capra, F. 1976. *The Tao of Physics*. London: Fontana.

Capra, F. 1978. In: *Psychology, science and spiritual paths: contemporary issues* (ed. J. Welwood). *Journal of Transpersonal Psychology* Vol. **10**, No. 2, pp. 93–111.

Capra, F. 1982. Foreword to: *Space, Time and Medicine*. (ed. L. Dossey) Boulder Colorado: Shambala Publications Inc.

Capra, F. 1983. *The Turning Point: science, society and the rising culture*. Glasgow: Fontana. First published 1982, London: Wildwood House.

Castaneda, C. 1970. *The Teachings of Don Juan: a Yaqui Way of Knowledge*. Harmondsworth: Penguin. First published 1968, Berkeley: University of California Press.

Castaneda, C. 1973. *A Separate Reality*. Harmondsworth: Penguin.

Castaneda, C. 1975. *Journey to Ixtlan*. Harmondsworth: Penguin.

Castaneda, C. 1976. *Tales of Power*. Harmondsworth: Penguin.

Castaneda, C. 1978. *The Second Ring of Power*. London: Hodder & Stoughton.

Castaneda, C. 1982. *The Eagle's Gift*. Harmondsworth: Penguin.

Castaneda, C. 1984. *The Fire Within*. London: Black Swan Books.

Chertok, L. 1981. *Sense and Nonsense in Psychotherapy: the challenge of hypnosis*. Oxford: Pergamon.

Chevalier, G. 1976. *The Sacred Magician: A ceremonial diary*. London: Paladin (Granada).

Child, I. L. & Iwao, S. 1968. Personality and esthetic sensitivity: extension of findings to younger age and different culture. *Journal of Personality and Social Psychology* March Vol. **8**, pp. 308–312.

Child, I. L. 1973. *Humanistic Psychology and the Research Tradition: their several virtues*. New York: Wiley.

Cohen, J. 1958. *Humanistic Psychology*. London: Allen & Unwin.

Combs, A. W. & Snygg, D. 1959. *Individual Behaviour: a perceptual approach*. New York: Harper & Row.

Conant, J. B. 1952. *Modern Science and Modern Man*. New York: Doubleday Anchor. First published 1929 New York: University of Columbia Press.

Cooper, D. 1967. *Psychiatry and Anti-Psychiatry*. London: Tavistock.

Cooper, J. C. 1981. *Yin and Yang: the Taoist harmony of opposites.* Wellingborough, UK: The Varsity Press.

Cosgrove, M. P. 1982. *Psychology Gone Awry: four psychological world views.* Leicester, UK: Inter-Varsity Press.

Crowley, A. 1922. *Diary of a Drug Fiend.* London: Collins.

Dass, R. 1978. *Journey of Awakening: a meditator's guidebook.* USA: Hanuman Foundations Inc.

Davis, J. D. 1972. Review of S. Rachman (1971). In: *The British Journal of Psychology* The Effects of Psychotherapy Vol. **63**, pp. 642-643.

Dawkins, R. 1976. *The Selfish Gene.* Oxford: Oxford University Press.

Daws, P. P. 1976. *Early Days: a personal review of the beginnings of counselling in English education during the decade 1964-74.* Cambridge: Hobson's Press.

De Mille, R. 1978. *Castaneda's Journey.* London: Abacus edition, Sphere Books.

De Mille, R. (ed.) 1980. *The Don Juan Papers: more Castaneda controversies.* Santa Barbara: Ross Erikson.

Dossey, L. 1982. *Space, Time and Medicine.* Boulder Colorado: Shambala Publications Inc.

Drury, N. 1978. *Don Juan, Mecalito and Modern Magic: the mythology of inner space.* London: Routledge & Kegan Paul.

Drury, N. 1979. *Inner Visions: explorations in magical consciousness,* London: Routledge & Kegan Paul.

Eddington, A. 1958. *The Philosophy of Physical Science.* Ann Arbor: University of Michigan Press.

Einstein, A. 1934. *Essays in Science.* New York: Philosophical Library.

Einstein, A., Podolsky, B., & Rosen, N. 1935. Can quantum mechanical description of reality be considered complete? *Physical Review* Vol. **47**, pp. 77ff.

Enroth, R. 1977. *Youth, Brainwashing and Extremist Cults.* Exeter, UK: Paternoster Press.

Evans, C. 1974. *Cults of Unreason.* London: Routledge & Kegan Paul.

Evans, R. I. 1981a. *Dialogue with Carl Rogers: Dialogues in Contemporary Psychology Series.* London: Praeger Publishing.

Evans, R. I. 1981b. *Dialogue with R. D. Laing: Dialogues in Contemporary Psychology Series.* London: Praeger Publishing.

Evans-Wentz, W. Y. 1976. *The Tibetan Book of the Dead* (3rd edn). Oxford: Oxford University Press.

Farson, R. 1981. Carl Rogers: quiet revolutionary. In: Evans, R. I. (1981). *Dialogue with Carl Rogers: Dialogues in Contemporary Psychology Series.* London: Praeger Publishing.

Ferguson, M. 1978. In: *Psychology, science and spiritual paths: contemporary issues* (ed. J. Welwood), *The Journal of Transpersonal Psychology* 1978, Vol. **10**, No. 2, pp. 93-111.

Ferguson, M. 1982. *The Aquarian Conspiracy: personal and social transformation in the 1980s*. London: Paladin (Granada).

Festinger, L. 1957. *A Theory of Cognitive Dissonance*. New York: Row Peterson.

Frankl, V. E. 1969a. *The Doctor and The Soul*. London: Souvenir Press.

Frankl, V. E. 1969b. *The Will to Meaning: foundations and applications of logotherapy*. London: Souvenir Press.

Frankl, V. E. 1973. *Psychotherapy and Existentialism: selected papers in logotherapy*. Harmondsworth: Penguin.

Freedman, S. & Clauser, J. 1972. Experimental test of local and hidden variable theories. *Physical Review* Vol. **28**, pp. 938ff.

Fromm, E. 1951. *Psychoanalysis and Religion*. London: Gollancz.

Fromm, E. 1979. *The Art of Loving*. London: Unwin paperbacks (4th impression).

Fromm, E. 1980. *The Greatness and Limitations of Freud's Thought*. London: Cape.

Gale, A. 1983. Biological approaches to personality. *Bulletin of the British Psychological Society* Vol. **36**, A6.

Gibran, K. 1978. *The Prophet* London: Book Club Associates.

Gibson, J. J. 1950. *The Perception of the Visual World*, Boston: Houghton Mifflin.

Giorgi, A. 1970. *Psychology as a Human Science: a phenomenologically based approach*. New York: Harper & Row.

Goldstein, K. 1940. *Human Nature in the Light of Psychopathology*. Cambridge Mass: Harvard University Press. Reprinted 1950.

Goodman, P. 1960. *Growing Up Absurd: problems of youth in the organized system*. New York: Random House.

Grof, S. 1979. *Realms of the Unconscious*. London: Souvenir Press.

Gurdjieff, G. 1974. *Views From the Real World: the early talks of Gurdjieff*. London: Routledge & Kegan Paul.

Gurdjieff, G. 1976. *All And Everything; First series — an objectively impartial criticism of the life of man* (in three books). London: Routledge & Kegan Paul.

Gurdjieff, G. 1978. *Meetings with Remarkable Men*. London: Pan Books.

Hamilton, V. 1973. Psychology in society: ends or end? *The Bulletin of the British Psychological Society* Vol. **20**, pp. 185–189.

Happold, F. C. 1970. *Mysticism: a study and an anthology*. Harmondsworth: Penguin.

Harré, R. 1983. *The Social Construction of Mind*. Lecture given at the University of Keele, Dec. 8th.

Harré, R. & Secord, P. F. 1972. *The Explanation of Social Behaviour*. Oxford: Blackwell.

Heather, N. 1976. *Radical Perspectives in Psychology*. London: Methuen.

Heider, F. 1958. *The Psychology of Interpersonal Relations*. New York: Wiley.

Herndon, J. 1965. *The Way Its Spozed To Be*. New York: Simon & Schuster.

Heron, J. 1979. Co-counselling. In *A Visual Encyclopaedia of Unconventional Medicine: a health manual for the whole person* (ed. A. Hill), p. 212. London: New English Library.

Heron, J. 1981. Experiential research methodology. In: *Human Inquiry: a sourcebook of new paradigm research* (eds P. Reason & J. Rowan) pp. 152-67. Chichester: Wiley.

Heron, J. 1982. *Empirical Validity in Experiential Research.* London: British Postgraduate Medical Federation, University of London.

Hetherington, R. 1983. Sacred cows and white elephants. *The Bulletin of the British Psychological Society* Vol. **36**, pp. 273-280.

Heutzer, C. S. 1984. The power of meaning: from quantum mechanics to synchronicity. *The Journal of Humanistic Psychology* Vol. **24** (Winter), pp. 80-94.

Hildgard, E. 1965. *Hypnotic susceptibility.* New York: Harcourt, Brace & World.

Hirai, T. 1975. *Zen Meditation Therapy.* Tokyo: Japan Publications Inc.

Holland, R. 1977. *Self and Social Context.* London: Macmillan. Reprinted 1979.

Holt, J. 1964. *How Children Fail.* New York: Pitman.

Hora, T. 1960. The process of existential therapy. *Psychiatric Quarterly* Vol. **34**, pp. 495-505.

Hudson, L. 1966. *Contrary Imaginations: a psychological study of the English Schoolboy.* London: Methuen.

Hudson, L. 1972. *The Cult of the Fact.* London: Cape. Reprinted in 1978. Paperback 1976.

Hudson, L. 1978. *Human Beings: an introduction to the psychology of human experience.* England: Triad/Paladin (Granada).

Huxley, A. 1954. *The Doors of Perception.* London: Chatto and Windus.

Huxley, A. 1976. *Island.* London: Triad/Panther. First published 1962, Chatto and Windus.

Huxley, A. 1979. *Brave New World.* London: Panther (Granada).

Huxley, A. 1977. *Moksha; writings on psychedelics and visionary experience* (eds M. Horowitz & C. Palmer). New York: Stonehill Publishing Co.

Huxley, J. Sir, 1971. *Vedanta and Modern Science: correspondence between Sir J. Huxley and Swami Ranganathananda on the 'Message of the Upanishads'.* Bombay: Bharatiya Vidya Bhavan.

Illich, I. 1970. *Celebration of Awareness: a call for institutional revolution.* Harmondsworth: Penguin.

James, W. 1890. *Principles of Psychology.* Vols I and II. New York: Holt.

James, W. 1892. *Psychology: the briefer course.* New York: Holt.

James, W. 1902. *The Varieties of Religious Experience.* London: Longman.

Janov, A. 1973. *The Primal Scream.* London: Abacus.

Jones, E. E. & Davis, K. E. 1965. From acts to dispositions: the attribution process in person perception. In: *Advances in Experimental Social Psychology* Vol. **2** (ed. L. Berkowitz). New York: Academic Press.

Jones, E. E. & Nisbett, R. E. 1971. The actor and the observer: divergent perceptions of the causes of behaviour. In: *Attribution: perceiving the causes of Behaviour* (eds E. E. Jones, D. E. Kanouse, H. H. Kelley, R. E. Nisbett, S. Valins & B. Weiner). Morristown: General Learning Press.

Jourard, S. M. 1967. Experimenter-subject dialogue: a paradigm for a humanistic psychology. In: *Challenges of Humanistic Psychology* (ed. J. F. T. Bugenthal). New York: McGraw Hill.

Jourard, S. M. 1969. The effects of experimenter's self-disclosure on subject's behaviour. In: *Current Topics in Clinical and Community Psychology* (ed. C. Speilberger) pp. 109-150. New York: Academic Press.

Jourard, S. M. 1971. *The Transparent Self.* New York: Van Nostrand.

Joynson, R. B. 1974. *Psychology and Common Sense.* London: Routledge & Kegan Paul.

Jung, C. G. 1946. *Psychology and Religion.* New Haven: Yale University Press, Oxford: Oxford University Press.

Jung, C. G. 1972. *Synchronicity: An acausal connecting principle.* Translated from the German by R. F. C. Hull. London: Routledge & Kegan Paul.

Jupp, A. C. 1976. *Parapsychology and the Counsellor.* Unpublished dissertation (Diploma of Advanced Study in Education), University of Keele, UK.

Kaufman, W. 1956. *Existentialism from Dostoevsky to Sartre.* London: Meridan.

Kelley, H. H. 1967. Attribution Theory in social psychology. In: *Nebraska Symposium on Motivation* (ed. D. Levine). Lincoln: University of Nebraska Press.

Kelly, G. A. 1955. *The Psychology of Interpersonal Constructs.* New York: Norton.

Kelly, G. A. 1963. *A Theory of Personality: the psychology of personal constructs.* New York: Norton.

Kelly, G. A. 1969. Humanistic methodology in psychological research. *Journal of Humanistic Psychology* Vol. **9**, pp. 53-65.

Koch, S. 1964. Psychology and emerging conceptions of knowledge as unitary. In: *Behaviourism and Phenomenology* (ed. T. W. Wann) pp. 1-41. London & Chicago: Chicago University Press.

Koestler, A. 1975. *The Ghost in the Machine.* London: Pan Books.

Koestler, A. 1976. *The Call Girls: a tragi-comedy with prologue and epilogue.* London: Pan Books.

Kohl, H. 1967. *Thirty-six Children.* New York: American Library.

Kozol, J. 1967. *Death At An Early Age.* Boston: Houghton-Mifflin.

Kuhn, T. S. 1962. *The Structure of Scientific Revolutions.* (2nd edn). International Encyclopaedia of Unified Science Vol. 2 No. II. London & Chicago: University of Chicago Press. Reprinted 1970.

Laing, R. D. 1959. *The Divided Self: an existential study of sanity and madness.* London: Tavistock.

Laing, R. D. 1967. *The Politics of Experience and the Bird of Paradise.* Harmondsworth: Penguin.

Laing, R. D. 1983. *The Voice of Experience: experience, science and psychiatry.* London: Allen Lane.

Laing, R. D. & Esterson, A. 1973. *Sanity, Madness and the Family: families of schizophrenics.* Harmondsworth: Penguin.

Lasch, C. 1978. *The Culture of Narcissism: American life in an age of diminishing expectations.* New York: Norton.

Leary, T. 1970. *The Politics of Ecstasy.* London: Granada.

Leary, T. 1983. *Flashbacks: an autobiography.* London: Heinemann.

Leiberman, M. A., Yalom, I., & Miles, M. 1973. *Encounter Groups: first facts.* New York: Basic Books.

Leonard, G. 1968. *Education and Ecstasy.* New York: Delacorte.

Le Shan, L. 1969. Physicists and mystics: similarities in world view. In: *The Journal of Transpersonal Psychology* Vol. **I**(2) pp. 1-20.

Le Shan, L. 1974. *The Medium, the Mystic and the Physicist: toward a general theory of the paranormal.* New York: Viking Press.

Lewin, K. 1952. *Field Theory in Social Science.* New York: McGraw Hill. Reprinted 1963.

Lilly, J. C. 1973. *The Centre of the Cyclone: an autobiography of inner space.* London: Paladin (Granada).

Llewelyn, S. & Fielding, G. 1984. Judging the Cults; *Report of the Symposium held at the British Psychological Society Conference.* London, December.

Lowen, A. 1975. *Bioenergetics.* Harmondsworth: Penguin.

MacKinnon, D. 1965. Personality and the realization of creative potential. *American Psychologist* April 1965, Vol. **20**, pp. 273-281.

MacQuarrie, J. 1973. *Existentialism.* Harmondsdworth: Penguin. Reprinted 1980.

Maslow, A. H. 1954. *Motivation and Personality.* New York: Harper & Row.

Maslow, A. H. 1968. *Toward a Psychology of Being.* New York: Van Nostrand.

Maslow, A. H. 1969. Existential Psychology—what's in it for us? In: *Existential Psychology.* (2nd edn) (ed. R. May) pp. 49-54. New York: Random House.

May, R. 1958. *Existence: a new dimension in psychiatry and psychology.* New York: Basic Books.

May, R. 1967. *Psychology and the Human Dilemma.* New York: Van Nostrand.

May, R. 1969. *Existential Psychology* (2nd edn). New York: Random House.

Mehta, G. 1981. *Karma Cola: marketing the mystic.* London: Fontana.

Milgram, S. 1974. *Obedience to Authority: an experimental view.* New York: Harper & Row.

Minogue, K. 1980. The guru. In: *The Don Juan Papers: more Castaneda controversies.* (ed. R. De Mille). Santa Barbara: Ross-Erikson.

Mintz, A. L. 1973. Encounter groups and other panaceas. *Commentary* pp. 1-8 The American Jewish Committee.

Morse, S. J. & Watson, R. I. (eds) 1977. *Psychotherapies: a comparative casebook.* New York: Holt, Rinehart & Winston.

Naranjo, C. 1974. *The One Quest.* London: Wildwood House.

Needleman, J. 1978. In: *Psychology, science and spiritual paths: contemporary issues* (ed. J. Welwood) *The Journal of Transpersonal Psycholgy* Vol. **10** No. 2, pp. 93-111.

Neisser, U. 1976. *Cognition and Reality.* San Francisco: W. H. Freeman.

Ollendorff-Reich, I. 1969. *Wilhelm Reich: a personal biography*. London: Elek Books.

Oppenheimer, R. 1956. Analogy in Science. *American Psychologist* Vol. **II**, pp. 127–133.

Orne, M. T. 1959. The nature of hypnosis: artefact and essence. *Journal of Abnormal Social Psychology* Vol. **58**, pp. 277–299.

Orne, M. T. 1962. On the social psychology of the psychological experiment; with particular reference to demand characteristics and their implications. *American Psychologist* Vol. **17**, pp. 776–783.

Ornstein, R. E. (ed) 1973a. *The Nature of Human Consciousness: a book of readings*. San Francisco: W. H. Freeman.

Ornstein, R. E. 1973b. The traditional esoteric psychologies. In: *The Nature of Human Consciousness* (ed. R. E. Ornstein). San Francisco: W. H. Freeman.

Ornstein, R. E. 1975. *The Psychology of Consciousness*. Harmondsworth: Penguin.

Ornstein, R. E. 1976. *The Mind Field*. Oxford: Pergamon.

Patel, A. 1980. *Man and Transformation in Ancient Indian Culture: an introductory study of some of the traditions in early Buddhism of the Theravada school dealing with aspects of personal growth and enhancement*. Unpublished dissertation (Diploma of Advanced Study in Education) University of Keele, UK.

Patterson, C. H. 1973. *Humanistic Education*. Englewood Cliffs, New Jersey: Prentice Hall.

Patterson, C. H. 1974. Humanistic education: the challenge to the counsellor. *British Journal of Guidance and Counselling* Vol. **2**, No. I, January pp. 2–14.

Patterson, C. H. 1980. *Theories of Counselling and Psychotherapy* (3rd edn). New York: Harper & Row.

Pelletier, K. R. 1978. *Mind as Healer, Mind as Slayer: a holistic approach to preventing stress disorder*. London: Allen & Unwin.

Perls, F. S. 1969. *Gestalt Therapy Verbatim*. New York: Bantam. Reprinted 1976.

Perls, F. S. 1976. *The Gestalt Approach and Eye Witness to Therapy*. New York: Bantam Books.

Perls, F. S., Hefferline, R. & Goodman, P. 1973. *Gestalt Therapy*. Harmondsworth: Penguin.

Peters, F. 1964. *Boyhood With Gurdjieff*. London: Dutton.

Peters, F. 1965. *Gurdjieff Remembered*. London: Gollancz.

Peters, F. 1978. *Balanced Man: a look at Gurdjieff fifty years later*. London: Wildwood House.

Pirsig, R. M. 1974. *Zen and The Art of Motorcycle Maintenance: an inquiry into values*. London: The Bodley Head.

Polanyi, M. 1958. *Personal Knowledge: towards a post critical philosophy*. London: Routledge & Kegan Paul.

Postman, N. & Weingertner, C. W. 1969. *Teaching as a Subversive Activity*. New York: Delacorte Press.

Prabhupado, Swami 1968. *Bhagavad Gita As It Is*. New York & London: The Bhaktivedanta Book Trust.

Pribram, K. H. 1971. *Languages of the Brain: experimental paradoxes and principles in neuropsychology*. Englewood Cliffs, New Jersey: Prentice-Hall.

Pribram, K. H. 1976. *Consciousness and the Brain*. New York: Plenum.

Pribram, K. H. 1978. In: *Psychology, science and spiritual paths: contemporary issues* (ed. J. Welwood). *Journal of Transpersonal Psychology* Vol. **10**, No. 2, pp. 93-111.

Prigogine, I. & Stengers, I. 1985. *Order Out Of Chaos: man's new dialogue with nature*. London: Fontana.

Rachman, S. 1971. *The Effects of Psychotherapy*. New York: Pergamon.

Radhakrishnan, S. 1948. *Indian Philosophy*. Vol. **I**. London: Allen & Unwin.

Rajneesh, Bhagwan Shree 1978. *Neither This Nor That; reflections on a Zen Master*. London: Sheldon Press.

Rajneesh, Bhagwan Shree 1979. *Take It Easy*. Vol. **II** Poona: Rajneesh Foundation Ltd.

Rajneesh, Bhagwan Shree 1983. *The Orange Book: the meditation techniques of Bhagwan Shree Rajneesh*. Oregon, USA: Rajneesh Foundation International.

Ranganathananda, S. 1971. *Vedanta and Modern Science: correspondence between Sir Julian Huxley and Swami Ranganathananda on the 'Message of the Upanishads'*. Bombay: Bharatiya Vidya Bhavan.

Reason, P. and Rowan, J. (eds) 1981. *Human Inquiry: a sourcebook of new paradigm research*. Chichester: Wiley.

Reibel, L. 1984. A homeopathic model of psychotherapy. *Journal of Humanistic Psychology* Winter Vol. **24** No. I. pp. 9-48.

Reps, P. 1978. *Zen Flesh, Zen Bones*. Harmondsworth: Penguin.

Rhinehart, L. 1976. *The Book of Est*. New York: Holt, Rhinehart and Winston.

Richer, J. 1975. Two types of agreement—two types of psychology. *Bulletin of the British Psychological Society* Vol. **28**, pp. 342-345.

Roe, A. 1953. A psychological study of eminent psychologists and anthropologists and a comparison with biological and physical scientists. *Psychological Monographs* **67**, No. 352.

Rogers, C. R. 1961. *On Becoming A Person: a therapist's view of psychotherapy*. London: Constable.

Rogers, C. R. 1964. Toward a science of the person. In: *Behaviourism and Phenomenology* (ed. T. W. Wann) pp. 109-133, London & Chicago: Chicago University Press.

Rogers, C. R. 1967. Two divergent trends. In: *Existential Psychology* (2nd edn) (ed. R. May) pp. 84-92, New York: Random House.

Rogers, C. R. 1969. *Freedom To Learn*. Columbus Ohio: Chas. E. Merrill Publishing Co.

Rogers, C. R. 1973. *On Encounter Groups*. Harmondsworth: Penguin.

Rogers, C. R. 1976. *Client-Centred Therapy*. London: Constable.

Rogers, C. R. 1980. *A Way Of Being*. Boston: Houghton Mifflin.

Rogers, C. R. & Stevens, B. 1967. *Person to Person: the problem of being human*. New York: Real People Press.

Rose, S., Kamin, L. J. & Lewontin, R. C. 1984. *Not In Our Genes: biology, ideology and human nature*. Harmondsworth: Penguin.

Rosenthal, R. 1966. *Experimenter Effects in Behavioural Research*. New York: Appleton Crofts.

Roszak, T. 1970. *The Making of a Counter Culture: reflections on the counter culture and its youthful opposition*. London: Faber & Faber.

Roszak, T. 1975. *Unfinished Animal: the aquarian frontier and the evolution of consciousness*. New York: Harper & Row.

Rowan, J. 1976. *Ordinary Ecstasy: Humanistic psychology in action*. London: Routledge & Kegan Paul.

Rowan J. 1983. *The Reality Game: a guide to humanistic counselling and therapy*. London: Routledge & Kegan Paul.

Ruitenbeek, H. (ed) 1972. *Going Crazy: the radical therapy of R. D. Laing and others*. New York: Bantam Press.

Russell, B. 1948. *History of Western Philosophy: and its connection with political and social circumstances from the earliest times to the present day*. London: Allen & Unwin.

Russell, B. 1959. *Mysticism and Logic and other essays*. London: Allen & Unwin.

Rychlak, J. F. 1977. *The Psychology of Rigorous Humanism*. New York & London: Wiley.

Sagan, C. 1976. Foreword to: R. Story (1976) *The Space Gods Revisited*. London: New English Library.

Sartre, J-P. 1984. *Existentialism and Humanism*. London: Methuen. Originally published in French 1946.

Schacter, S. and Singer, J. E. 1962. Cognitive, social and physiological determinants of emotional state. *Psychological Review* Vol. **69**, pp. 379–399.

Scharfstein, B-A. 1973. *Mystical Experience*. Oxford: Blackwell.

Schofield, W. 1964. *Psychotherapy: the purchase of friendship*. Englewood Cliffs, New Jersey: Prentice-Hall.

Schrodinger, E. 1957. *Science Theory and Man*. New York: Dover.

Schutz, W. C. 1967. *Joy: expanding human awareness*. New York: Grove.

Schutz, W. C. 1973. *Elements of Encounter*. USA: Joy Press.

Shaffer, J. B. P. 1978. *Humanistic Psychology*. Englewood Cliffs, New Jersey: Prentice-Hall.

Shah, I. 1973. *The Exploits of the Incomparable Mulla Nasrudin*. London: Pan Books.

Shah, I. 1975. *The Pleasantries of the Incredible Mulla Nasrudin*. London: Pan Books.

Shapiro, D. A. & Shapiro, D. 1977. The double standard in evaluation of psychotherapies. *The Bulletin of the British Psychological Society* Vol. **30**, pp. 209–210.

Shotter, J. 1975. *Images of Man in Psychological Research*. London: Methuen.

Shotter, J. 1980. Human Being, Being Human: psychology. In: 1970s Paper given at *Humanistic Psychology Conference*, Chester, England, Easter 1980.

Shotter, J. 1981. Telling and reporting: prospective and retrospective uses of self-ascriptions. In: *The Psychology of Ordinary Explanations of Social Behaviour* (ed. C. Antaki) pp. 157–181, London: Academic Press.

Silberman, C. 1970. *Crisis in the Classroom*. New York: Random House.

Silcock, B. 1985. The Cosmic Gut. *Sunday Times* March 24th, p. 13.

Silverman, D. 1975. *Reading Castaneda: a prologue to the social sciences*. London and Henley: Routledge & Kegan Paul.

Simonton, O. C., Matthews-Simonton, S. & Creighton, J. 1978. *Getting Well Again*. Los Angeles: Tarcher.

Skinner, B. F. 1962. *Walden Two*. New York: MacMillan (Paperback edition). First published MacMillan 1948.

Skinner, B. F. 1973. *Beyond Freedom and Dignity*. Harmondsworth: Penguin.

Snygg, D. and Combs, A. N. 1959. *Individual Behaviour*, revised edition. New York: Harper & Row (first published 1949).

Staal, F. 1975. *Exploring Mysticism*. Harmondsworth: Penguin.

Stapp, H. P. 1971. S-Matrix interpretation of quantum theory. *Physical Review* Vol. **D3** (March 15th), pp. 1303–1320.

St. Exupery, de, A. 1974. *The Little Prince*. London: Pan Books.

Story, R. 1976. *The Space Gods Revealed*. London: New English Library.

Szasz, T. S. 1972. *The Myth of Mental Illness*. London: Paladin (Granada).

Szasz, T. S. 1973. *The Manufacture of Madness*. London: Paladin (Granada).

Szasz, T. S. 1979. *The Myth of Psychotherapy: mental healing as religion, rhetoric and repression*. Oxford: Oxford University Press.

Targ, R. & Puthoff, H. 1977. *Mindreach: positive proof that ESP exists*. London: Cape.

Tart, C. 1969. *Altered States of Consciousness*. San Francisco: W. H. Freeman.

Tart, C. 1975. *Transpersonal Psychologies*. London: Routledge & Kegan Paul.

Taylor, J. 1975. *Superminds: an investigation into the paranormal*. London: Macmillan.

Tillich, P. 1952. *The Courage To Be*. Nisbett and Co. Reprinted London: Collins, 1980.

Toffler, A. 1985. Science and change. Foreword to Prigogine, I. and Stengers, I. *Order Out of Chaos: man's dialogue with nature*. London: Fontana.

Truax, C. 1963. Effective ingredients in psychotherapy. *Journal of Counselling Psychology*, Vol. **10**, pp. 256–263.

Truax, C. 1971. Effectiveness of counselor and counselor aides. *Journal of Counselling Psychology*, Vol. **18**, pp. 365–367.

Truax, C. & Carkhuff, R. 1967. *Toward Effective Counselling and Psychotherapy.* Chicago: Aldine Atherton.

Vine, I. 1977. What we teach—and don't teach—to psychology students. *Bulletin of the British Psychological Society.* (Nov.) Vol. **30**, pp. 376–377.

Von Daniken, E. 1969. *Chariot of The Gods: was god an astronaut?* London: Souvenir Press.

Von Daniken, E. 1970. *Return To The Stars: gods from outer space.* London: Souvenir Press.

Von Daniken, E. 1973. *The God of the Gods.* London: Souvenir Press.

Von Daniken, E. 1974. *In Search of Ancient Gods: my pictorial evidence for the impossible.* London: Souvenir Press.

Von Daniken, E. 1975. *Miracles of the Gods: a hard look at the supernatural.* London: Souvenir Press.

Wann, T. W. (ed.) 1964. *Behaviourism and Phenomenology.* London & Chicago: University of Chicago Press.

Warnock, M. 1970. *Existentialism.* Oxford: Oxford University Press. Reprinted 1979.

Watson, J. B. 1913. Psychology as the behaviourist views it. *Psychological Review* Vol. **20** (15), pp. 8–15.

Welwood, J. (ed.) 1978. Psychology, science and spiritual paths: contemporary issues *Journal of Transpersonal Psychology.* Vol. **10**, No. 2, pp. 93–111.

Westland, G. 1978. *Current Crises in Psychology.* London: Heinemann.

Wheatley, D. 1973. *The Devil and All His Works.* London: Arrow.

Whitehead, A. N. 1958. *The Function of Reason.* Boston: Beacon.

Whitehorn, K. 1981. *View From a Column.* London: Eyre Methuen.

Wilber, K. 1977. *The Spectrum of Consciousness.* Wheaton, Illinois: Theosophical Publishing House.

Wilhelm, R. 1978. *The I Ching or Book of Changes.* (3rd edn) London: Routledge & Kegan Paul.

Wilson-Ross, N. 1973. *Hinduism, Buddhism, Zen.* London: Faber & Faber.

Wittgenstein, L. 1978. *Tractatus Logico-Philosophicus.* London: Routledge & Kegan Paul. First English translation published 1922.

Yalom, I. D. 1980. *Existential Psychotherapy.* New York: Basic Books.

Zimbardo, P. G. 1969. *The Cognitive Control of Motivation.* Scott, Foresman.

Zukav, G. 1980. *The Dancing Wu-Li Masters: an overview of the new physics.* London: Fontana.

INDEX

A

Abelson, P. H., 30
Absolute truth, 4
Abstraction, 39, 73
Absurdity, 71
Acceptance, 56, 127
Action-at-a-distance, 117
Acupuncture, 90
Adam and Eve, 6
Adorno, T., 98
Agency, 26, 50, 106–107
Aichorn, A., 41
Akaido, 92
Alcoholic psychoses, 45
Alexander F. Matthias, 91
Alexander Technique, the, 92
Alienation, 27, 72
Allport, G. W., 74, 81
Alpert, R., 40
Alternative society, 30
America, 29, 33, 76
Ancient Greeks, the, 1, 3, 17, 168
Ancient Wisdom, the, 9–10, 23, 131
Anderson, M., 37
Animal rights, 28
Anthropology, 38
Anti-psychiatry, 77–8
Antiquity, 30, 121, 131
Anxiety, 13, 46, 47, 51, 60, 71, 75, 92, 95
Apter, M., 106
Aquinas, T., 18
Arica (see Ichazo), 37
Aristotle, 17
Armouring, 89–90, 91
Art, 23, 43
Asceticism, 63
Ashe, G., 9, 23
Aspect, A., 117, 118
Assaglioli, R., 58, 97
Association for Humanistic Psychology, 66

Astronomy, 18
Atman, 122
Atomic physics, 119
Attendant, 45
Attention, 15, 59
Authenticity, 50, 69
Authoritarianism, 7
Authority, 9, 17, 19, 32, 48, 87, 108–9
Automata, 27
Avidja, 12, 69, 122
Awareness, 39, 56, 67, 84, 87, 92, 131

B

Bacon, F., 18, 24, 26
Bad faith, 75
Baigent, M., 38
Balance, 3, 13, 14, 15, 21, 39, 40, 43, 52, 90, 92, 117, 131
Bancroft, A., 38
Baptism, 7
Bardo Thodol (see also Tibetan Book of the Dead), 33
Barlow, W., 92
Barnes, H., 68, 83
Barnes, M., 79
Beatles, the, 40, 41
Becket, S., 72
Becoming, 5, 53, 67
Behaviour, 20, 26, 27, 36, 48, 50, 55, 76
  group, 50
Behaviour modification, 48
Behaviourism, 26, 27, 28, 36, 48, 50, 55, 76
Being, 39, 46, 67, 85–6, 102
  change of, 58
  in the world, 68–9, 129
  patterns of, 58, 129
  psychology of, 50, 51, 53
Bell's Theorem, 117, 130
Berke, J., 79
Berne, E., 94

144

Berner, C., 96
Bhagavad Gita, the, 33
Bhagwan Shree Rajneesh (*see also* Rajneesh),
    8, 11, 12, 33, 41
Binswanger, L., 76, 77-8
Biodynamic Therapy, 90-1
Bioenergetics, 58, 90
Biofeedback, 88, 130
Blavatsky, H., 33
Bohm, D., 3, 113, 118, 119-121, 122
Book of Changes, the (*see also* Tao Te
    Ching, I Ching), 14
Boss, M., 76
Boucouvoulas, M., 53
Boyeson, G., 90-91
Brahman, 122
Brain sciences, 45
Breakdown, 60, 70
Breathing, 90, 91
    exercises, 123
Brentano, F., 74
Brujo, 37
Buber, M., 71
Buddha, the, 8, 12, 13, 15, 127
Buddhism, 7, 12, 15, 16, 33, 34, 39, 46
Burge, J., 124
Burt, C., Sir, 27
Business studies, 66

C

Cabbalism, 38-9
Calvinists, 7
Campbell, E., 98, 128
Campaign for Nuclear Disarmament, 28
Camus, A., 1, 29, 71, 72
Cancer, 129
Cannabis (*see* Marijuana), 34
Capra, F., 18, 26, 104, 113, 114, 119, 128,
    130
Castaneda, C, 37, 38, 39, 40, 70, 122
Catharsis, 58, 62, 92
Central America, 38
Centre, 12, 15, 16, 74, 131
Centredness, 16
    client, 56
    person, 56, 57
CERN, 125
Chakra (*see* wheel), 12
Change, 13, 14, 56, 99, 127
Character analysis, 89
Chesterton, G. K., 32

Chevalier, G., 38
Chi, 90
Child, I., 25, 81, 102, 105
Children, 42
Children of God, the, 35
China, 15
Chinese culture, 5, 14
    mythology, 16
Chinese naturalism, 15
Choice(s), 16, 29, 56, 68, 72, 73, 75, 79
Christ, Jesus, 8
Christianity, 6, 8, 15
Chuang Tsu, 14, 15
Church, the, 17, 18, 44
Classical Period, the, 3, 4, 7, 17
Classroom, 56
Clinical psychology, 46, 50
Co-counselling, 88, 96
Cognitive psychology, 27, 105
Cohen, J., 66
Combs, A. W., 74
Common sense, 105, 106, 115, 118, 125
Complementarity, principle of, 115, 116,
    119
Conditioning, 28, 49
Confession, 58, 62
Confidentiality, 109
Conformity, 29, 45
Confucius, 8, 13
Congruence, 54, 85
Consciousness, 2, 17, 19, 20, 27, 30, 31, 34,
    35, 73-4, 97, 111, 123, 125, 126, 128
    altered states of, 6, 29, 30, 37, 43, 52, 79,
        86, 128
    bimodal, 130
    cosmic, 122, 125
    expanded, 39, 52
    movement, 30, 49
    mystical, 38
    objective, 20
    pedestrian, 124
    pure, 123
    research, 130
    visionary, 39
Conservation, 28
Control, 26, 27, 29, 48, 108
Cooper, D., 76-8, 81
Cooper, J. C., 16
Co-operative enquiry, 109
Copernicus, N., 18
Cosgrove, M. P., 52, 126

Cosmic vision, 2
Cosmology, 11, 15, 17, 18, 19, 37, 131
Cosmos, 17, 18, 44, 131
Counselling, 56-7, 81, 85, 86
  re-evaluation, 96
Counsellor training courses, 57
Counter-culture, 29, 31, 32, 33, 35, 49, 52,
  57, 62, 65, 78, 79
Courage, 69
Creativity, 14, 51, 66, 69, 105
Creator, 19
Crowley, A., 34
Cults, 30, 32, 35, 41

D

Dance, 16, 43, 88
Dasein, 68
Daseinanalysis, 77
Dawkins, R., 26
Daws, P. P., 56-7
Death, 13, 38, 39, 46, 68, 69-71, 97
de Beauvoir, S., 29, 72
Defence(s), 51, 54, 60, 71, 75, 87, 108,
  127
deMille, R., 38
Dervishes, 16, 36
Descartes, R., 18
Deschooling, 42
Desensitization, 48
Determinism, 51, 68, 73, 75, 76
Disease, 45, 53, 129
Disequilibrium, 60
Dialogue, 71, 109, 128
Disorder, 48, 127
Dissection, 4
Dissipative structures, 126-8
Divine Light Mission, the, 35
Divine proportion, the, 3
Doing, 31, 86-7, 92, 98
Don Juan (Matus), 37, 40, 70, 122
Dossey, L., 113, 129
Doubling, 93
Dread, 46, 79
Drugs, 29, 30, 35, 39, 79, 113, 123, 124,
  129
Drury, N., 6, 30, 38
Dualism, 24
Duality, 116, 131
Dukka (see also Sorrow, Suffering), 13
Dürkheim, K., 33

E

Eastern culture, 5, 8, 11, 21
Education, 8, 41, 43, 50, 56, 67, 85
  American, 42
  in Europe, 42
Ego, 12, 26, 39, 79, 94, 130, 131
Einstein, A., 114, 115, 117, 124
Einstein-Podolsky-Rosen Theorem, 117
Electron(s), 115 ff.
Eliade, M., 33
Elvis, 36
Emotion(s), 20, 43, 58, 61, 66, 70, 95, 96
Empathic understanding, 55
Empathy, 57, 86
Empedocles, 3
Empirical Method, 18, 20, 107
Empiricism, 103
Encounter, 57, 61, 70, 86, 88, 95, 96, 129
Enfoldment, 123
Engineering, 27
Enlightened One, the, 8, 17, 37, 39
Enlightenment, the, 17
Enlightenment, 12, 15, 16, 39, 40, 62, 64,
  70, 73, 95, 96
  intensive, 96-7
Entropy, 68, 115, 127
Environment, 59, 60, 75, 128
Epimenides paradox, 115
Erhard, W., 95
Esalen Institute, the, 43, 58, 62, 63, 67, 91,
  130
Est, 95-6
Esterson, A., 76, 77, 81
Ethics, 18, 46
Ethnomethodology, 38
Europe, 29, 43
Existence, 13, 16, 20, 23, 43, 46, 67
Existential (psycho) analysis, 75, 83
Existentialism, 67-82, 84, 103
Existentialists, 46, 68, 69, 71
Experience, 20, 27, 48, 51, 65, 72, 76, 104,
  111, 129
  group, 49
Experimental method, 25, 103
Experimentation, 32, 34, 110
Eysenck, H., 27

F

Fact(s), 4, 5, 7, 9, 20, 25, 30, 46, 73, 107,
  124, 129
Faith, 6, 7, 63

Family, 44
Family Life, 78
Fasting, 123
Ferguson, M., 102, 113, 126
Festinger, L., 105
Field Theory, 59
Flower Power, 29
Flux, 5, 12, 14, 107
Frankl, V., 24, 28, 45, 48, 49, 71, 72, 76
Freedom, 12, 29, 39, 41, 49, 56, 65, 67, 72, 86, 88
  psychology of, 74, 83
Free will, 98
Freud, S., 20, 47, 51, 65, 75, 76, 89, 92, 129
Fromm, E., 7, 17, 48, 71
Frustration, 46, 72

G

Gale, A., 110
Galileo, 18, 24, 129
Genes, 26
Gestalt, 58-9, 75, 93, 95, 99
  approach
  Prayer, 63
  psychology, 57, 74
  school, 121
  switch, 113
  therapy, 58, 60, 61, 93-4
Gesture, 58
Gibran, K., 8, 9, 69, 121
Gibson, J. J., 73
Gimmicks, 87, 93
Ginsberg, A., 33
Giorgi, A., 107
God, 6, 7, 19, 32, 37, 63
Godel's Incompleteness theorem, 115
Gods, 6, 33
Goekel, R., 17
Golden mean, 3, 13, 43
Golden section, the, 3
Goldstein, K., 59, 74
Goodman, P., 42
Gravity, 91, 124
Greeks, 4, 7, 73
Grof, S., 123, 130
Groundedness, 16
Groups, 50, 61
Growth, 43, 50, 51, 55, 61, 66, 87, 93
  centre, 43
Guilt, 7, 69, 72, 96
Gunther, B., 56

Gurdjieff Foundation, the, 37
Gurdjieff, G., 8, 33, 36, 37, 118
Guru, 17, 36, 37, 40, 63

H

Hahnemann, S., 53
Hallucinogens, 29
Hamilton, V., 63, 99
Happold, F. C., 4
Hare Krishna Foundation, 35
Harmony, 3, 21, 38
Harre, R., 106
Healing, 53, 129
Heather, N., 25, 27, 79, 104
Hebrews, 7
Heidegger, M., 46, 68, 69, 72
Heider, J., 105
Heisenberg, W., 115, 116
Hemianopia, 21
Heraclites, 3
Herbalism, 90
Here-and-now, 12, 39
Hermeneutic approach, the, 107
Heron, J., 97, 109
Hetherington, R., 24, 100, 107, 110, 130
Heutzer, C., 118
Hinduism, 7
Hippies, 40
Hippocrates, 118
Holistic psychology, 66, 75
Holland, R., 76, 82
Hologram, 120
Holographic theory, 128
  universe, 120-1
Holomovement, 121
Holt, J., 42
Holy Grail, the, 16
Homeopathic model, the, 129
Homeostasis, 60
Hubris (*see* Pride), 6, 51
Hudson, L., 30, 42, 105
Humanism, 67, 72, 74
Humanistic psychology, 52, 64, 66, 72, 75, 79, 81, 82, 88, 97, 98, 100, 101, 110, 130
Humanities, 67
Human potential, 3, 8, 40, 43, 58, 130
  movement, 58-64, 67, 70
Human rights, 28
Humphreys, C., 33
Husserl, E., 46, 72, 73, 74, 77

Huxley, A., 7, 27, 34, 35, 43, 123
Huxley, J., Sir, 34
Hypnosis, 41, 88, 127, 130

I

Ichazo, O., 33
I Ching (see Tao Te Ching), 33
Iconoclasm, 32
Id, 26, 48, 94
Ideology, 27, 49, 103, 104
Ignorance, 12, 17, 69
Illich, I., 42
Illusion(s), 6, 22, 34, 44, 73, 98, 121
Illusionist, 39
Imagery, 127
Impermanence (see Anicca), 13, 39, 127
India, 21, 40
Indian culture, 5
    thought, 21
Insight, 2, 4, 12, 15, 16, 17, 21, 37, 73, 131
Instability, 126
Integration, 59, 92
Intentionality, 66, 72, 74
Institute for Bioenergetic Analysis, 90
Intellect, 21, 29, 30, 39, 41, 43, 97
Introspection, 19, 20
Intuition, 2, 3, 4, 8, 15, 39, 74, 97
Irrationality, 3
Isherwood, C., 33
Islam, 15
Isolation, 68, 70-1, 123

J

Jackins, H., 96
James, W., 20, 31, 52, 66, 74, 110, 123
Janov, A., 86
Japan, 15
Jaspers, K., 46, 72
Jourard, S., 87, 93, 109
Journal of Humanistic Psychology, 66, 130
Journal of Transpersonal Psychology, 53, 130
Joy, 7
Joynson, R. B., 106
Jung, C. G., 20, 31, 47, 52, 118
Jupp, A. C., 86

K

Karma, 33
Katchalsky, A., 127
Kaufman, W., 73

Kelly, G. A., 74, 81
Kelley, H., 105
Kepler, J., 3, 18
Kerouac, J., 33
Khaos, I., 68
Kierkegaard, S., 46, 72, 73
Kingsley Hall, 78-9
Koan(s), 15, 60, 96, 113, 125, 127
Koch, S., 26, 103
Koestler, A., 27, 48, 81, 126
Kofka, K., 59, 74
Kohl, H., 42
Kohler, W., 59, 74
Korea, 15
Kosmos, 1
Kozol, J., 42
Krishnamurti, J., 8, 33
Kubrick, S., 35
Kuhn, T., 76, 112-3
Kundalini, 66

L

Laboratory(ies) (see also National Training
    Laboratories), 20, 50, 102, 104, 106,
    108
Laing, R. D., 20, 28, 45, 47, 48, 76-9, 81,
    88, 127
Lama Govinda, 33
Lao Tsu, 8, 14, 85
Lasch, C., 44, 45, 47, 49, 50
Laughter, 39
Leary, T., 35, 40, 59, 79, 123, 128
Leonard, G., 42
LeShan, L., 119
Lewin, K., 49, 105
Light, 114, 116, 118, 120, 121, 123, 130
Lilly, J., 37, 123, 130
Listening, 55
Llewelyn, S., 35
Loach, K., 78
Logotherapy, 72
Love, 23, 81
Lowen, A., 58, 90, 91
LSD, 30, 34, 124

M

Machine(s), 19, 25, 26, 49, 79, 125, 129
MacQuarrie, J., 65, 72
Madness, 79
Magic, 2, 34, 37, 121
Maharaj Ji, 35, 41

Maharishi Mahesh Yogi, 40, 41
Majhim nikaya, 13
Mandala, 2
Marathon(s), 5, 8, 88
Marcel, G., 72
Marijuana (see Cannabis), 79
Martial arts, 8, 43
Marx, K., 129
Maslow, A. H., 6, 24, 50, 51-3, 54, 58, 60,
    63, 66, 70, 80, 83, 104, 110, 129
Massachusetts Institute of Technology, 49
Massage, 91
Master(s), 2, 8, 127
Materialism, 18, 126
Mathematics, 3, 123, 124
Matter, 18, 19, 20, 115, 116, 117
May, R., 76, 79, 81, 104
Maya, 5, 34, 69, 121
Meaning(s), 32, 36, 46, 49, 71, 106, 131
Meaninglessness, 23, 29, 32, 62, 68, 71-2
Measure, 3-4, 116, 102
Measurement, 3, 111, 118
Mechanics, 19
Medicine, 47, 128, 129
  homeopathic, 129
  humanistic, 129
  oriental, 90
Medical science, 45
Meditation, 12, 13, 15, 16, 17, 33, 34, 36,
    38, 39, 41, 43, 127
Mehta, G., 40
Memory, 121-2, 127
Mental health, 47, 71
Mental illness, 45, 46, 51, 62, 76, 77, 127
Mental life, 17
Merleau-Ponty, M., 72
Mescaline, 34, 123
Metaphor(s), 45, 76
Method(s), 20, 25, 28, 47, 72, 82
Mexico, 38
Middle Ages, the, 17, 18
Middle East, the, 15
Middle way (or path), 13, 43, 131
Milgram, S., 108
Mind, 18, 19, 21, 26, 27, 39, 48, 69, 90,
    92, 124, 129, 130-1
Mindfulness, 15, 69
Minkowski, J., 76
Minogue, K., 25, 36
Mintz, A. L., 58, 62
Mirroring, 93

Mohammed, 8
Moon, Rev. Sun Myeung, 35, 36
Morality, 73, 106
Moreno, J., 92
Moslems, 15
Motivation, 54, 105
Motives, 49, 106
Murphy, M., 43
Mysticism, 3, 6, 8, 21, 30, 31, 34, 40, 119,
    124, 129, 131
Mystics, 2, 38, 121, 124, 126
Myth, 37, 128, 131
Mythology, 2

N
Naranjo, C., 32, 36, 41
Narcissism, 50, 98
Nasrudin, 16
National Training Laboratories, 50, 66
Nausea, 79
Needleman, J., 103, 4
Neill, A. S., 41
Neiser, U., 105
Neurosis, 51, 59, 72, 89
New biology, 128
New paradigm research, 109-111
Newton, I., 19, 124
Nietzsche, F., 19, 20, 72, 73
Nikhilananda, Swami, 33
Nineteenth Century, the, 19, 25, 44, 46
Non-being, 69
North America, 66
Nuclear arms, 28
  power, 28
Nudity, 62, 99

O
Objectivity, 19, 20, 73, 102, 105, 107
Occult, 8, 28, 30, 37, 119
Occultism, 36
Oedipus, 36
Opium, 34, 123
Orage, A. R., 37
Order, 119-22, 127
  implicate, 120-2
  explicate, 119-120
Orange Book, the, 11
Orange Movement, the, 35, 41
Organismic Theory, 59
Orgone Therapy, 89
Orne, M., 108

Ornstein, R. E., 12, 20, 21, 41, 130
Orthodox scholasticism, 17-8
Ouspensky, P., 37

P

Pain, 63, 84
Paradigm(s), 31, 112-131
  shift, 110, 113, 130
Parapsychology, 130
Pascal, B., 67
Patel, A., 5, 12
Pavlov, I., 28
Peace, 29
Peak experience, 51
Perception, 2, 6, 53, 54, 73, 104, 114, 115, 122
Perls, F. S., 53, 58-64, 74, 93
Permissiveness, 42
Personality, 11, 54, 70, 83, 91, 107
Perturbation, 127
Peters, F., 37
Peyote, 34, 123
Phenomenological method, 74, 76, 100, 107
Philadelphia Association, the, 78
Phenomenological approach, the, 38, 110
Phenomenology, 73-4, 82
Philosophy, 9, 17, 18, 20, 31, 33, 43, 46, 65, 72, 73, 103
Physicality, 30
Physics, 20, 112, 114, 125, 128, 130, 131
Pirsig, R. M., 33
Plato, 3, 107
Polanyi, M., 125
Politics, 23, 128
  of Ecstasy, 35
  of psychotherapy, 49
  radical, 45
Pollution, 28
Positivism, 20, 73
Postman, N., 42
Power(s), 7, 16, 18, 39, 48, 87
Powerlessness, 7
Prana, 90
Precognition, 130
Pribram, K., 113, 121, 124
Price, R., 43
Pride, 6, 19
Prigogine, I., 99, 113, 126-8
Primal Therapy, 94-5, 96
Problems in living, 46
Prometheus, 6, 28

Pseudo-science, 33
Psilocybin, 123
Psychedelic(s), 29, 123, 124, 129
  revolution, 34, 35
Psychiatric taxonomy, 45
Psychiatry, 46, 47, 50, 79
Psychic phenomena, 130
Psychoanalysis, 26, 48, 65, 66, 75, 92
Psychodrama, 88, 92, 95, 99
Psychokinesis, 117, 130
Psychology, 11, 17, 20, 21, 24, 31, 33, 43, 46, 65, 72, 73, 103
  empirical, 107
  industrial, 66, 75, 129
  organisational, 66
Psychopathology, 45, 46, 51
Psychosynthesis, 58, 97
Psychotherapy, 43, 44, 46, 49, 53, 56, 62, 92, 98, 103, 119, 127
Psychotrophic drugs, 34, 35, 37
Pythagorus, 3, 7

Q

Quantum leap, 115
  mechanics, 115
  physics, 86, 116-119
  theory, 115, 117, 120, 130

R

Radhakrishnan, 8
Radicalism, 32
Rajneesh (*see also* Bhagwan Shree Rajneesh), 8, 11, 12, 13, 21, 41, 84, 87, 131
Ram Dass, 33, 40, 53
Ranganathananda, Swami, 34
Ratio, 3, 4
Rationality, 4, 5, 9, 21, 30, 31, 73
Reason, 3, 5, 9, 17, 29, 30, 39, 73
Rebirth, 38
Rebirthing, 95
Reductionism, 19, 20, 23, 25, 29, 47, 65, 75
Reflexology, 90
Reibel, S., 53
Reich, W., 89-90, 91
Relationship skills, 50
Relativity Theory (*see also* Einstein), 117
Relaxation, 91
Renaissance, the, 18, 67, 118
Replicability, 103
Reps, P., 84
Research tradition, the, 20

Responsibility, 26, 29, 48, 50, 59, 65, 67, 69, 72, 95, 99, 129
Reversal Theory, 106-7
Rhinehart, L., 88, 95
Richer, J., 24
Robot, 31
Rogers, C. R., 31, 47, 49, 50, 53-8, 59, 61, 62, 63, 66, 74, 79, 81, 86, 93, 104, 110
Roleplaying, 58, 91
Rolf, I., 58, 91
Rolfing, 91, 99
Roman(s), 4
    empire, 8
Rosenthal, R., 108
Roszak, T., 23, 27, 28, 29, 30, 34, 35, 37
Rowan, J., 87, 88, 109-111
Ruitenbeek, H., 78
Rumi, Jalal-al, 16
Russell, B., 2, 3, 5, 7, 19
Russia, 24
Rychlak, J. F., 103, 112

S

Sagan, C., 33
Sai Baba, 8
Salvation, 44, 47
Samsara, 12
Samyaktva (see Tranquility), 13
Sanskrit, 5
Sarnath Sermon, the, 12
Sartre, J-P., 29, 46, 68, 69, 71, 72, 74-6, 83, 98, 99
Satori (see Enlightenment), 15
Scepticism, 19
Schacter, J., 105
Scharfstein, B-A., 16
Scheler, M., 74
Schizophrenics, 49, 76, 78
Schofield, W., 46
School, 45
Schools
    British, 41, 57
    American, 42
    English Secondary, 56
Schutz, W., 62, 63
Science, 4, 9, 18, 19, 20, 23, 24, 25, 28, 29, 31, 33, 43, 47, 80, 100, 114, 119, 124, 129
Scientific method, 20, 26-27, 48, 100
Scientific research, 23, 58
Scientism, 73

Scientology, 35
Self-actualization, 51, 54, 59, 66, 81, 88
Self-awareness, 8, 12
Self-concept, 50, 54
Self-determination, 42
Self-development, 50
Self-discovery, 54, 62
Self-dislike, 51
Self-esteem, 50
Self-expression, 8, 92
Self-indulgence, 34
Self-knowledge, 41
Self-organization, 127
Self-perception, 12, 55
Self-realization, 7
Self-respect, 51
Self Theory, 54
Self-understanding, 93
Senile dementia, 45
Sensitivity, 2, 50
    training, 95
Sensory deprivation, 123
Seventeenth Century, the, 17, 29, 67
Shah, I., 16, 33
Shaffer, J. B. F., 64, 76, 79, 85, 86, 108, 109
Shaman, 2
Shamanism, 37
Shapiro, D., 100
Shiatsu, 90
Shotter, J., 106, 107
Siddharta Gautama (see Buddha), 8, 12
Silberman, C., 42
Silverman, D., 38
Sin(s), 7, 48, 110
Skinner, B. F., 25, 26, 27, 48
Snygg, D., 74
Social psychology, 105
Sociobiology, 26
Sociological analysis, 38
Sociology, 75
Soliloquy, 93
Sorcery, 2, 37-9
Sorrow (see Dukka), 13
Soul, 3, 11, 17, 20, 21, 27, 50
Spectrum psychology (see Wilber), 131
Spontaneity, 51, 66
Sputnik, 24
Staal, F., 119
Standard(s), 4, 9, 102, 111
Story, R., 30
Stress, 53, 90, 91

Structural Integration, 58
Student(s), 28, 29, 42, 50
Subjectivity, 13, 16, 38, 65, 66, 73, 102, 107
Suffering (see Dukka), 13, 24, 25
Sufi(ism), 12, 15, 16, 33, 36
Summerhill, 41
Super-ego, 26, 48, 94
Supernatural, 5, 30
Super-symmetry, 125
Suzuki, T., 33, 34
Synchronicity, 118, 130
Szasz, T. S., 45, 47, 76

T
T'ai Chi, 90, 92
Tao, 43, 83, 122, 128
  of physics, 119–20
Taoism, 7, 12, 14, 38
Tao Te Ching (see Book of Changes, I
  Ching), 14
Tart, C., 12, 29, 30, 52, 112, 113, 130
Teacher, 8, 9, 42
Techniques, 41, 43, 48, 58, 61, 62, 87, 92,
  98
Technocracy, 29, 30, 32, 37
Technology, 21, 23, 24, 26, 27, 42, 83, 88,
  99
Telepathy, 117
Theology, 18, 73, 101
Theory of Special Relativity, 114, 124, 125
Theosophists, 33
Therapy (see also Psychotherapy), 55, 63, 76,
  88, 91, 95, 129
Third Force Psychology, 52, 65–6, 104, 131
Tibetan Book of the Dead, the (see Bardo
  Thodol), 33, 35
Tillich, P., 45, 68, 81
Toffler, A., 4, 128
Touch, 58
  therapy, 58
Training, 49
  training or T-groups, 50, 99
Tranquility (see Samyaktva), 13
Transactional Analysis, 94, 96, 99
Transcendence, 7, 11, 12, 13, 15, 34, 36,
  40, 66, 67, 69, 131
Transcendental Meditation, 35, 40
Transformation, 13, 102, 127, 129
Transformation theory, 126–7
Transparency, 55
Transpersonal Psychology, 52

Trust, 42, 61
Twentieth Century, the, 20, 22, 23, 26, 31,
  33, 37, 41, 44, 114, 126, 130

U
Ultimate concerns, 68, 101
  oneness, 12, 14
  reality, 15
  truth, 7, 16, 124
Ultimate unity, 14–15
Uncertainty, 13, 46, 47, 115
  principle, 115, 116–7
Unconditional positive regard, 55
Unification Church, the, 35
Unification Theory, 125
United States of America, 24, 33, 41, 43
Unity, 2, 16, 38, 119
Uranium, 28

V
Values, 27, 29, 47, 63, 66, 67, 69, 73, 74,
  128
Vegetotherapy, 89
Verification, 102, 103, 104
Vietnam, 28
Villa, 21, 78
Vine, I., 111
Virgin Mary, the, 36
Von Daniken, E., 32, 33, 35
Vital force, 53

W
War (see World War Two and Vietnam), 28,
  29
Warnock, M., 68, 72, 74, 82, 84
Watson, J. B., 26, 65
Watts, A., 33, 34, 58
Weingartner, C. W., 42
Welwood, J., 129
Wertheimer, M., 59, 72
West, Ellen, 77
Western civilisation, 3, 4, 5, 6, 18
  culture, 4, 9, 11, 19, 27, 29, 30, 31, 32,
    37, 40, 41, 44, 62, 87, 97, 131
  thought, 67
Westland, G., 83, 103, 104, 105, 107
Wheatley, D., 2
Wheel (see Chakra), 12, 16
Wheels, 19, 26
Whitehorn, K., 36
Wholeness, 36

Wilber, K., 130-1
Will, 7, 9, 11, 16, 20, 39, 40, 72, 99
Wisdom, 1, 9, 14, 15, 16, 131
Wittgenstein, L., 25
Workshop(s), 63, 88
World War Two, 24, 50

Y

Yalom, I. D., 71, 75, 76, 81, 95, 99, 100, 103
Yang, 14, 15, 119

Yaqui knowledge, 38, 39
Yin, 14, 15, 119
Yoga, 33, 43, 66, 79, 90, 92

Z

Zazen, 15
Zen, 12, 15, 33, 34, 36, 38, 41, 60, 79, 84, 92, 96, 97, 113, 125, 127
    events, 125
Zimbardo, P., 105
Zukav, G., 117-9